The Crucifixion

of

Jesus

A Medical Doctor Examines the Death and Resurrection of Christ

Joseph W. Bergeron, M.D.

With a Foreword by Gary Habermas, Ph.D.

The Crucifixion of Jesus

A Medical Doctor Examines the Death and Resurrection of Christ

by Joseph W. Bergeron

ISBN: 1-947707-19-1
ISBN-13: 978-1-947707-19-1

Library of Congress Control Number: 2018946437

Published by St. Polycarp Publishing House
www.stpolycarppublishinghouse.com
info@stpolycarppublishinghouse.com

Printed in the United States of America

DEDICATION

To my son, Matthew, a man of good character.

To my son, Joseph, who teaches us all trust and humility.

To my wife, Magdalen, my love and companion.

And to my Lord Jesus Christ, the blessed and only Sovereign, the King of Kings and Lord of Lords. Amen.

CONTENTS

ACKNOWLEDGMENTS

I would like to thank Roger Bailey, M.D. His help has been invaluable.

I would also like to thank Aaron Simms and the staff of St. Polycarp Publishing House for their professionalism and sense of mission.

That a few simple men should in one generation have invented so powerful and appealing a personality, so lofty an ethic and so inspiring a vision of human brotherhood, would be a miracle far more incredible than any recorded in the Gospels. After two centuries of Higher Criticism, the outlines of the life, character, and teaching of Christ, remain reasonably clear, and constitute the most fascinating feature in the history of Western man. [1]

- Will Durant, Historian

---

[1]From THE STORY OF CIVILIZATION, VOL. III: CAESAR AND CHRIST by Will Durant. Page 557. Copyright © 1944 by Will Durant. Copyright renewed 1972 by Will Durant. Reprinted with the permission of Simon & Schuster, Inc. All rights reserved.

Joseph W. Bergeron

FOREWORD
BY DR. GARY HABERMAS

The occasion of this introduction is to introduce the publication of a well-researched volume by physician Joseph W. Bergeron, my friend and coauthor in a related study on a similar topic.[2] Entitled *The Crucifixion of Jesus: A Medical Doctor Examines the Death and Resurrection of Christ*, Dr. Bergeron delves chiefly into circumstances pertaining to the end of Jesus' life, bringing his medical interests and expertise to bear on dozens of separate details.

As such, this volume investigates events from the life of Jesus, beginning with aspects like Jesus' claims regarding his personal identity (Chapter 1), information concerning Jesus' life and what might be known about him (Chapter 2), and the political situation in which Jesus lived (Chapter 3). This paves the way for the crux of this text, which Bergeron begins by detailing the surrounding circumstances that led to Jesus' death (Chapter 4). As indicated by the title, the bulk of the book concerns the general nature of Roman crucifixion (Chapter 5), the specifics of Jesus' own crucifixion (Chapter 6), the medical cause of Jesus' death (Chapter 7), and his resurrection (Chapter 8). We will return to the specific details below.

The Center of the Christian Faith

The majority of Joe Bergeron's volume, then, is concerned with the truths of the Christian Gospel message as it was originally communicated, located at the very center of the Christian faith. Taken in its narrower sense, when the Gospel particulars were actually defined in the New Testament book of Acts and the Epistles, three indispensable factual elements are almost always

---

[2] Joseph W. Bergeron and Gary R. Habermas, "The Resurrection of Jesus: A Clinical Review of Psychiatric Hypotheses for the Biblical Story of Easter," *Irish Theological Quarterly*, 80, no. 2 (2015) 157-172.

mentioned in tandem--what we might term God's side of the Gospel. These three rudiments are that Jesus was Deity (usually indicated by Jesus' identification by titles such as Messiah or Christ, Lord, or the Son of God,[3] along with a few other lofty comments like Jesus being exalted to the Father's right hand). Additionally, Jesus died by crucifixion and then rose from the dead and appeared to his followers. Other items (such as Jesus being David's son or his burial after death) are sometimes mentioned in these same contexts, too, but they are not cited as uniformly or consistently.

Many representative New Testament passages identify consistently these three central foci when the Gospel particulars are itemized and preached.[4] The encouraged human response to this Gospel message in terms of a life faith-commitment to Jesus Christ is likewise emphasized in many texts, often being offered to the original hearers and later readers in the very same context.[5] The identification and preaching of this message was the dominant proclamation in the early church.

Probably the best-known example that this declaration was central is Paul's detailed declaration in 1 Corinthians 15:1-22. Perhaps the most direct comment is that this Gospel message (15:1-2) was "of first importance" (15:3). Further, if this message were not true, then preaching (15:14) and other testimony (15:15) are vain or even false. Moreover, our loved ones who have died trusting in Christ have perished (15:18). Perhaps most stunning are the comments that even our personal faith is in vain, and our sins have not been forgiven (15:14, 17). Apart from Jesus' and the believer's

---

[3] These matters are multi-faceted, such as Son of God and Lord being the loftier of these three titles. But the particulars cannot be unpacked here. The comments above are well-represented in the relevant literature, though.

[4] Such texts would include Acts 1:21-22; 2:22-28; 3:12-21; 4:2, 8-12; 4:33; 5:29-32; 10:34-43; 13:26-39; 17:1-4; Romans 1:1-4; 4:24-25; 10:9; 1 Corinthians 15:3-7; Philippians 2:6-11; 2 Timothy 2:8-9; 1 Peter 1:3-9; 1:18-21; Revelation 2:8; 5:6-14.

[5] In the above texts, compare the offers of salvation and commitment in Acts 2:37-41; 3:22-23; 4:2; 8:12; 5:32; 10:43; 13:26, 39; 17:3-4; Rom. 1:5-6; 4:24; 10:9; 1 Cor. 15:1-2, 11; Phil. 2:10-11; 2 Tim. 2:10; 1 Pet. 1:6-9; 1:13, 17, 21; 2:21; 1 Jn. 2:6; Rev. 2:10-11.

resurrections, Christians may as well turn into "party animals" (15:32b). In sum, apart from the message of the Lord Jesus Christ's death and resurrection, believers would be the most miserable of all human beings (15:19)!

It would be very difficult to think of a New Testament passage that expresses in more graphic terms the absolute crucial nature of this central message! Yet, Paul goes on to correct this negative impression by asserting that because Christ has been raised from the dead (15:20), we can now reverse each of these previous sentiments. Thankfully, none of these earlier proclamations of Christian futility is true!

But this is not the only New Testament passage that proclaims this centrality, as just a few examples indicate. When asked what sign would demonstrate that he was God's chosen one and spokesman, Jesus himself more than once referred to his death and resurrection (Matt. 12:38-40; 16:1-4). Jesus' being alive is the basis for the believer's afterlife (John 14:19; cf. 1 John 3:2). In his own words, this Gospel message was the crux of Jesus' entire story (Luke 24:25-27; 44-48). Coming out of the gate with their earliest preaching, the resurrection was the center of the apostle's message (Acts 4:2, 33; 17:31). The resurrection also grounded both Christian theology (1 Peter 1:3-5) as well as Christian practice (1 Corinthians 15:58-16:2).

Specific Details of Bergeron's Positions

Beginning with the cogs of this central Christian proclamation and moving to the details of crucifixion in general (Chapter 6), Joe Bergeron's volume is packed full of intriguing, insightful, and documented medical information. He treats such subjects as hematidrosis or sweating blood (129-133), along with medical shock and both early and late signs that Jesus was suffering from it (140-141, 163-167). Bergeron also includes several modern explanations of the details regarding the type and results of Jesus' beating, along with his own analysis (134-138). Lastly, explanations of the likely extent of Jesus' lung injuries (138-139) and the chest wound (139-140) were exceptionally insightful.

Concerning his own views of what occurred to Jesus during his crucifixion (Chapter 7), Bergeron first spends an exceptional amount of time listing several of the most popular medical views on the cause of Jesus' death (142-167), devoting the most space to the most popular view today, that of suffocation/asphyxiation (147-156). Apparently favoring pleural effusion (the presence of fluid from the lungs—139-140), Bergeron moves on to his own positions. His position centers on shock (156-159) and then moves forward to Trauma-Induced Coagulopathy, which is a complication of shock (167), where the individual loses the ability to clot blood flow (159-167).[6] Throughout the evaluative process, Bergeron remains careful, nuances his material, acknowledges the presence of other possible positions, and makes a good case for his final conclusion.

Bergeron then addresses Jesus' resurrection appearances in Chapter 8. He moves from an overview and synopsis of biblical material (172-176), to addressing briefly the ever-present question of variations in the accounts (176-177). Introducing the resurrection appearances leads to a thorough examination of the natural alternative views regarding this event (176-193). Then Bergeron considers the Minimal Facts Argument for Jesus' resurrection appearances (193-200), which uses only those historical data that even critical scholars will almost always recognize. He ends the chapter by applying Differential Diagnosis to the possibilities (200-201).

A brief Epilogue (203-206) recounts the centrality of the death and resurrection message for the New Testament, as well as some personal ramifications. This last portion is reminiscent to the first

---

[6] Joseph W. Bergeron, "The Crucifixion of Jesus: Review of Hypothesized Mechanisms of Death and Implications of Shock and Trauma-Induced Coagulopathy," *Journal of Forensic and Legal Medicine* 19 (2012):113–116.

section of this introduction above. Altogether, Bergeron has presented a vast number of scholarly theses for consideration, making this a highly intriguing investigation.

Gary R. Habermas, PhD
Distinguished Research Professor
Chair, Department of Philosophy
Liberty Baptist Theological Seminary
www.garyhabermas.com

Joseph W. Bergeron

PROLOGUE

Some of the most intelligent people I've met in education and professional life have had limited or no knowledge about Jesus Christ or how the events of his life gave rise to the world's largest major religion. One reason must be the general animus that exists toward Christianity in colleges and universities. This was true when I was in college and continues today. A general disregard of Christianity among educators and a dearth of cogent teaching about the life of Jesus have created measurable effects. An estimated sixty percent of young people who have grown up in church leave their faith during college years.[7] This is an epidemic.

Is the significance of Jesus Christ so easily debunked? Can Christian beliefs about Jesus' death and resurrection withstand logical scrutiny? The answers lie in painstaking explication of the facts about Jesus' execution and of his disciples' belief that Jesus was resurrected from the dead to bodily life.

The Bible contains the most detailed accounts of Jesus' life and message. In referring to biblical texts we are forced to consider the question of whether or not they are accurate. If we cannot establish the reliability of the biblical accounts of Jesus' life, further discussion has little value. That being said, there is considerable evidence that Jesus' life and teachings were recorded by those who knew him best and that the texts have been handed down through time without error. Within this present book, evidence for the validity of the biblical accounts of Jesus' life is discussed as well as historical references to Jesus from outside the Bible.

Jesus lived in Judaea and Galilee, areas that were part of the Kingdom of Herod the Great. Herod ruled the Jewish kingdom as a

---

[7]Barna Group Staff, "The Priorities, Challenges, and Trends in Youth Ministry," The Barna Group, April 6, 2016. https://www.barna.com/research/the-priorities-challenges-and-trends-in-youth-ministry/ (accessed November 12, 2017).

client state of the Roman Empire from 37 BC until his death, around 4 BC. The Romans divided the kingdom among Herod's sons after his death.[8] While the borders of the first century Jewish kingdom differ from those of modern Israel, regions within the Herodian kingdom are collectively referred to as "Israel" within this book for simplicity's sake.[9]

The politics in Jesus' time were complex and can be missed with a casual reading of the Bible. Jewish leaders attempted to preserve a tenuous favorable relationship with Rome plus maintain internal political stability within Israel. Class tensions existed among the Jews, in addition to a palpable disdain for their foreign rulers. The threat of a Roman police state and seizure of Israel's monetary reserves loomed large. The common citizenry hoped for a dynamic leader sent by God who would free them from Roman occupation and reestablish Israel as an autonomous theocratic nation state. Many thought Jesus would be that leader. Jewish religious leaders felt differently. They rejected the idea that Jesus was God's Messiah and imminent leader. More than that, they feared Jesus' rising popularity would attract Roman attention and trigger martial law. Their personal wealth and social status were at risk. Understanding the political turmoil in Jesus' time sheds light on why killing Jesus seemed so important.

Many find it difficult to accept the biblical accounts of Jesus' life as trustworthy historical documents. Still, the biblical passages describing Jesus' crucifixion have stand-alone historical importance. By Jesus' time, Romans had used crucifixion as their most severe form of capital punishment for three centuries.

---

[8]After the death of Herod the Great, the Romans divided Herod's kingdom among his children. Herod Antipas became the ruler of Galilee, and Archelaus initially ruled Judea, both were client rulers within the Roman empire. See Chapter 3 for further discussion.

[9] Staff writer, "The Herodian Period: 37 BCE – 73 CE" Israel Ministry of Foreign Affairs, 2013, http://www.mfa.gov.il/mfa/aboutisrael/maps/pages/kingdom%20of%20herod-%2030%20bce%20to%2070%20ce.aspx/ (accessed July 3, 2018). See also Chapter 3 for further discussion.

Crucifixion was a perfected method of execution. There are no compelling reasons to question the accuracy of the biblical descriptions of Jesus' execution. Roman crucifixion practices are well known and will be discussed in detail here.

Death by crucifixion was the result of slow torture, without a mortal wound or direct injury to vital organs. What ultimately caused Jesus to die? Did Jesus' heart rupture from emotional agony? Did hanging on the cross cause Jesus to suffocate? Was he killed when a Roman soldier impaled his chest with a spear? Did he die from shock? The plausibility of each is examined in light of current medical understanding.

It is an inescapable fact that Jesus' disciples experienced *something* that made them believe he had been resurrected to bodily life after dying on the cross. The martyrdom of his disciples and the rapid expansion of Christianity in the first century defy explanation otherwise. The litmus test that they experienced something that for them was *real* is that they would not recant their belief in Jesus' resurrection even though for many it meant torture and death.

Were the disciples tricked somehow? Was Jesus' body snatched? Did they go to the wrong tomb? Could psychiatric illness explain the disciples' belief in Jesus' resurrection? Were the disciples hallucinating when they saw Jesus after his crucifixion? Hallucination hypotheses for the disciples' belief in Jesus' resurrection have largely escaped commentary by medical professionals yet the medical implications are significant.

Many physicians have written about the crucifixion of Jesus. I do not seek to supplant their work. Rather, I humbly stand on the shoulders of the distinguished medical scholars who have sought to understand and explain how Jesus died. I am indebted to their scholarship.

I do not endorse any particular church or denomination. Rather, I have focused on the most foundational beliefs common to all traditional orthodox Christians, the death and bodily resurrection of Jesus Christ.

May you find the reading insightful. To Christians, I trust you will appreciate the detailed descriptions and better understand what happened to Jesus the day he was crucified. To those unsure of what they think about Jesus, I applaud your academic integrity and desire to seek further knowledge. To all, I trust you will apprehend the logical basis for belief in the death and resurrection of Jesus Christ.

Joseph W. Bergeron, M.D.

CHAPTER 1
WHO DID JESUS CLAIM TO BE?

"You have a teacher who says he came from God and we have a teacher who says he came from God. What's the difference? Jesus never said he was God, did he?" My friend grew up in India in a faith tradition other than Christianity. He is a scientist, an expert in investigation and analysis. His questions were logically directed and struck to the core of orthodox Christianity. Who did Jesus claim to be?

Jesus was clear in stating that he was a human being yet he also claimed a supernatural identity. He said he was the Son of God, meaning in his culture that he *was* God. Moreover, he claimed to be the Messiah, a supernatural deliverer and King foretold in Hebrew prophecy. Jesus' statements can seem enigmatic today, but they were clearly understood in his time and culture.

Jesus said and did things as if he *were* God. For example, Jesus said he had the power to forgive sins and assure life after death in heaven for his followers. Moreover, Jesus' reputation as a miracle worker appeared to validate his claims of identity.

Son of Man

Jesus referred to himself as the "Son of Man," that is to say, *a human being*. The title of Son of Man is meant to contrast the lowly state of a human from the exalted position of God. In using the moniker "Son of Man" Jesus was clear in stating he was a human being. It would not have been understood any other way. Son of Man was Jesus' most utilized self-descriptive term yet it seems paradoxical to his declarations of being the Son of God and Messiah.

Prior to Jesus, the title "Son of Man" was used only once in the Bible to describe a divine figure. This is found in Daniel's prophecy of a King who would come from God at the end of time and rule the entire Earth for eternity, the Messiah (Dan. 7:13–14). The "Son of Man" who Daniel saw is human but not an ordinary mortal.

Daniel's prophecy thus foretold an immortal human (Son of Man) who came from God to rule over the entire earth in an eternal kingdom:

And with the clouds of the sky one like a son of man was approaching. He went up to the Ancient of Days [God] and was escorted before him. To him was given ruling authority, honor, and sovereignty. All peoples, nations, and language groups were serving him. His authority is eternal and will not pass away. His kingdom will not be destroyed (Dan. 7:13–14).

Daniel's Son of Man-Messiah is unlike any other human and shares characteristics unique to God. The Son of Man comes from God, rides on the clouds, and presides over the whole Earth for eternity. Coming in the clouds is reserved for God, "He [God] makes the clouds his chariot, and travels along on the wings of the wind" (Ps. 104:3). In Hebrew culture, God is the ultimate ruler of the Earth, "For God is king of the whole earth! Sing a well-written song! God reigns over the nations! God sits on his holy throne!" (Ps.47:7–8).

The Messiah

Jesus unmistakably identified himself as the Messiah of Hebrew prophecy.[10] He said, "No one has ascended into heaven except the one [Jesus referring to himself] who descended from heaven—the Son of Man" (John 3:13). In this reference to himself as the *Son of Man,* Jesus clearly points to Daniel's prophecy.

In talking with his disciples, Jesus quizzed them as to who they thought he was. He then confirmed to them that he was the Messiah

---

[10]Messianic expectations in Jesus' time are discussed in Chapter 3.

and the Son of God:

When Jesus came to the area of Caesarea Philippi, he asked his disciples, "Who do people say that the Son of Man is?" They answered, "Some say John the Baptist, others Elijah, and others Jeremiah or one of the prophets." He said to them, "But who do you say that I am?" Simon Peter answered, "You are the Christ, the Son of the living God." And Jesus answered him, "You are blessed, Simon son of Jonah, because flesh and blood did not reveal this to you, but my Father in heaven! (Matt. 16:13–17).

A rabbi would often proclaim a blessing upon a student who made a particularly wise or insightful comment.[11] Jesus pronounced a blessing on Peter for his answer, specifically for correctly identifying him as the Messiah and Son of God. Jesus further dignified Peter's words by stating he received this revelation directly from God.

Peter's revelation that Jesus was the Son of God and Messiah was so important to Jesus that he commemorated the moment by changing Peter's name from Simon to Peter (Latin: *Petrus*, English: Stone). In doing so, Jesus signified that the bedrock of his Messianic community, the Christian Church at large, was the understanding and acceptance that he was the Messiah and the Son

---

[11]Jesus was Jewish, had studied the Hebrew scriptures, attended and taught in the Synagogue, and had disciples who sought to learn from him. In this sense he was a *rabbi*, literally meaning "my teacher" or "my master." Ordination by the laying on of hands (*semichah*) and "Rabbi" as a certified title did not exist until the Mishna (rabbinical literary record oral tradition compiled in the early centuries of the Common Era). Jesus was not a rabbi in this sense since formal ordination and certification of rabbinic title had not yet been instituted. Michael L. Brown, *60 Questions Christians Ask About Jewish Beliefs and Practices*, (Bloomington: Chosen Books, 2011), 36-37. In modern times, rabbis are professional clergy who have generally completed multiple years of study including rabbinic seminary. My Jewish Learning Staff, "What does It Mean to Be a Rabbi?" *myjewishlearning.com*. My Jewish Learning, https://www.myjewishlearning.com/article/rabbi-teacher-preacher-judge-but-not-priest/. (accessed February 21, 2018).

of God (Matt. 16:18).[12]

Jesus said he had a father-son relationship with God. He said:

I tell you the solemn truth, a time is coming—and is now here— when the dead will hear the voice of the Son of God, and those who hear will live. For just as the Father has life in himself, thus he has granted the Son to have life in himself, and he has granted the Son authority to execute judgment, because he is the Son of Man.

Do not be amazed at this, because a time is coming when all who are in the tombs will hear his voice and will come out—the ones who have done what is good to the resurrection resulting in life, and the ones who have done what is evil to the resurrection resulting in condemnation (John 5:26–29).

Jesus again places himself in the context of Daniel's prophecy as the Son of Man-Messiah. According to Jesus, the Son of Man-Messiah is also Son of God.

What did it mean to be the Son of God?

In Jesus' time and culture, claiming to be the Son of God was one and the same as claiming to be God himself. People gathered in the Temple one day to ask Jesus questions, specifically to find out if he claimed to be the Messiah. His response exceeded their expectations. Rather than an affirmation that he was the Messiah, Jesus replied that he was literally the Son of God and that he was one with his father, God.

".... The Father and I are one." The Jewish leaders picked up

---

[12]In Roman Catholic theology, Jesus' statements and the renaming Simon as Peter signified that Peter was designated the leader of the Church at its formation, in effect the first Pope. Catholic Answers staff, "Origins of Peter as Pope," *Catholic.com*. Catholic Answers, August 4, 2008, https://www.catholic.com/tract/origins-of-peter-as-pope. (accessed January 3, 2018).

rocks again to stone him to death. Jesus said to them, "I have shown you many good deeds from the Father. For which one of them are you going to stone me?" The Jewish leaders replied, "We are not going to stone you for a good deed but for blasphemy, because you, a man, are claiming to be God" (John 10:30–33).

The Jewish leaders' reaction leaves no doubt as to precisely what Jesus' statements meant. Claiming to be the Son of God was literally the same as claiming to be God himself. According to the crowd, Jesus was guilty of blasphemy and deserved to be stoned to death.[13]

Jesus spoke about God as his father in a way that was unprecedented in Hebrew culture. Jews might have spoken of God as their father in a figurative and collective sense (John 8:41). However, Jesus spoke about God differently. He was assuming a oneness with God as a direct offspring. To Jewish listeners, Jesus was identifying himself as God. The crowd clearly understood what he meant.

Authority over the Law of Moses

Perhaps the most revered prophet in Jewish history was Moses. Moses' relationship with God was unrivaled, "The Lord would speak to Moses face to face, the way a person speaks to a friend" (Ex. 33:11). Moses received the Ten Commandments directly from God.

The Fourth Commandment in the Ten Commandments is to "Remember the Sabbath day to set it apart as holy" (Ex. 20:8). God himself "blessed the Sabbath day and set it apart as holy" (Ex. 20:11). Religious leaders criticized Jesus for not properly observing

---

[13]Blasphemy of the name of God was punishable by execution by stoning. "Whoever blasphemes the name of the LORD, he shall surely be put to death, and the entire congregation shall certainly stone him. The foreigner as well as the native in the land, when he blasphemes the name, then he shall be put to death" (Lev. 24:16, MEV).

the Sabbath (Mark 3:1-6, Matt. 12:1-2, Luke 13:13-15).   For
example, Jesus healed a man with an atrophied hand on the Sabbath.
This made some Pharisees so angry that they plotted how to
assassinate him (Mark 12:9-14).

Jesus declared that he had authority over the Sabbath day, "For
the Son of Man is Lord of the Sabbath" (Matt. 12:8).   Only God
could override the Law of Moses!

Preexistence

Abraham founded the Hebrew nation centuries before Jesus was
born.   Yet, Jesus told the Pharisees that Abraham had seen him.
Speaking to the Pharisees, Jesus said:

*"Your father Abraham was overjoyed to see my day, and he saw
it and was glad."*

*Then the Judeans replied, "You are not yet fifty years old! Have
you seen Abraham?" Jesus said to them, "I tell you the solemn truth,
before Abraham came into existence, I am!" Then they picked up
stones to throw at him, but Jesus was hidden from them and went
out from the temple area (John 8:56-59).*

Not only did Jesus say he existed before Abraham was born, but
he said it this way, "before Abraham came into existence, *I am!*"
The Greek term used here is *ego eimi (ἐγὼ εἰμί)*, "I am", but the
syntax indicates meaning outside the bounds of the usual mundane
sense of the term, "I am."

God first spoke to Moses from a bush that was on fire but did not
incinerate.   When Moses asked his name, God said, "I AM that I

AM" (אֶהְיֶה אֲשֶׁר אֶהְיֶה) (Ex. 3:2,14).[14]   The name "I AM" defines God's identity as the uncreated creator, eternally self-existent, independent of time and requiring no external validation.[15] Moses encountered Almighty God. The Hebrew pronunciation of God's name is thought to have been "Yahweh," which was a reflection of the name "I AM."   In Hebrew culture, however, the name of God was too sacred to ever be spoken.[16]

When Jesus said "before Abraham existed 'I am'" he evoked remembrance of Moses' meeting with God. Jesus was referring to himself as Almighty God. The crowd clearly understood this. They rejected Jesus' assertion that he was God and attempted to stone him to death for the blasphemy.

The evening before he was arrested, Jesus met and prayed with his disciples. Part of his prayer included the declaration that he was the Son of God and that he existed before the creation of the earth. Jesus prayed:

When Jesus had finished saying these things, he looked upward to heaven and said, "Father, the time has come. Glorify your Son, so that your Son may glorify you— just as you have given him authority over all humanity, so that he may give eternal life to everyone you have given him. Now this is eternal life—that they know you, the only true God, and Jesus Christ, whom you sent. I glorified you on earth by completing the work you gave me to do. And now, Father, glorify me at your side with the glory I had with you before the world was created" (John 17: 1–5).

---

[14]The name of God was considered so sacred that it was not spelled out completely. Rather, it was expressed in a tetragrammaton transliterated as "YHWH." It is generally considered that it would have been pronounced "Yahweh" even though speaking the name of God was prohibited. When a reader encountered the tetragrammaton they would substitute *Adonai* (the Lord) or *HaShem* (the name). David Bivin, *New Light on the Difficult Words of Jesus: Insights from His Jewish Context* (Holland: En Gedi Resource Center, 2005),55–56, 57 fn 1.

[15]Rev 4:8–11 seems a corollary passage.

[16] J. Julius Scott, *Jewish Backgrounds of the New Testament* (Grand Rapids: Baker Books, 1995), 63-64.

Jesus asks God to glorify him and restore him to his rightful exalted position side by side with God himself, namely to his divine status as it was prior to the creation of the world. This is astounding, since in Jewish theology God does not glorify anyone, "I am the Lord! That is my name! I will not share my glory with anyone else..." (Isa. 42:8). Jesus' prayer also affirmed the promise of eternal life to those believing in him.

Almighty God

Polytheism and pantheism are commonplace throughout the world. Concepts of God differ among religions. For someone to say that they are part of God, come from God, or that they are *a god* is normal in some religions. For a Swami in India to claim that he is the incarnation of a particular *Hindu God* does not seem out of place, for example. However, in Judaism God exists on a higher plane and separate from humanity. In Jewish theology there is only one Almighty God, the omnipotent creator of the universe and all life.

The cornerstone declaration of Jewish monotheism is the *Shema Yisrael, "Listen, Israel: The Lord is our God, the Lord is one! You must love the Lord your God with your whole mind, your whole being, and all your strength"* (Deut. 6:4–5). Jesus illustrated the importance of the *Shema Yisrael* to Jewish religious thinking in his time:

*Now one of the experts in the law came and heard them debating. When he saw that Jesus answered them well, he asked him, "Which commandment is the most important of all?" Jesus answered, "The most important is: '**Listen, Israel, the Lord our God, the Lord is one. Love the Lord your God with all your heart, with all your soul, with all your mind, and with all your strength** '" (Mark 12:28–30).*

Jesus said the foremost commandment in Judaism is the *Shema*

Yisrael. The *Shema Yisrael* is a creed and a profession of absolute devotion to the one and only Almighty God. Jewish boys were taught the *Shema* as soon as they were able to speak. It was recited twice daily, once in the morning and evening.[17] It would have been the first scripture passage Jesus learned.

When Jesus said he was God, it was completely different from the claims of a Swami in India. He wasn't claiming that he had become the incarnation of a particular god. Such a claim would not be astonishing. Many gods are worshipped, each with dedicated devotees. Rather, Jesus identified himself as the one and only Almighty God who had become a human being.

Jesus' Trial Testimony

Perhaps Jesus' most striking declarations of supernatural identity occur after his arrest. Jesus was taken to the home of Annas, father-in-law of the Jewish High Priest, Joseph Caiaphas, for a secret trial late at night. Some members of the Sanhedrin, the Jewish ruling tribunal were also present.

The high priest said to him, "I charge you under oath by the living God, tell us if you are the Christ, the Son of God." Jesus said to him, "You have said it yourself. But I tell you, from now on you will see the Son of Man sitting at the right hand of the Power [God] and coming on the clouds of heaven." Then the high priest tore his clothes and declared, "He has blasphemed! Why do we still need witnesses? Now you have heard the blasphemy! What is your verdict?" They answered, "He is guilty and deserves death." Then they spat in his face and struck him with their fists. And some slapped him, saying, "Prophesy for us, you Christ! Who hit you?" (Matt. 26: 63–68).

---

[17]Marin R. Wilson, *Our Father Abraham: Jewish Roots of the Christian Faith* (Grand Rapids: Eerdmans, 1989), 122–125.

Image 1 - *He is Guilty of Death*. Vasily Polenov.

Jesus' answers might seem obscure to non-Jewish readers, but his meaning was unmistakable to the High Priest and others present. When asked if he was the Christ [Messiah] and the Son of God, Jesus answered, "You have said it yourself..." In essence Jesus was saying, ...*it is exactly as you have stated.* But to remove all ambiguity, Jesus also cited two messianic prophecies and states that he is the person the prophets were referring to.

First, he told the High Priest and others judging him they would see him at the right hand of Power [God] and coming in the clouds. Caiaphas and those present understood that Jesus was pointing to Daniel's messianic prophecy of the eternal King who would come from Heaven riding on clouds and rule the world for eternity (Dan 7:13–14).

Secondly, Jesus declared his rightful position was being seated at the right hand of God.[18] This is also a reference to a messianic prophecy:

---

[18]In Jewish culture, God's right hand is symbolic of God's power, deliverance and salvation, Ex 15:6, Ps 20:6, Ps 89:13, Ps 98:1, Ps 138:7. Neil and Amy Lash, "The Lord's Right Hand – April 2016", Jewish Jewels, April 1, 2016. Jewish Jewels, http://www.jewishjewels.org/news-letters/the-lords-right-hand-april-2016/. (accessed March 21, 2017)

Here is the Lord's proclamation to my lord:
Sit down at my right hand until I make your enemies your
footstool! (Ps. 110:1)

This psalm's authorship is attributed to David, the most revered king in Jewish history who was also considered a prophet. David states "the Lord" (*Hashem* or "the Name" [of God]) proclaims to "my Lord" (*Adonai*) sit down at my right hand..." This prophetic psalm describes a supernatural person obviously greater than David, the author. It has a peculiar juxtaposition of words. God refers to the person seated next to him on the right as *Adonai*, "the Lord."

In effect, Jesus told Caiaphas that he was *Adonai* (the Lord-God) and that he would see him seated at God's "right hand." Caiaphas became so angry that he tore his clothes as a sign of outrage and declared Jesus guilty of blasphemy. The High Priest and Jewish leaders acted as an *ad hoc* jury. They found Jesus guilty of blasphemy and therefore worthy of the death penalty by Hebrew law (Image 1: *He is Guilty of Death*). It is noteworthy that Jesus made no effort to correct any misunderstanding. There was no mistake.

The Jews brought charges against Jesus before the Roman Prefect, Pontius Pilate. Blasphemy within the Jewish religion was irrelevant to the Romans. Pilate didn't want to be bothered with religious disagreements. Plus, he knew Jewish leaders were motivated by jealousy. Pilate "knew that they had handed Him over because of envy" (Matt. 27:18). Pilate attempted to deflect the Jews and told them to judge Jesus themselves by Hebrew law. However, since they were seeking the death penalty Pilate was obligated to hear the charges against Jesus. Roman courts had sole jurisdiction over capital punishment.

Pilate told them, "Take him yourselves and pass judgment on him
according to your own law!" The Jewish leaders replied, "We
cannot legally put anyone to death." (This happened to fulfill the

word Jesus had spoken when he indicated what kind of death he was going to die.[19]) So Pilate went back into the governor's residence, summoned Jesus, and asked him, "Are you the king of the Jews?" Jesus replied, "Are you saying this on your own initiative, or have others told you about me?" Pilate answered, "I am not a Jew, am I? Your own people and your chief priests handed you over to me. What have you done?" Jesus replied, "My kingdom is not from this world. If my kingdom were from this world, my servants would be fighting to keep me from being handed over to the Jewish authorities. But as it is, my kingdom is not from here." Then Pilate said, "So you are a king!" Jesus replied, "You say that I am a king. For this reason I was born, and for this reason I came into the world—to testify to the truth. Everyone who belongs to the truth listens to my voice" (John 18:31–37).

Even in the midst of Roman legal proceedings on trumped up charges of sedition, Jesus made no attempt to seek a pardon from Pilate or to correct misunderstandings about accusations against him. Pilate's interrogation of Jesus found him innocent of any capital offense under Roman law.

Interestingly, when Pilate heard that Jesus claimed to be the Son of God it startled him; "when Pilate heard what they said, he was more afraid than ever" (John 19:8). Pilate again went to speak with Jesus:

... and he [Pilate] went back into the governor's residence and said to Jesus, "Where do you come from?" But Jesus gave him no answer. So Pilate said, "Do you refuse to speak to me? Don't you know I have the authority to release you, and to crucify you?" Jesus replied, "You would have no authority over me at all, unless it was

---

[19] Jesus foretold that he would be killed by crucifixion (John 12:32). To fulfill Jesus' prediction he had to be executed by the Romans since Jews did not use crucifixion as a form of capital punishment. Roy A. Stewart, "Judicial Procedure in New Testament Times" The Evangelical Quarterly, 100.

given to you from above. Therefore the one who handed me over to you is guilty of greater sin" (John 19:9-11).

Pilate sought to release Jesus from that point on, but the Jewish crowd shouted, "If you release this man, you are no friend of Caesar! Everyone who claims to be a king opposes Caesar!" (John 19:12). Pilate would not accept the political risk of accusations of disloyalty to Caesar. He was cornered. Pilate had no recourse but to order Jesus' execution.

Life after Death

Through religion we may seek peace of mind, perhaps a code of conduct or ethics, but more than anything else we look to religion to answer the question of what happens at the moment of death. Medical science provides no insight into what happens after the cessation of biological life. It is not intended to. Is it possible to form any logical conclusions about life after death?

The fascination with life after death is inescapable. Descriptions of near death experiences are too numerous to explain away even though they are difficult to scientifically verify. Even I have encountered a number of patients through the years who have reported near death experiences to me. Many physicians have.

There are many platitudes about life after death. *He or she was a good person* (at least more good than bad); *I'm sure they went to heaven. All religions lead to God, don't they? If I follow my religion things will be OK in the end. If I am the best person I can be, surely God will accept me into heaven. How could a loving God send anyone to hell?*

If we stand before God at the moment of death, what will he think? How does God judge humans? Will God judge mankind on our terms? The idea that God would place an individual's life deeds on some sort of scale and accept that person into heaven if the scale leans a bit more to the *good* than *bad* seems comforting. Most people would place themselves on the positive side of that scale, even if they lacked adequate basis to do so. Can we safely assume God analyzes humans this way?

It seems inherently self-evident that *a loving God would not send anyone to hell.* It may feel comfortable and politically correct to say that *all religions lead to God* and *everything will be all right in the end.* Yet, this is counterintuitive. Most religions would reject this notion and require adherence to their particular belief system. If a loving God sought to provide a remedy for Man's most primal fear, the *fear of death*, wouldn't he take a specific course of action and provide specific instructions to mankind?

Matters of faith are generally inaccessible to scientific inquiry. For this reason, many choose to abandon the study of religion. True, science is incapable of comprehensive study or quantification of the supernatural. Is this a logical basis to conclude God does not exist? To forsake the study of religion because scientific proofs are unobtainable is not a logical position. To deny the existence of God and life-after-death requires special assumptions that are unverifiable. As such, atheism is a faith-system [religion] of its own.

Jesus on Life after Death

Jesus spoke to his disciples about life after death. He assured them he would protect them at the moment of death and take them to eternal life with God in heaven.

Jesus said to his disciples:

My sheep listen to my voice, and I know them, and they follow me. I give them eternal life, and they will never perish; no one will snatch them from my hand. My Father, who has given them to me, is greater than all, and no one can snatch them from my Father's hand (John 10:27–29).

Do not let your hearts be distressed. You believe in God; believe also in me. There are many dwelling places in my Father's house. Otherwise, I would have told you, because I am going away to make ready a place for you. And if I go and make ready a place for you, I will come again and take you to be with me, so that where I am you may be too (John 14:1–3).

The prospect of eternity without God is frightening. Jesus said that it was *not believing* in him that alienated people from God. According to Jesus, eternity in hell is self-inflicted. Eternal damnation is not God's desire for humanity. Jesus said:

For this is the way God loved the world: He gave his one and only Son [Jesus referring to himself], so that everyone who believes in him will not perish but have eternal life. For God did not send his Son into the world to condemn the world, but that the world should be saved through him. The one who believes in him is not condemned. The one who does not believe has been condemned already, because he has not believed in the name of the one and only Son of God. Now this is the basis for judging: that the light has come into the world and people loved the darkness rather than the light, because their deeds were evil (John 3:16–19).

Indifference to Jesus places people on the wrong side of eternity by default. Jesus framed the decision in straightforward and certain terms. Believing in him brought God's compassion, forgiveness, and eternal life in heaven. Rejection or ambivalence about Jesus has perilous consequences.

Can Jesus Be Taken Seriously?

People will often dismissively say, "Jesus was a good moral teacher" as if to acquiesce that Jesus was a sage who made a positive contribution to philosophy. It is, of course, true that Jesus taught morality. This does not set Jesus apart, however. History has known other worthy moral teachers.

Jesus went far beyond that. His claims were polarizing and at times incendiary. Jesus claimed that he was Almighty God who became a human being and was the fulfillment of Hebrew Messianic prophecies. His purpose was to bring forgiveness to humanity. He said that faith in him was the *only* the pathway to heaven. Rejecting him sealed a fate of eternal separation from God.

If Jesus was not who he said he was, what kind of a man must he have been? Peter Kreeft framed the dilemma this way:

A measure of your sanity is the size of the gap between what you think you are and what you really are. If I think I am the greatest philosopher in America, I am only an arrogant fool; if I think I'm Napoleon, I'm probably over the edge; if I think I am a butterfly, I am fully embarked from the sunny shores of sanity. But if I think I am God, I am even more insane because the gap between anything finite and the infinite God is even greater than the gap between any two finite things, even a man and a butterfly.[20]

Was Jesus a lunatic? There is no literary evidence to suggest Jesus suffered from psychiatric illness. Jesus was hugely popular among the common citizenry. When religious leaders attempted to entrap Jesus with questions it typically ended in their embarrassment. He was not considered a lunatic, either by the Jews or the Romans. Rather, the Gospel accounts show that Jesus possessed superior intellect and organizational leadership.

Was Jesus a liar? People may lie and willfully propagate known falsehood in an attempt to gain something or to protect themselves from negative consequences. Had Jesus been a liar, the utility of doing so ceased once proceedings began for his execution. Jesus

---

[20]Peter Kreeft, *Fundamentals of the Faith: Essays in Christian Apologetics* (San Francisco: Ignatius Press, 1988), 59.www.ignatius.com. Used with permission.

did not waver or recant, however. He continued to affirm his identity to his death.

People will sometimes die for a cause they truly believe in, even if it seems misguided to others but no one persists in a lie when doing so means certain torture and death. Jesus' willingness to suffer an ignominious death by crucifixion rather than recant signifies he was not lying.

C.S. Lewis encapsulated the conundrum of Jesus and his claims this way:

I am trying here to prevent anyone saying the really foolish thing that people often say about Him: "I'm ready to accept Jesus as a great moral teacher, but I don't accept His claim to be God." That is the one thing we must not say. A man who was merely a man and said the sort of things Jesus said would not be a great moral teacher. He would either be a lunatic – on a level with the man who says he is a poached egg – or else he would be the Devil of Hell. You must make your choice. Either this man was, and is, the Son of God: or else a madman or something worse. You can shut Him up for a fool, you can spit at Him and kill Him as a demon; or you can fall at His feet and call Him Lord and God. But let us not come with any patronizing nonsense about His being a great human teacher. He has not left that open to us. He did not intend to.[21]

There are only two alternatives. Either Jesus is who he said he was, or he was morally or intellectually deranged. A careful examination of the facts is imperative.

---

[21]Clive Staples Lewis, *Mere Christianity* (New York: Harper Collins, 1980), 52. MERE CHRISTIANITY by C.S. Lewis copyright © C.S. Lewis Pte. Ltd. 1942, 1943, 1944, 1952. Extract reprinted by permission.

CHAPTER 2
HOW WE KNOW ABOUT JESUS

His life and teachings gave rise to the largest major world religion, *Christianity*. But how do we know Jesus really existed? Can we be certain who wrote the biblical accounts of Jesus' life? Aren't there a lot of inconsistencies between the different accounts of Jesus' life in the Bible? Did the information about Jesus in the New Testament morph over time and become mythological?

Orthodox Christianity derives its understanding of Jesus from the New Testament part of the Bible. The New Testament is a collection of books and letters. The first four books in the New Testament are called the *Gospels*.[22] They profess to be eyewitness records of Jesus' life and teachings. Can we trust the Gospels as eyewitness accounts?

Since the Gospels are relied upon to understand what Jesus did and taught, the integrity of the biblical texts is critical. If we cannot establish that the Gospels are uncorrupted eyewitness testimonies, an accurate understanding of Jesus becomes difficult. However, there is considerable evidence to support that the Gospels are accurately preserved eyewitness accounts. There is also evidence outside the Bible that verifies Jesus was an influential historical figure.

Evidence of the life of Jesus outside the Bible

Literary evidence exists outside the Bible confirming the historicity and influence of Jesus. Some were written by Christians. Perhaps the most interesting, however, are works of authors unfriendly to Christianity. References to Jesus and his crucifixion by those who did not revere him are perhaps the best evidence of his historicity.

---

[22]*Gospel* is derived from the Old English, *gōd-spell* meaning "good story" or good news. It was substituted for Greek word, *euaggelion* (εὐαγγέλιον), "good news." J. Warner Wallace, "What does 'Gospel' Really Mean?", ColdCaseChristianity.com, May 16, 2014, http://coldcasechristianity.com/2014/what-does-gospel-really-mean/ (accessed December 6, 2017).

Pontius Pilate

Pontius Pilate was the Roman Prefect presiding over Judea when Jesus was crucified. He became the pawn of Jewish leaders in their plot to kill Jesus. Pilate was manipulated into ordering Jesus to be crucified.[23]

Pontius Pilate is a known historical figure, attested to both in the Bible as well as in non-biblical sources. Physical evidence of Pontius Pilate as a historical figure was discovered in 1961. A stone bearing the Latin inscription, *Tiberium, Pontius Pilatus, Praefectus Judea,* was found in Caesarea, Israel, dating to the period of 26 to 37 AD. The stone appears to commemorate Pontius Pilate's dedication of a temple to the Emperor Tiberius. The temple was named *Tiberium.* The rest of the inscription further reading, *Pontius Pilatus, Praefectus Judea,* simply means "Pontius Pilate, Prefect of Judea."[24] (Image 2: *Pilate Stone*). Caesarea is a coastal city and was the local seat of Roman government in Israel during Jesus' time.[25]

Image 2 - *Pilate Stone.* The inscription reads, "Tiberium, Pontius Pilate, Prefect of Judea."

---

[23]See Chapters 4 and 6 for a detailed discussion.

[24]Joseph M. Holden and Norman Geisler, *The Popular Handbook of Archaeology and the Bible* (Eugene: Harvest House, 2013), 347.

[25]When Judea was converted into a Roman province in 6 AD, the Romans moved the governmental residence and military headquarters from Jerusalem to Caesarea. Haim Hillel Ben-Sasson, ed., *A History of the Jewish People*(Cambridge: Harvard University Press, 1976), 246-247.

Archived records are known to have existed in ancient Rome. Among them are the *Commentarii principis*, which contained communications to the Emperor from officials throughout the Roman Empire. These would have contained records of Pilate's governance in Judea.[26] In the digital age data lasts forever, but in Jesus' time written documents had a shelf-life and many no longer exist.

The Roman Empire was an extensive and intricate political machine with a well-developed legal system. Governmental records were maintained of all regions in the empire. Day to day governmental records of Pilate's political career have not survived to the present time. However, there are ancient literary references to the political career of Pontius Pilate and of his sentencing Jesus to death by crucifixion.

Publius Cornelius Tacitus (56 – 117 AD)

Tacitus was a Roman orator and senator during the reign of Emperor Vespasian. He was also proconsul or Roman governor of Asia from 112-113 AD. He wrote in his *Annals*, a 116 AD text on Roman history, that Nero blamed Christians for the great fire of Rome in AD 64 in order to dispel rumors that the fire had been deliberately set by Nero's operatives. This was Nero's justification for the mass persecution of Christians (Image 3: *The Christian Martyrs' Last Prayer*). Tacitus writes:

But all human efforts, all the lavish gifts of the emperor, and the propitiations of the gods, did not banish the sinister belief that the conflagration was the result of an order. Consequently, to get rid of the report, Nero fastened the guilt and inflicted the most exquisite tortures on a class hated for their abominations, called Christians by the populace. Christus, [Christ] from whom the name had its origin, suffered the extreme penalty [crucifixion][27] during the reign

---

[26]Gary Habermas, *The Historical Jesus: Ancient Evidence for the Life of Christ* (Joplin: College Press, 1996), 215-216.

[27] "The extreme penalty" (*summa supplica*) is a reference to crucifixion. Martin Hengel, *Crucifixion in the Ancient World and the Folly of the Message of the Cross* (London: Fortress Press, 1977), 33.

of Tiberius at the hands of one of our procurators, Pontius Pilatus, and a most mischievous superstition, thus checked for the moment, again broke out not only in Judaea, the first source of the evil, but even in Rome, where all things hideous and shameful from every part of the world find their centre and become popular. Accordingly, an arrest was first made of all who pleaded guilty; then, upon their information, an immense multitude was convicted, not so much of the crime of firing the city, as of hatred against mankind. Mockery of every sort was added to their deaths. Covered with the skins of beasts, they were torn by dogs and perished, or were nailed to crosses, or were doomed to the flames and burnt, to serve as a nightly illumination, when daylight had expired.[28]

Tacitus was not a Christian. He referred to Jesus Christ as *Christus* (Latinization of the Greek word, *Christ*) and referred to his followers as Christians. Tacitus' knowledge of Christianity would have come from communications within the Roman government. Being a Roman of high political standing, he would have had access to legal and political records, official reports, and contemporary historical literature while preparing his own historical text, *the Annals*.

Roman archives must have contained information on Jesus and his followers. Tacitus specifically refers to the crucifixion of Jesus by Pontius Pilate as well as the "mischievous superstition" of Christians, no doubt referring to the Christian belief that Jesus resurrected from the dead after being crucified. Tacitus provides a very early attestation to the historicity of Jesus and his crucifixion by Pontius Pilate, that Christians believed Jesus had been resurrected from the dead, and that Christianity had spread rapidly through the Roman Empire.

An official Roman dossier on Christianity must have been the basis for Roman perspectives on Christianity's origin, beliefs and practices. Tacitus verifies that Jesus was crucified by Pontius Pilate and that Christians were a hated minority. Making Christians out to be a group of eccentric religious heretics would be of particular

---

[28]Tacitus, Annals 15:44 in *The Works of Tacitus*, Alfred John Church and William Jackson Brodribb translators, (London: Macmillan, 1864, 1877). http://www.sacred-texts.com/cla/tac/a15040.htm. Public Domain (accessed January 8, 2018).

importance in seeking to justify their brutal mass persecution.[29] To Tacitus, as well as to other Romans, Christians would have been considered weird heretics because of their belief that Jesus had risen from the dead. Christian refusal to worship the emperor or any accepted Roman god also caused acrimony. Tacitus' pejorative reference to Jesus and his followers is compelling evidence of Jesus' historicity and influence.

Image 3 - *The Christian Martyrs' Last Prayer.* Jean-Léon Gérôme.

Justin Martyr (c. 100-165 AD)

Justin Martyr, born in *Flavia Neapolis*, was a second century Gentile convert to Christianity. He was beheaded, around 165 AD, rather than recant his Christian faith and worship Roman gods, hence his surname "Martyr."

As a Christian apologist,[30] Justin wrote in his *First Apology* to the then Roman Emperor, Antoninus Pius and his sons, explaining

---

[29]Tacitus' commentary was that the brutality of execution was "to glut one man's (Nero's) cruelty." Ibid.

[30]Apologetics is the field of Christian theology focused on presenting a logical basis for the Christian faith, answering objections and defending against theological error. *Apology*, in this context, refers to the ancient meaning arising from the Greek (ἀπολογία) meaning, "to give a reasoned defense" such as in a court of law, used with similar meaning in 1 Pet. 3:15, Acts 16:16. Strong's Concordance, "apologia," Helps Ministries, Inc., http://biblehub.com/str/greek/627.htm. (accessed December 6, 2017).

that Christianity was a fulfillment of Jewish prophecy. Justin also pointed out that Jesus' crucifixion had been foretold in Hebrew prophecy (Ps. 22:16, 18). He appealed to Caesar, asking him to refrain from persecuting Christians. He sought to convince the Emperor that Christians were model citizens and that their beliefs were valid.

Justin cites a document entitled *the Acts of Pontius Pilate,* which appears to have been a record of Pilate's governance of Judea. He asked Caesar to look for himself in official government records to verify that Jesus was an actual historical figure who had been executed by Pontius Pilate. He pointed out that the crucifixion of the Messiah by foreigners had been foretold in Hebrew prophecy (Ps. 22:16, 18). (Jews did not use crucifixion as a method of capital punishment).[31] Justin also noted that Jesus' reputation as a miracle worker was attested to in the *Acts of Pontius Pilate.*[32]

Justin wrote:

And the expression, "They pierced my hands and my feet," was used in reference to the nails of the cross which were fixed in His hands and feet. And after He was crucified they cast lots upon His vesture, and they that crucified Him parted it among them. And that these things did happen, you can ascertain from the Acts of Pontius Pilate.[33]

Advising Caesar to *look it up for himself* would be incredibly daring, if not foolhardy, if the records did not exist or if they were contrary to Justin's description of them. Justin was well aware that the very act of writing his *First Apology* imperiled his own life. We must conclude that Justin, as well as Tacitus and others, were aware of governmental records entitled *the Acts of Pontius Pilate* and their contents.

---

[31]Stewart, "Judicial Procedure in New Testament Times," 100.

[32]Josh McDowell and Bill Wilson, *Evidence for the Historical Jesus: a compelling case for his life and his claims* (Eugene: Harvest House, 1988, 1993), 22.

[33]Justin Martyr, First Apology, chapter 35, trans. Marcus Dods, (Edinburgh: Clark, 1867). Ante-Nicene Christian Library, Wikisource.org. https://en.wikisource.org/wiki/Ante-Nicene_Christian_Library/The_First_Apology_of_Justin_Martyr. Public Domain. (accessed January 8, 2018).

Ancient References to Jesus Outside the Bible

Titus Flavius Josephus (c. 37-100 AD)

Josephus, birth name *Joseph ben Matityahu*, was Jewish and initially fought against the Romans in the First Jewish-Roman war (66 to 73 AD). He later defected and became a servant of Emperor Vespasian who granted him freedom and Roman citizenship. Josephus was a historian and wrote several volumes of Jewish history primarily for a Roman audience. He was not a Christian. Josephus made two references to Jesus.

Testimonium Flavianum

What is called the *Testamonium Flavianum* is the most famous yet controversial passage in Josephus' writings.

Now there was about this time Jesus, a wise man, if it be lawful to call him a man; for he was a doer of wonderful works, a teacher of such men as receive the truth with pleasure. He drew over to him both many of the Jews and many of the Gentiles. He was [the] Christ. And when Pilate, at the suggestion of the principal men amongst us, had condemned him to the cross, those that loved him at the first did not forsake him; for he appeared to them alive again the third day, as the divine prophets had foretold these and ten thousand other wonderful things concerning him. And the tribe of Christians, so named from him, are not extinct at this day.[34]

While some consider the *Testamonium Flavianum* authentic, it has likely been tampered with in some way. Josephus went to great lengths as a defector to curry favor with the conquering Romans, including adopting part of the name of the Emperor *Vespasian*, whose full name was *Titus Flavius Caesar Vespasianus Augustus.* It is therefore counterintuitive to believe that Josephus would have

---

[34]Flavius Josephus, The Antiquities of the Jews, book 18, chapter 3.3, trans. William Whiston, (London: Blackie and Son 1866).
https://en.wikisource.org/wiki/The_Antiquities_of_the_Jews/Book_XVIII. Public Domain. (accessed January 8, 2018).

come out with such a declarative statement of Christian faith. In Josephus' time Christians were hated and persecuted.

Most scholars concur that the *Testamonium Flavanium* existed in some form in Josephus' original text, even though it appears to have been altered.[35] The importance of this passage is that it points to very early non-Christian historical reference to Jesus, whatever it may have stated in its original form.

Another reference by Josephus to Jesus is much more matter of fact and refers to the execution of James, the brother of Jesus:

Festus was now dead, and Albinus [Procurator of Judea after Porcius Festus] was but upon the road; so he assembled the Sanhedrin of judges, and brought before them the brother of Jesus, who was called Christ, whose name was James, and some others, [or, some of his companions]; and when he had formed an accusation against them as breakers of the law, he delivered them to be stoned.[36]

Josephus' account of the execution by stoning of James is generally unchallenged and considered unaltered.[37]

Josephus had no sympathy for Jesus or Christians. The *Testamonium Flavanium* may have been altered, but Josephus' reference to the killing of Jesus' brother, James, is generally uncontested. The fact that these references are present, at all, is evidence of the historicity and influence of Jesus. Josephus' *Antiquities of the Jews* was written in the 13th year of reign of Emperor Flavius Domitian around 93 AD, and within the living memory of Jesus and his disciples. Josephus' work provides very early non-Christian literary reference to Jesus outside the Bible.

[35]Josh McDowell and Bill Wilson, *Evidence for the Historical Jesus* (Eugene: Harvest House Pub, 1993) 38-43.

[36]Josephus, *Antiquities of the Jews*, book 20, chapter 9:1, https://en.wikisource.org/wiki/The_Antiquities_of_the_Jews/Book_XX. Public Domain. (accessed January 8, 2018).

[37]McDowell and Wilson, *Evidence for the Historical Jesus*, 37.

Eyewitnesses

In Peter's first recorded sermon to non-Jewish listeners, he said:

We are witnesses of all the things he [Jesus] did both in Judea and in Jerusalem. They killed him by hanging him on a tree, but God raised him up on the third day and caused him to be seen, not by all the people, but by us, the witnesses God had already chosen, who ate and drank with him after he rose from the dead (Acts 10: 39-41).

Peter stated he and other disciples were *eyewitnesses* of Jesus' life, teachings, death and bodily resurrection. The value of eyewitness testimony cannot be understated. Peter further said that he, as well as the other Apostles, were divinely appointed witnesses to testify about of Jesus' life, teachings and his resurrection from the dead.[38]

Jesus had many followers. Yet, the Gospels describe Jesus being intentional about selecting an inner circle of twelve disciples and mentoring them closely. He then commissioned them with preaching, teaching and the organizational leadership of the church.[39] Jesus was not haphazard in selecting leaders for his movement. The status of the Apostles and the authority of their teaching was recognized and deeply revered even by early Christians (Act 2:42-43).

---

[38]Jesus' inner circle of twelve disciples are also referred to as the twelve apostles. Apostle comes from the Greek word apostolos (ἀπόστολος), meaning "messenger" or" delegate." Strong's Concordance, "Apostolos", Helps Ministries, Inc. http://biblehub.com/greek/652.htm. (accessed December 6, 2017).

[39]Matt. 24:14, Mark 3:14, Luke 24:46-48, Acts 5:42

Can the Gospels be Traced to Eyewitness Authors?

Testimony of Apostolic and Church Fathers

The term "Church Fathers" refers to early Christian theologians and church leaders. They generally do not date beyond the fourth century depending on tradition. The term "Apostolic Fathers" refers to a more select group of Church Fathers dating to the first century and first half of the second century. Apostolic Fathers were one or two generations from Jesus' inner circle of twelve disciples. The Apostolic Fathers were in a position to know who wrote the Gospels.

Papias (c. 60-130 AD)

Papias was Bishop of Hierapolis in Asia Minor, modern day Turkey, who lived in the generation immediately following Jesus. He was a student of the Apostle John, one of Jesus' original twelve disciples. Papias' writings have not survived but he is quoted by other early writers. Eusebius (260-340 AD), Church Father, author and historian, quoted Papias' as stating that the Gospel of Mark was a transcription from Peter about the life of Jesus. Mark had been a close companion of Peter's and someone Peter referred to as a son (1 Pet. 5:13).

Eusebius, quoting Papias, wrote:

Mark, having become the interpreter of Peter, wrote down accurately, though not in order, whatsoever he remembered of the things said or done by Christ. For he neither heard the Lord nor followed him, but afterward, as I said, he followed Peter, who adapted his teaching to the needs of his hearers, but with no intention of giving a connected account of the Lord's discourses, so that Mark committed no error while he thus wrote some things as he remembered them. For he was careful of one thing, not to omit any of the things which he had heard, and not to state any of them falsely.[40]

---

[40]Eusebius, *The Writings of Papias*, in *Ecclesiastical History*, book 3, chapter 39. http://rbedrosian.com/Eusebius/euch3.htm. Public domain. (accessed December 28, 2017).

Concerning the Gospel of Matthew, Eusebius again quotes Papias, "So then Matthew wrote the oracles in the Hebrew language, and every one interpreted them as he was able."[41] Papias' writings provide very early documentation of the authenticity and known authorship for the Gospels of Matthew and Mark. It is thought that Matthew also wrote his Gospel in Greek to speak to a wider audience.[42]

Justin Martyr (c. 100-165 AD)

Justin Martyr gives us valuable insight into Christian worship in his time. Christian church services specifically included readings from the "memoirs of the apostles."

And on the day called Sunday, all who live in cities or in the country gather together to one place, and the memoirs of the apostles or the writings of the prophets are read, as long as time permits; then, when the reader has ceased, the president verbally instructs, and exhorts to the imitation of these good things.[43]

Justin also directly quoted the Gospel of John, "For Christ also said, 'Except ye be born again, ye shall not enter into the kingdom of heaven'" (cf. John 3:3; *First Apology* 61).[44] John's Gospel must have been in Justin's possession and read during Christian meetings. We cannot be certain what Justin was referring to as the *memoirs of the apostles*, but more likely than not he was referring to the four Gospels in the New Testament. Justin's reference to *memoirs of the apostles* denotes apostolic authority. Accordingly, they were used in Christian worship and revered as scripture just as the Old

---

[41]Ibid.

[42]Ron Jones, "The Hebrew and Greek Gospels Written by Matthew the Apostle of Jesus Christ" Ron Jones and the Titus Institute. Hebrew Gospel.com. http://hebrewgospel.com/Matthew%20Two%20Gospels%20Main%20Evidence.php (accessed 1/2/2018).

[43]Justin Martyr, *First Apology*, 67, https://en.wikisource.org/wiki/Ante-Nicene_Christian_Library/The_First_Apology_of_Justin_Martyr. Public Domain. (accessed December 28, 2017).

[44]Ibid.

Testament prophets. Justin's writings contain literary evidence that he possessed the Gospels of Matthew, Mark, Luke, and most likely the Gospel of John.[45]

Irenaeus (120-190 AD)

Irenaeus was a Church Father, scholar and apologist who was also a Bishop in what is now Lyon, France. He was a student of Polycarp, who had been a student of the Apostle John, an original disciple of Jesus. The Apostle John was in a position to verify the authenticity and authorship of the Gospels; *Matthew, Mark* and *Luke*. We must assume he passed that information on to Polycarp, who in turn taught Irenaeus. Irenaeus wrote:

Matthew also issued a written Gospel among the Hebrews in their own dialect, while Peter and Paul were preaching at Rome, and laying the foundations of the Church. After their departure, Mark, the disciple and interpreter of Peter, did also hand down to us in writing what had been preached by Peter. Luke also, the companion of Paul, recorded in a book the Gospel preached by him. Afterwards, John, the disciple of the Lord, who also had leaned upon His breast, did himself publish a Gospel during his residence at Ephesus in Asia.[46]

Irenaeus names the Gospel authors. Luke was noted to be a close friend and travel companion of the Apostle Paul. Luke's Gospel was transcribed from Paul according to Irenaeus. Interestingly, Irenaeus tells us John wrote his Gospel when living in Ephesus, Greece.

The authors of the Gospels were well-known in the first century and attributed the same as they are in Bibles today. Had the authorship of any of the Gospels been questionable or erroneously

---

[45] Michael Kruger, *The Question of Canon: Challenging the Status Quo in the New Testament Debate* (Downers Grove: Intervarsity Press, 2013) 170.

[46] Irenaeus, *Against Heresies*, book 3, chapter 1:1, in *Ante-Nicene Fathers*, Vol. 1. Translators Alexander Roberts, James Donaldson, and A. Cleveland Coxe. (Buffalo: Christian Literature Publishing Co., 1885.) https://en.wikisource.org/wiki/Ante-Nicene_Fathers/Volume_I/IRENAEUS/Against_Heresies:_Book_III/Chapter_I. Public domain. (accessed December 28, 2017).

attributed, Papias, Irenaeus, Justin Martyr, and others would have known and rejected them.

Paul's Trial before the Roman Supreme Court

The Apostle Paul said his conversion to Christianity was the result of meeting the resurrected Jesus. Paul had a specific assignment: to preach about Jesus among non-Jewish people groups (Acts 9:1-6, 26:12-17).

Paul had been a Pharisee, a Jewish religious leader, and an effective persecutor of Christians. After his meeting with Jesus he became an outspoken and prolific advocate of Christianity. Jewish leaders hated him. Paul was arrested and held in custody in Caesarea. Jewish leaders asked Porcius Festus [Roman procurator of Judea] to send Paul to Jerusalem for trial. The Jews plotted to assassinate Paul on the way (Acts 25:1-3). Paul, however, requested the venue of his trial be changed to Rome and specifically appealed to the Court of Caesar, the highest court in the Roman Empire.

Paul speaking to the Roman Procurator, Porcius Festus:

Paul replied, "I am standing before Caesar's judgment seat, where I should be tried. I have done nothing wrong to the Jews, as you also know very well. If then I am in the wrong and have done anything that deserves death, I am not trying to escape dying, but if not one of their charges against me is true, no one can hand me over to them. I appeal to Caesar!" (Acts 25:10-11).

Paul was sent to the Supreme Court of Rome. In special cases, Caesar himself presided over the court. Rome had jurisdiction over a far-reaching empire and had a developed legal and court system, including courier and record keeping capabilities. Paul was transferred to Rome under armed guard where charges against him were to be investigated and adjudicated (Acts 27:1-2).

Documents had to be prepared and submitted to answer charges against Paul. There would have been pre-trial fact-finding efforts and required documents filed responding to questions about the charges against Paul, similar to *Interrogatories* prior to modern court proceedings. Imprecise facts would be recognized and potentially harmful to Paul's defense. Moreover, falsifying data submitted to the Roman Supreme Court would have been hazardous, if not foolhardy, both to Paul and the preparer of such documents.

Luke was a Greek physician, Christian convert, and friend of Paul's. He was part of Paul's traveling missionary team beginning with Paul's second missionary journey (Acts 16:10).[47] Luke and Paul were seemingly inseparable. Luke stayed with Paul while he was held under house arrest in Rome and appears to have been Paul's only companion at times (2 Tim. 4:11). Paul referred to Luke as a "dear friend" (Col. 4:14). By virtue of his education, cultural background and close association with Paul, Luke was best positioned to prepare documents for submission to the Supreme Court.[48]

Luke wrote the Gospel that bears his name as well as the *Acts of the Apostles.* Luke's writings comprise the largest contribution to the New Testament in terms of volume of text from a single author. Both of Luke's books were written to a Roman official named *Theophilus,* the precise identity of whom is lost. It is clear that Theophilus was not a Christian. The *Gospel of Luke* and the *Acts of the Apostles* appear to be a two-volume set addressed to Theophilus, a non-Christian Roman official. Luke's writings stand out among other entries in the New Testament in that they are not written to Christians.[49]

John Mauck, in his book *Paul on Trial,* makes a compelling case that Luke's purpose of extensive research and chronicling the lives of Jesus and the apostles was to prepare a legal brief for Paul's trial before the Roman Supreme Court, and probably a hearing before Caesar himself. Mauck concludes that Theophilus most likely held the office of *cognitionibus,* a special investigator who collected information in preparation for trial, and that he was likely a member

---

[47]Paul had three missionary journeys recorded by Luke in the *Acts of the Apostles*, Acts 13-14, Acts 15:26-18:22, and Acts 18:23-20:38.

[48]It is noteworthy that the term "Christian" originated as a name for Greek converts in Antioch (Acts 11:26). Luke, a Greek physician, may have been a member of the early group of converts in Antioch and became part of the missionary team traveling with the Apostle Paul.

[49]Mark's Gospel also appears to have been written to a Gentile audience. However unlike Luke's Gospel, Mark's Gospel was written to Christians. Delbert Burkett, *An Introduction to the New Testament and the Origins of Christianity* (Cambridge: Cambridge University Press, 2002) 157.

of Caesar's *consilium*, or special advisory council.[50] Luke seems to have gotten to know Theophilus and addressed him informally in the opening of his second document, *the Acts of the Apostles* (Acts 1:1).

Luke, having more education than most and having a Gentile perspective of Jewish tradition, would have also been an obvious choice to write Paul's legal defense for Roman readership. Luke makes the case that charges against Paul were motivated by jealousy among Jewish leaders who charged that Paul was propagating an illegal religion (*religio illicita*). Luke responds to these allegations by arguing that Christianity was a sect of Judaism thus providing basis for Paul's acquittal. Judaism was a sanctioned religion in the Roman Empire and therefore permissible under Roman law.[51] Judaism was excused from the designation of *religio illicita*. Luke's writing ends with Paul in prison awaiting trial, indicating Luke wrote prior to Paul's death.

Luke affirms to Theophilus that he completed careful investigation of eye witness accounts and that his written narrative of the life and teaching of Jesus was precise and verifiable. Luke's close association with Paul afforded him the opportunity to meet people who actually knew Jesus, including James the brother of Jesus and possibly some of the other Apostles (Acts 21:17-18). Luke tells Theophilus that his documents were carefully investigated and that he could rely on their accuracy. Luke wrote:

Now many have undertaken to compile an account of the things that have been fulfilled among us, like the accounts passed on to us by those who were eyewitnesses and servants of the word from the beginning. So it seemed good to me as well, because I have followed all things carefully from the beginning, to write an orderly account for you, most excellent Theophilus, so that you may know for certain the things you were taught (Luke 1:1-4).

If Luke could establish that Christians were a sect within Judaism and part of a religion permitted by Rome, it would provide grounds

---

[50]John W. Mauck, *Paul on Trial: The Book of Acts as a Defense of Christianity*, (Nashville: Thomas Nelson, 2001), 26-28.

[51]Ibid., 113-115.

for Paul's acquittal and possibly alleviate Roman persecution of Christians. Instead, if Christianity were viewed as a new rogue religion, accusations against Paul would be indefensible and Christians would be subject to continued persecution. Stakes were high.

Luke was submitting documents to Rome's highest court. He knew that his reported facts were subject to further investigation and verification. Misleading the Roman Supreme Court would have dire consequences. Luke would have gone to great length to accurately document the events of Jesus' life and Paul's work as a Christian advocate. Luke's defense of Paul may have worked. There is some historical evidence that Paul was released from prison after trial but later recalled to Rome and eventually executed.[52]

Luke stated "many have undertaken" to compile a record of the life of Jesus. This implies that written accounts of Jesus' life existed in addition to the New Testament Gospels, according to Luke "many" of them. Luke must have collected them. Some passages in Matthew's Gospels are also found in Luke's Gospel, for example.[53] Whatever the case, Luke wrote during a time when eyewitness were still living and able to verify or refute the facts. For Luke, detailed accuracy was imperative.

True to his avocation as an evangelist, Luke did not miss the opportunity to provide his Roman readers a clear dissertation of the life and teachings of Jesus. Luke would have also understood the importance of his research to Christians. Luke's writings were known to early Christian leaders and circulated among churches. Luke's authorship of the *Gospel of Luke* and *the Acts of the Apostles* was well known prior to the time of Irenaeus. Furthermore, Luke's

---

[52]Eusebius indicates that it was traditionally held that Paul was not martyred at the close of Luke's book *Acts of the Apostles*, rather that he was released and continued preaching but was later returned to Rome and executed. Eusebius, *Church History*: L.1, C22. http://www.documentacatholicaomnia.eu/03d/02650339,_Eusebius_Caesariensis,_Chu rch_History,_EN.pdf (accessed June 14, 2017).

[53]Some hypothesize that a separate text about Jesus' life may have existed referred to as "Q" (from *Quille*, German for "source"), and that it was the source of the similar verses found in the Gospels of Matthew and Luke. If so, it is thought to have been a very early orally-derived recorded text. Richard Horsley and Jonathan Draper, *Whoever Hears You Hears Me: Prophets, Performance, and Tradition in Q*, (Harrisburg: Trinity Press, 1999) 150.

writings were considered handed down from Paul. Irenaeus considered *Luke-Acts* a two-volume set.[54] These are very early references pointing to Luke's writings being accepted with Apostolic authority and having known and verified authorship.[55]

Intrinsic Evidence of Authenticity

In the first Jewish-Roman War, the Roman army leveled and burned the city of Jerusalem in 70 AD. Jerusalem and the Temple were looted and destroyed. Yet, the siege of Jerusalem is absent from the New Testament. This is empirical evidence that the Gospels were written prior to 70 AD and within the lifetimes of the attributed authors.

The Gospels contain minor variations in detail. This would be expected of individuals writing about the same events, but separated from each other by time and location. If the Gospels were identical in every detail, it would suggest collaboration. With minor variation in detail, all the Gospels report the same overarching story of Jesus' death and resurrection. This offers further empiric evidence of their authenticity. Additionally, scribal practices and textual criticism offer evidence that the Gospel manuscripts have been transmitted through time without error.

The Temple in Jerusalem

The Temple in Jerusalem was the national center of Jewish faith and worship in Jesus' time. It took decades to build (John 2:20) and was fully completed in AD 64 [Image 4: *Herod's Temple*]. It was awe inspiring to gaze upon. It was built of marble with a succession of terraces. Josephus likened its appearance to a snow-covered mountain.[56] The Temple was renowned for large holds of precious

---

[54]Andrew Gregory, "The Reception of Luke and Acts in the Period Before Irenaeus "*Tyndale Bulletin*, 53, no. 1, (2002): 153-156.

[55]References attributed to Luke are also found in the *Didache*, a late first or early second century catechism and worship manual. Jonathan A. Draper, *The Didache in Modern Research* (Leiden: Brill Academic Pub, 1996), 126-127.

[56]Josephus, "Wars of the Jews" book 5, chapter 5:7, in *The Works of Josephus*, 708

metals.[57] Portions of the external facade were plated with gold. The gates were plated with gold and silver, except the most inner gate which was plated with brass. The outward face of the front wall was covered with gold plate, which according to Josephus, reflected the daybreak sunlight so brightly one had to turn their eyes away.[58] To say the Temple was the pride of the Jewish people would be an understatement. The Temple was the paramount symbol of national identity and the center of religious life in Israel.

The Temple had important significance in Jesus' life. Jesus was taken there eight days after birth to be dedicated to God by his parents. While at the Temple that day, the baby Jesus was blessed by a prophet and prophetess (Luke 2:25-36). When Jesus was age twelve, his parents lost track of him while traveling home after the Passover feast. (Passover marked the beginning of the week-long Feast of Unleavened Bread, collectively referred to as Passover week). Upon returning to Jerusalem to search for him, they found the young Jesus in the Temple questioning members of the Sanhedrin (Luke 2:41-49) [Image 5: *The Finding of the Savior in the Temple*]. As an adult, Jesus taught in the Temple (John 18:20, Matt. 21:23, Mark 12:35). Additionally, Jesus threw concession merchants out of the Temple (John 2:13-17, Matt. 21:12).

Image 4 - *Herod's Temple*. Herod the Great enlarged the Temple Mount to twice its previous size and built a new Temple. There were four gates in the western wall and two gates in the southern wall. The Antonia Fortress in the northwest corner guarded the Temple. Image by Dr. Leen Ritmeyer, used with permission.

---

[57]In Jesus' time it was considered binding to swear an oath by the gold of the Temple, but not by swearing an oath by the Temple itself, even though the Temple was considered God's dwelling place. Jesus rebuked religious leaders for venerating temple gold of greater importance than God. (Matt. 23:16-17).

[58]Josephus, "Wars of the Jews" book 5, chapter 5:7 in *The Works of Josephus*, 707-708

Image 5 - *The Finding of the Savior in the Temple*. William Holman Hunt.

The boy Jesus in the Temple: During religious festivals, Sanhedrin members would publicly teach on terraces by the Temple. Common citizens had the rare opportunity to listen to and question members of the Sanhedrin. In Jesus' time, at twelve he could be considered at the age of Bar Mitzvah and expected to attend Passover activities in the Temple. It would have been his first time to do so. (The traditional Bar Mitzvah age of 13 is from the Mishna which was written after Jesus' time). Attending the first two days of Passover week was obligatory but many families left after that, seemingly the case with Jesus' parents.[59] Jesus was intrigued by the Temple and stayed, unbeknownst to his parents. Not finding Jesus in their group of travelers, his parents returned to Jerusalem to find him in the Temple listening and asking questions of the Rabbis (Luke 2:41-50).

---

[59]Leen Ritmeyer, "Twelve-year-old Jesus in the Temple at Passover," *www.ritmeyer.com*. Ritmeyer Archaeological Design, April 7, 2017,https://www.ritmeyer.com/2017/04/08/twelve-year-old-jesus-in-the-temple-at-passover/. (accessed February 8, 2018).

Jesus Prophesies the Siege of Jerusalem

Two days before his execution, Jesus made a startling prediction to his disciples that Jerusalem would be surrounded by armies and destroyed. The Jews would be taken into captivity. The Temple would be completely destroyed not leaving one stone upon another (Luke 21:5-6, 20-24, Mark 13:1-2, Matt. 24:1-2).[60] Jesus' prophecy was fulfilled in 70 AD when Jerusalem was overrun by the Roman army.[61] Jerusalem was sacked and burned. The slaughter was relentless [Image 6: *The Destruction of the Temple of Jerusalem*].

Josephus was an eyewitness to the siege of Jerusalem. He wrote that so many civilians were killed that their blood stifled flames of the burning of the city. Endless killing "made the whole city run

---

[60]The Western Wall, also known as the "Wailing Wall", is a remnant of the Temple mount still standing in Jerusalem. Some question whether this is an indication that Jesus' prophecy was inaccurate, namely his prophecy that the Temple would be completely destroyed, "not one stone will be left on another. All will be torn down!" (Matt. 24:2). Actually, the Wailing Wall is part of Herod's expansion of the Temple Mount and not part of the Temple structure proper. In actual fact, the Temple was razed to the ground as Jesus had prophesied. Wayne Jackson, "Jesus' Prophecy and the Destruction of the Temple." *ChristianCourier.com*. Christian Courier Publications. https://www.christiancourier.com/articles/1302-jesus-prophecy-and-the-destruction-of-the-temple (access April 9, 2018).

[61]The Jewish War against Rome began in 66 AD leading to the catastrophic siege of Jerusalem in 70 AD. According to Josephus, the War against Rome was provoked by the brutal rulership of Gessius Florus, the Roman procurator of Judea from 64-66 AD. Israeli public frustration peaked when Florus claimed 17 talents of gold from the Temple treasury ostensibly for Caesar [At a gold valuation of $1290 per ounce current valuation would approximate $30.8 million. Hirsch, Emil G. and others, "Weights and Measures" Jewish Encyclopedia.com http://www.jewishencyclopedia.com/articles/14821-weights-and-measures#217. (accessed April 2, 2017).]. The Jews protested and appealed to Caesar to remove him. Florus was also mocked by the Israeli public which infuriated him. He commanded his soldiers to plunder an area called *the upper marketplace.* This lead to the slaughter of 3,600 men, women and children. Florus also crucified equestrian class Jewish Roman citizens which was unprecedented. The Jewish citizenry felt the consequences of War with Rome could not be worse than persisting under the rule of Florus. Josephus, *Wars of the Jews*, book 2, Chapter 14: 5,6,9 in *The Works of Josephus,* 616-617. See also, Josephus, *Antiquities of the Jews*, book 20, Ch 11: 1 in *The Works of Josephus*, 541. The War culminated in the siege of Jerusalem in 70 AD but ultimately came to a close when the Romans overran the fortress city of Masada in 73 AD. According to Josephus, all the families in Masada committed suicide rather than be captured by the Romans. Josephus, *Wars of the Jews*, book 7, Ch 9 in The Works of Josephus, 769.

down with blood, to such a degree indeed that the fire of many of the houses was quenched with these men's blood."[62] Josephus stated that ninety-seven thousand young and strong were taken away in captivity and 1.1 million civilians were killed, mostly Jerusalem residents but also others visiting for Passover.[63] The Temple was looted and destroyed [Image 7: *Remnants of the Destruction of the Temple*]. The entire city was razed.   According to Josephus, Jerusalem would have looked like a desert to anyone that had seen it previously and new visitors to the area would not have known where the city had been.[64]

In 71 AD the destruction of Jerusalem was celebrated in Rome with a triumphal parade displaying captives and the spoils of war. The celebration culminated in the execution of the leader of the Jewish uprising, Simon bar Giora.[65]   The Arch of Titus, completed in AD 82, still stands depicting the spoils from the siege of Jerusalem being brought to Rome (Image 8: *Arch of Titus*).

After the siege of 70 AD, Jerusalem no longer existed as major population center in the Middle East. Jews became a persecuted minority without a sovereign capital until Israel was reestablished as a nation state in modern times.

How is it that such a horrible cataclysmic event in Jewish history is not mentioned anywhere in the Bible? Had the Gospels been written after 70 AD the authors surely would have mentioned it. This is empirical evidence that the Gospels were written prior to the siege of Jerusalem.   It is noteworthy that the destruction of Jerusalem was the fulfillment of a prophecy from Jesus himself. Contributing authors to the New Testament would not have missed this point. It would also have been tempting for copyists to add the destruction of the Temple to the Gospels as validation of Jesus'

---

[62]Josephus, *Wars of the Jews*, book 6, chapter 8:5 in *The Works of Josephus,* 748.

[63]Josephus, *Wars of the Jews*, book 6, chapter 9:3 in *The Works of Josephus,* 749.

The number of Israelis killed and taken captive reported by Josephus are considered inaccurate by some scholars, but the net effect of the siege of Jerusalem is clearly understood. Seth Schwartz, "Political, social and economic life in the land of Israel," in Steven T. Katz, and others, eds., *The Cambridge History of Judaism. vol. 4, The Late Roman-Rabbinic Period* (Cambridge: Cambridge University Press, 2006), 24.

[64]Josephus, Wars of the Jews, book 6 chapter 1:1 in *The Works of Josephus,* 727.

[65]Richard A. *Horsley, Bandits, Prophets, and Messiahs: Popular Movements in the Time of Jesus* (Philadelphia: Trinity Press. 2000), 126–127.

prophecy. Rather, the absence of any mention of the Siege of Jerusalem or the destruction of the Temple is intrinsic evidence that the Gospels were written before 70 AD and also that the Gospel texts were not altered by copying scribes.

Image 6 - *The Destruction of the Temple of Jerusalem.* Francesco Hayez.

Image 7 - *Remnants of the Destruction of the Temple*. Excavation near the Western Wall revealed stones from the Temple that had been knocked to the street below by a Roman battering ram.[66]

Image 8 - *Arch of Titus*. The Arch of Titus shows a military parade bringing the spoils of war to Rome including gold from the Temple in Jerusalem. Note the Menorah among the spoils.

---

[66]Wikimedia Commons contributors, "File:NinthAvStonesWesternWall.JPG," *Wikimedia Commons, the free media repository*, https://commons.wikimedia.org/w/index.php?title=File:NinthAvStonesWesternWall.JPG&oldid=200746420 (accessed April 10, 2018).

What about variations in the Gospel accounts?

The Gospels vary in detail when describing the same events in some instances. For example, John's Gospel states Mary Magdalene went to Jesus' tomb on Easter morning, Luke mentions Mary Magdalene and others (some of whom are unnamed), Mark names three women (Mary Magdalene among them), and Matthew mentions Mary Magdalene and another women named Mary.[67] Minor variations in the Gospel accounts, however, do not alter the overarching story of Jesus' life and teachings.

Yet, some would take this as a point of criticism to question the validity of the Gospel accounts altogether. Such criticisms are without adequate basis, however. It would be peculiar if the Gospels were identical in every respect and did not contain some minor differences.

Separate authors writing about the same events will express individual perspectives of their recollection. J. Warner Wallace, a cold case forensic detective and one-time atheist, examined the Gospels with the discipline of *Forensic Statement Analysis*, as is done with testimonies collected during criminal investigations. Wallace concludes that the Gospels are consistent with separately obtained eye-witness testimonies.[68] If the Gospels were identical in every detail, it would be suspicious of collusion or literary corruption. Instead, the minor discrepancies in story details are exactly what would be expected from different eyewitnesses separately describing the same events.

What about Copy Errors?

Imagine a world without printing presses, copy machines or digital storage devices. Scribes were trained professionals and necessary in every aspect of life requiring a written record, from literature to legal documents. They were doubly careful when copying the Bible. Jewish scribes had a tradition of exacting precision, particularly when handling words they believed came

---

[67] John 20:1, Luke 24:1, Mark 16:1, and Matt. 28:1

[68] J. Warner Wallace, *Cold-Case Christianity: A homicide detective investigates the claims of the Gospels* (Colorado Springs: David C. Cook, 2013), 89-98.

from God. Every copy of biblical text was reviewed within thirty days and if errors were found on three pages the entire copy was discarded.[69]

In 1947 a shepherd boy found a cave west of the Dead Sea containing multiple scrolls of books from the Old Testament Hebrew Bible. The Dead Sea Scrolls date between 100 B.C and 100 A.D and include nearly every book from the Old Testament part of the Bible. The Dead Sea scrolls showed very few discrepancies from tenth century texts from which modern translations are derived.[70] For example, the Dead Sea scrolls included a copy of the Book of Isaiah which was written 1000 years earlier than any manuscript which was then available; that is, the Dead Sea copy of Isaiah was a millennium older than other known Isaiah manuscripts at the time. However, the words of Isaiah are said to be "word for word identical with our standard Hebrew Bible in more than ninety five percent of the text. The five percent of variation consisted chiefly of obvious slips of the pen and variations in spelling."[71] It is remarkable to consider that the Book of Isaiah was unaltered while being passed from one generation of scribes to the next for a thousand years.

In 1970, archeologists discovered a scroll in the Holy Ark of an ancient synagogue at En-Gedi, Israel. The scroll had been so badly charred in a fire that it could not be opened. Recently, through a complex process of computerized tomography and image reconstruction, scientists have been able to read the scroll without unrolling it. It proved to be the earliest copy of the Pentateuch (the first five books of the Bible) found in a synagogue. It dates to the third or fourth century by carbon dating, possibly to the first or second century based on paleographic indications. Like the Dead Sea Scrolls, the En-Gedi scroll is identical to the Medieval texts from which most modern translations of the Old Testament Hebrew

---

[69]Scott Manning, "Process of copying the Old Testament by Jewish Scribes," *Historian on the Warpath*. March 17, 2007, http://www.scottmanning.com/content/process-of-copying-the-old-testament-by-jewish-scribes/. (accessed February 12, 2017).

[70]Ibid.

[71]Gleason L. Archer, *A Survey of Old Testament Introduction* (Chicago: Moody Press, 1974), 25.

Bible are derived.[72] It is astounding that Hebrew scribal practices were so precise that the Bible we read today is exactly the same as what was read in the En-Gedi synagogue nearly two thousand years ago. Were early Christian scribes equally exacting when copying Apostolic writings?

Evidence indicates Christian scribes understood the imperative of copy accuracy. Eighty-five to ninety percent of the first century Greco-Roman world was illiterate. Yet, Christianity stands out among ancient religions for its proliferation of doctrinal literature.[73] Christian scribes must have understood the importance of their work to the spread of Christianity and its Apostolic teachings. The Bible even contains a greeting from a scribe, Tertius, the original transcriptionist for Paul's letter to the Roman churches (Rom. 16:22).[74] The spread of Christianity depended on the work of scribes.[75]

The New Testament is a collection of books and letters written by the Apostles to teach Christian converts. Their writings were to be copied, circulated among churches and openly read to congregants. Paul expressly directed churches to circulate his letters for public reading. Paul addressed his Galatian letter, "To the churches of Galatia" (Gal. 1:2) expressing his directive that the letter be copied and read in churches in that region. Paul likewise opens his letter to the Romans addressing "all those loved by God in Rome" indicating that copies were to be sent to all the churches in Rome (Rom. 1:7). Paul's instructions to the Colossians were, "after you have read this letter, have it read to the church of Laodicea. In turn, read the letter from Laodicea as well." (Col. 4:16). Justin

---

[72]William Brent Seales, et al., "From damage to discovery via virtual unwrapping: Reading the scroll from En-Gedi." *Science Advances*, September 2016,http://advances.sciencemag.org/content/advances/2/9/e1601247.full.pdf. (accessed September 23, 2017).

[73]Andreas Kostenberger and Michael J. Kruger, *The Heresy of Orthodoxy* (Wheaton: Crossway, 2010), 183.

[74]Ibid., 188-189.

[75]The earliest known New Testament document is *The John Rylands Fragment*, a papyri fragment containing a portion of the *Gospel of John* found in Alexandria, Egypt. It dates to between 117 AD and 138 AD. The Rylands Fragment attests to the prolific scribal activity and dissemination of New Testament literature among early Christians. By the very early second century the *Gospel of John* was circulating in Egypt. Holden and Geisler, *Handbook of Archeology of the Bible*, 112.

Martyr noted that reading the *Memoirs of the Apostles* was an integral part of church services in his time.[76]

A telling feature of early Christian scribal tradition is the use of *Nomina Sacra* (Sacred Name). *Nomina Sacra* are abbreviations used for names considered Holy. Typically, they were a contraction of the revered name using the first and last letter of the name with a line over the top (Image 9: *Nomina Sacra*). *Nomina Sacra* were most commonly substituted for the names *Jesus, Christ, Lord* and *God*. This practice was standard protocol and is almost universally observed in early Christian texts dating back to the earliest Greek manuscripts. Use of *Nomina Sacra* was not a space saving tactic. Rather, it was a uniform practice pointing to a culture of quality and reverence embraced by Christian scribes.[77] Christian scribes believed Apostolic writings were Holy. The ubiquitous scribal practice of incorporating *Nomina Sacra* from the earliest manuscripts onward indicates their long-standing commitment to flawless accuracy.

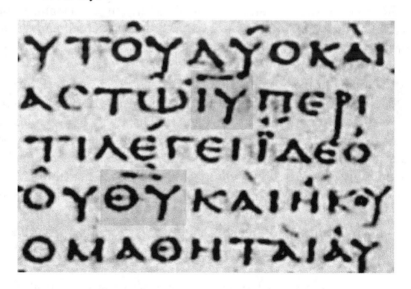

Image 9 - *Nomina Sacra*. Two nomina sacra are highlighted, ΙΥ and ΘΥ, representing Jesus and God respectively, in this passage from John chapter 1 in Codex Vaticanus, 4th century.

---

[76]See fn 43

[77]Kostenberger and Kruger, *The Heresy of Orthodoxy*, 191-192, 191 fn 51.

Is Jesus Misquoted in modern Bibles?

Bart Erhman's book *Misquoting Jesus: The Story Behind Who Changed the Bible and Why* became a *New York Times* best seller. Erhman's book title appears to have been selected for its sensationalism, which paid off commercially. Yet, the title is misleading. His premise is really not that Jesus was "misquoted," rather that variations in the texts were entered and transmitted through time by copyists, eventually damaging the stories of Jesus and corrupting the basis of modern orthodox Christian faith. As a main point, he cites two passages in the New Testament; the first being the story of Jesus writing in sand to stop a crowd from stoning to death a women caught in adultery (John 8:3-11), and the second being the longer version of the closing verses in Mark's Gospel (Mark 16:9-20). These two passages are questioned by scholars as possible later additions to the texts.[78] Additionally, he cites a handful of passages, less than 2 verses in length, in which there are differences in wording and alternate meanings in some manuscripts. These hardly support the assertion that Jesus was actually *misquoted* or that the texts were altered in a way that theologically changes the orthodox understanding of Jesus, as Erhman proposes.[79]

Erhman further notes that there are thousands of textual variations among early New Testament manuscripts. The thousands of variations reported by Erhman are not disputed. New Testament copyists would either directly copy books and letters, or copy by transcription during oral readings. There would have been abundant opportunity for error, misspelling, and word swapping from reading or listening errors.[80] Does this mean the literary connection to Jesus has been lost?

Daniel Wallace, a biblical scholar dedicated to the discipline of New Testament textual criticism, notes that Erhman's observations

---

[78]Erhman presents no new information here. Scholars are divided as to the authenticity and placement of these two passages, with varying opinions well footnoted in modern printings of the Bible. Craig L. Bloomberg, *Can We Still Believe the Bible?*(Grand Rapids: Brazos Press, 2014), 18-21.

[79]Daniel B. Wallace, "The Gospel according to Bart," *Bible.org*, April 24, 2006.https://bible.org/article/gospel-according-bart. (accessed October 23, 2016).

[80]Doug Powell, *Holman Quicksource Guide to Christian Apologetics* (Nashville: Holman Reference, 2006), 153.

of textual variation are correct, but they do not lead to the conclusions he proposes. Textual criticism is a centuries old discipline of analyzing documents when the originals are not available. Biblical texts from various regions and time periods are compared, as well as references to biblical quotations by Church Fathers. This enables logically-based textual reconstruction and validation. There are over 5700 ancient Greek texts, with fragments dating to the second century, in addition to over twenty thousand ancient transcripts in other languages. There are over one million quotations of biblical texts by Church Fathers. Wallace notes there is an "embarrassing" number of ancient biblical manuscripts, allowing an accurate and sound reconstruction of the originals in almost every verse.

Wallace categorizes textual variations in the New Testament into four groups: (1) spelling errors, (2) variants that do not affect translation, (3) meaningful variants that are not viable (dismissed as inconsistent in comparisons with early texts), and (4) meaningful and viable variants. Meaningful and viable variants do change the sense of meaning in a small number of passages, but these are rare, less than one percent of variants according to Wallace. Even so, meaningful and viable variants do not change foundational Christian beliefs.[81] (*Image 10*: Pie Graph, Quality of Variants Among New Testament Manuscripts). [82]

Wallace observes that Erhman's arguments are poorly nuanced and that he selects data supportive of his opinions without providing a comprehensive treatment of the subject and leaving out data or points of view contrary to his own. To those outside the discipline of textual criticism, it is difficult to objectively filter and assess the validity of Erhman's assertions.

However, the evidence is simply not present to establish that the

---

[81] J Ed Komoszewski, M. James Sawyer, and Daniel B. Wallace, *Reinventing Jesus: How contemporary skeptics miss the real Jesus and mislead popular culture* (Grand Rapids: Kregel, 2006), 54-63.

[82] Ibid., 63. Pie graph adapted and used with permission, courtesy of Kregel Publications. The vast majority of variants are either not viable or not meaningful. The *meaningful and viable variant* category is the smallest, most well-defined, and actually is far less than one percent. The pie graph reflects approximations of percentages of the variant categories. Personal communication, email from Daniel Wallace, Ph.D. May 2, 2018.

biblical texts have been corrupted to the point that our understanding of Jesus has been distorted. Rather, comprehensive textual criticism provides a high level of positive assurance that the accounts of Jesus' life that we have in the New Testament are intact and as written by the original authors.

Quality of Variants Among New Testament Manuscripts

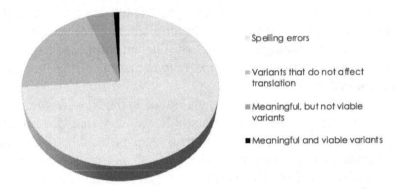

Spelling errors

Variants that do not affect translation

Meaningful, but not viable variants

Meaningful and viable variants

Image 10 - *Pie Graph: Quality of Variants Among New Testament Manuscripts.*

It is noteworthy that as earlier manuscripts of the Gospels have been discovered through time, they are found to be consistent with later texts. The earliest discovered Gospel manuscripts have failed to demonstrate wide divergence in meaning from later manuscripts. Evidence points to an accurate transmission of the Gospels to the present time; they have not been corrupted in any meaningful way since they were first written.

Erhman puts forth a *straw man fallacy*. He is less than comprehensive in his treatment of New Testament textual criticism, exaggerating the significance of textual variations when his actual aim is to invalidate the orthodox understanding of the life and teachings of Jesus.

To be sure, the Gospels are documents of faith. Their contents will always be controversial, accepted by some and rejected by others. Ehrman's arguments, however, do not provide a reasonable basis to invalidate the biblical description of Jesus. Textual criticism has failed to establish that the biblical understanding of Jesus has been corrupted through time. Ehrman himself acquiesces that "essential Christian beliefs are not affected by textual variants in the manuscript tradition of the New Testament."[83] One may choose not to believe them, but to say the Gospels state something different than what the original authors intended is unsupportable.

The bigger point is that modern translations make Erhman's argument mute. Erhman's criticisms are best leveled at older printings of the King James Version of the Bible. Today, textual variations and alternate wording of select New Testament passages are recognized and well documented. There has been no attempt to keep them secret. Rather, modern translations (particularly Study Bibles) have abundant footnotes pointing out alternate textual renderings. Variations identified through textual criticism have been fully incorporated into many current printings of the Bible.

In Summary

Jesus' life and the activity of his disciples did not occur in a vacuum. The events of Jesus' life, his crucifixion, and the testimony of his disciples were publicly well known. Jesus was a historical figure of considerable influence, well documented both inside and outside the Bible. The Gospels were written within living memory of Jesus by those who knew him best. The identities of the Gospel writers were known to first and second century Christian leaders. The accuracy of the Gospel accounts has been protected and their authenticity defended by scribes and Christian apologists from the very beginning. Textual Criticism has failed to find egregious flaws in Gospel transmission from one generation of scribes to the next. Rather, evidence indicates that the intended meaning of the Gospel writers has been accurately preserved and repeatedly authenticated through time as earlier manuscripts have been discovered.

With a reasonable degree of certainty, anyone today can pick up a modern printing of the Bible and gain a clear and accurate understanding of what Jesus' disciples saw and heard. The Gospels can be considered reliably preserved eyewitness testimony.

---

[83]Bart D. Ehrman, *Misquoting Jesus* (New York: HarperSanFrancisco, 2005), 252-253.

CHAPTER 3
THE POLITICS

The politics of any nation under foreign occupation becomes complex and precarious. The political tensions within Israel in Jesus' day were significant and can be missed with a casual reading of the Bible. Each clique and political faction had their own interests, the least influential among them being the common Israeli citizen. The ideal of Israel as a theological monarchy had been lost due to a long history of corrupt, often maniacal, political and religious leaders. The nation was further oppressed by a sometimes harsh Roman military occupation.

Common people struggled to survive, suppressed by a heavy tax burden from both their own countrymen as well as from Rome. In the midst of their struggles, however, the common citizen held on to a belief that God would ultimately free their country. How God would deliver Israel was less clear. Many believed the pathway to freedom was through armed resistance.

The Common Citizen

A small minority of people comprised the ruling class in Jesus' time. Common citizens were referred to as "People of the Land", the *Am ha'aretz* (עמהארץ), and had no particular distinction or social standing.[84] When self-aggrandizing was in order, the *Am har'aretz* were an easy target to discriminate against.

The *Am ha'aretz* were thought of as the uneducated lower rungs of society. Jesus and his followers were included. On one occasion, Pharisees ordered the arrest of Jesus but the Temple Guard failed to do so. The Pharisees chided the soldiers for being easily deceived just like the uneducated and low-class people that followed Jesus.

---

[84]Scott, *Jewish Backgrounds*, 234.

Then the officers returned to the chief priests and Pharisees, who said to them, "Why didn't you bring him back with you?" The officers replied, "No one ever spoke like this man!" Then the Pharisees answered, "You haven't been deceived too, have you? None of the rulers or the Pharisees have believed in him, have they? But this rabble who do not know the law are accursed!" (John 7:45-49)

"This rabble," the common people that followed Jesus, were considered accursed by the religious and socially elite.

Israel in Jesus time was an agrarian society.[85] The common people were typically farmers, truly *People of the Land*. No wonder Jesus often used farming parables in his teachings (e.g., Matt. 13:3-8, Mark 4:26-29). The common person's day to day life was about labor, trying to maintain the home, family, and pay their heavy tax burden.

The Romans

By the time Jesus was born, Caesar Augustus had consolidated his hold on Roman rule. Augustus was the nephew and adopted son of Julius Caesar. After Julius was assassinated in 44 BC, Augustus was able to consolidate power and secure his rule of the Roman empire through a complex sequence of events.[86] The Roman Senate had lost much of its power and became more or less window dressing to give the appearance of an ongoing republic. Ultimate authority rested with Caesar. This was not fully unwelcomed since it diminished political infighting and ostensibly restored the republic.[87]

---

[85]*Ibid.* 242.

[86]Christopher Mackay, *Ancient Rome: A military and political history* (Cambridge: Cambridge University Press, 2004) 165-169, 182-183.

[87]Ibid., 185.

Image 11 - Caesar Augustus: Augusto di Prima Porta, Vatican Museum.

Roman military might was well known and feared. Augustus had created a standing army of 150,000 legionaries plus auxiliary infantry and cavalry of 180,000 stationed throughout the empire.[88] Augustus understood that to maintain control of the empire plus seek further expansion could deplete military resources and potentially threaten the stability of the empire. He therefore recommended against ongoing imperialism and military conquest.[89] With Augustus and his policies came a prolonged period of stability known as the *Pax Romana* (Roman Peace) which lasted nearly two centuries.[90] The moniker *Pax Romana* had some propaganda-like qualities since *peace* was maintained by iron-fisted rule and depended on Roman military strength and presence.

Rome governed regions of the empire through governors or legates. Subordinate to the governors were proconsuls, typically of

---

[88]Stephen Dando-Collins, *Legions of Rome: The Definitive History of Every Imperial Roman Legion* (London: Quercus, 2010), 19.

[89]At his death, Augustus left a memorandum that his successors should be content with the boundaries of the empire and not pursue expansion the military imperialism. Mackay, *Ancient Rome*, 191.

[90]*Ibid.*

the equestrian class.[91] Augustus divided the empire into thirty-two regions (Image 12: *Map of the Roman Empire*). Politically stable regions were governed by proconsuls who answered to the senate and did not have military power. Where political instability or revolutionary elements were present, procurators (legates) governed larger regions and prefects smaller regions. Procurators and prefects had civil and military authority, were answerable directly to Caesar, and were to rule by Roman law.[92]

Whenever possible, Rome utilized local leadership. Client kingdoms, such as Israel, were allowed self-governance to a point and received Roman protection in exchange for taxation, military control and submission to Roman law as the final authority. By the time Jesus was born, the Romans had established alliances with Herod the Great and his family. Rome also exercised influence over the High Priest and the Sanhedrin.

Image 12 – *Map of the Roman Empire*, c. 117 AD.

---

[91]Owning a horse would indicate at least a modest position of wealth and social standing. The term "equestrian" became generalized to a class distinction, something like a "business-class" designation. Those of the equestrian class were restricted from advancement to the highest levels of government, however. Ibid., 186.

[92]Ibid., 183.

Herod the Great

Herod the Great ruled as King of Israel from 37 BC until his death.[93] Second to Caesar, he was the richest man in the Mediterranean.[94] He was Phoenician by ancestry, embraced Greek culture, was Roman by citizenship, but he was the King of Israel and Jewish by religion. He read Deuteronomy [the Hebrew Law] in the Temple every seven years and appointed the High Priest. He further secured his control over the High Priesthood by keeping the priestly garments in his possession.[95] He was reputed to be arrogant, calculating and ruthless.[96]

Herod was able to maintain a favorable relationship with Rome and continue to rule in Israel as monarch. He personally commanded his own multinational army estimated to be 15,000 soldiers. This allowed him to maintain cohesion and stability throughout his kingdom. As a client kingdom of Rome, Herod's army also served as auxiliary forces for the Roman army. Herod also had a praetorian guard of 2,000 men for personal security.[97]

He exhibited Stalin-like paranoia and ruthlessness. Killing anyone deemed suspicious or untrustworthy was typical. After having his first wife, Mariamme, executed Herod mourned with apparent mental repression of the facts, asking servants to search for her. He was noted to mourn for her with loud weeping. He later remarried eight times, plus kept a harem of 500.[98] Toward the end

---

[93] There is disagreement as to when precisely Herod died, but it is thought to have been in either 4 BC or 1 AD. Biblical Archeology Society Staff, "Herod's Death, Jesus' Birth and a Lunar Eclipse," www.biblicalarcheology.org, October 7, 2017, https://www.biblicalarchaeology.org/daily/people-cultures-in-the-bible/jesus-historical-jesus/herods-death-jesus-birth-and-a-lunar-eclipse/. (accessed June 22, 2018).

[94] Simon Sebag Montefiore, *Jerusalem: The Biography* (New York: Alfred A. Knopf, 2011), 89.

[95] *Ibid.*

[96] Scott, *Jewish Backgrounds*, 95.

[97] Samuel Rocca, *The Army of Herod the Great* (Oxford: Osprey pub., 2009), 9-22.

[98] Montefiore, *Jerusalem*, 90.

of his life Herod was in ill-health and suffered from progressive mental illness, perhaps dementia.[99]

The cruelty of Herod's personality is attested to in the New Testament. Shortly after Jesus' birth, three Magi inquired of Herod where the King of the Jews had been born, telling him that they had followed a star to Jerusalem to see the child. This kindled Herod's paranoia, perceiving a possible threat to familial succession to his thrown. Herod was furious after the Magi secretly departed the country without notifying him of the baby Jesus' whereabouts. Herod's reaction was to have all boys in Bethlehem under the age of two years killed (Matt. 2:1-18).[100]

Herod's pride was the Temple he built in Jerusalem. His aim was to have a legacy the magnitude of King Solomon's. Herod's Temple was a massive undertaking requiring eighty years to complete. He utilized Roman engineering and Egyptian building technology to build what became a wonder in the ancient world.[101]

Herod's Sons

After his death, Herod's kingdom was divided among his three sons. Archelaus was given rule over Samara and Judea but was replaced in 6 AD by a Roman procurator due to his incompetency and harsh dealing with the Jews. Philip, given the title Tetrarch,

---

[99]*Ibid.*, 88-89, 97.

[100]Magi, sometimes translated "wise men", and were thought to be skilled in astrology and have mystical ability to interpret omens. They often had high political standing (for example, Esther 1:13-14), and in some cases Magi were royalty. Jacob's son Joseph and the prophet Daniel functioned as Magi in their political settings and were both elevated to royal status (Gen. 41:37-40, 43 and Dan. 2:46-48). The Magi visiting the baby Jesus have traditionally been considered kings, most likely from Arabia. Tertullian believed the Magi were kings, in fulfillment of Isaiah's prophecy (Isa. 60:3,6) Chad Ashby, "Magi, Wise Men or Kings? It's Complicated." Christianity Today, August 8, 2008, Christianitytoday.com. http://www.christianitytoday.com/history/holidays/christmas/magi-wise-men-or-kings-its-complicated.html. (accessed December 28, 2017).

[101]Montefiore, *Jerusalem*, 90.

ruled over the region northeast of the Sea of Galilee.[102]

Herod Antipas, also referred to as Herod the Tetrarch in the New Testament, ruled over Galilee in the north and the region east of the Jordan River. Herod Antipas created controversy when he married his half-brother's wife while the half-brother was still living. This was a violation of Jewish law. John the Baptist publicly denounced him for this which resulted in John's imprisonment and eventual execution (Matt. 14:3-12). Jesus referred to Herod Antipas as a "fox" when he heard that Antipas was plotting to kill him also (Luke 13:32). Paradoxically, Herod Antipas heard of Jesus' miracles and wanted to meet him. Herod Antipas only met Jesus once, the morning of his crucifixion (Luke 9:7-9, 23:6-9).

The Herodians

The Gospels refer to a group called "Herodians." They are thought to have been pro-Roman Hellenistic Jews with close ties to the Herod dynasty during the time of Antipas. They may have been extended family members or cronies, and seem to have comprised a political faction or *ad hoc* political party.[103] Pharisees and Herodians had formed some kind of political alliance. At one point, Herodians conspired with Pharisees seeking a way to kill Jesus (Mark 3:6). On another occasion, Pharisees and Herodians jointly attempted to snare Jesus on the question of whether or not it was legitimate for Jews to pay taxes to Caesar. Any "yes" or "no" answer would certainly have incensed the crowd. Sensing their treachery, Jesus famously answered, "Give to Caesar the things that are Caesar's, and to God the things that are God's." (Mark 12:17).

---

[102]The term "tetrarch" indicates *ruler over a quarter*. However, Josephus records that Herod's kingdom was divided between his three sons. Josephus, *Antiquities*, book 17, chapter 11:4, in *Works of Josephus*, 473.

[103]Scott, *Jewish Backgrounds*, 208-209.

The High Priest

In Jewish tradition the office of High Priest began with Aaron, the brother of Moses, who was appointed by God himself. Succession of the High Priestly office was supposed to transition to Aaron's descendants (Ex. 29:4-9). Originally, the High Priest's office was a lifetime appointment (Num. 35:25,28). The High Priest was the ultimate ecclesiastical authority in Israel. By Jesus' time, however, the High Priest was an appointed job without regard to ancestral lineage and had rapid turnover directed by political leaders. Between 37 BC and 70 AD there were seventy-eight High Priests, typically appointed from aristocratic families.[104] Historically, the most famous was Joseph Caiaphas who was High Priest when Jesus was crucified.

In the first century, the High Priest's office was dominated by a handful of wealthy families. It was a prized position of influence and self-enrichment corrupted by greed and nepotism. Appointment was obtained by bribery. The High Priest's family could obtain enormous wealth profiting from the general population through the Temple Tax, graft, managing the concessions in the temple, stealing from the Temple treasury, taking tithes [monetary contributions] belonging to lower level priests, and profiting from the sale of skins of sacrificial animals.[105] To those in control of the Temple, opportunities for wealth seemed endless.

An estimated 300,000 to 500,000 lambs were sacrificed annually at Passover in Jesus time. Since a lamb was intended to provide for ten people at the Passover feast, it is estimated that three to five million people were in Jerusalem for the Passover festival.[106] Passover, as well as other festivals and religious services offered

---

[104]*Ibid.*, 92.

[105]Bruce David Chilton and Craig Evans, *Jesus in Context: Temple, Purity, and Restoration* (New York: Brill, 1997), 39-43.

[106]E. P. Sanders. *Judaism: Practice and Belief, 63 BCE-66CE* (London: Trinity Press International, 1992), 126.

huge potential for profit for ruling priestly families.[107]

The Sanhedrin

The tradition of a seventy member governing body of elders dates back to the time of Moses (Num. 11:16). The Sanhedrin was presided over by the High Priest. The Sanhedrin had both civil and religious authority. It had its own police force (the Temple Guard) and court system.[108]The Sanhedrin was comprised of two sects, Sadducees and Pharisees. About 80% of the Sanhedrin were Sadducees.[109] The Sadducees were more influential, but the Pharisees were considered orthodox and were more admired by the general public.

The influence of the Sanhedrin varied through time. When Herod the Great came to power, he executed forty five members of the Sanhedrin.[110]This eliminated the old nobility of the Sanhedrin and sent a chilling message of intimidation to newly appointed members. Sanhedrin influence was perhaps at its weakest during the reign of Herod the Great.[111]

Sadducees

There is no record in the Gospels of any Sadducee being sympathetic or accepting of Jesus. The Sadducees were politically well placed and had the backing of those with wealth and power. Sadducees were considered rude and argumentative. They were also more severe in rendering judgement and punishment than the Pharisees.

---

[107]Greed and corruption within the priesthood fueled Jesus' anger when driving out the concessions from the Temple. This profitable industry would have been controlled by ruling priests (Luke 19:45, John 2:13-17).

[108]Scott, *Jewish Backgrounds*, 95.

[109]Steven W. Allen, *The Illegal Trial of Christ* (Mesa: Legal Awareness Series, 2005), 39.

[110]Montefiore, *Jerusalem*, 84.

[111]Scott, *Jewish Backgrounds*, 94.

Sadducees accepted only the written law, rejecting other sacred writings or oral traditions. They also had their own beliefs and interpretations of religious protocol.[112] Sadducees did not accept the idea of an end-time resurrection of the dead, a commonly held belief in Jesus' time (Mark 12:18, Luke 20:27, Matt. 22:23).[113]

Unlike the Pharisees, they did not adhere to Jewish religious traditions outside the written law (Mark 7:3). They considered God largely dissociated from the affairs of mankind. Their disbelief in an end-time resurrection excluded any consideration of fate, eternal judgment, or anything beyond this physical life. Sadducees were also accepting of Greco-Roman culture. In short, they were religious secularists having the apparent goal of securing their position of power while maintaining their religious-political cult.[114]In Jesus' time, Sadducees had considerable influence in the Sanhedrin and were closely aligned with the High Priest, Joseph Caiaphas. Caiaphas himself was a Sadducee (Acts 5:17-18, 33).

Pharisees

In Jesus' time, there were about six thousand Pharisees. They were scholars dedicated to the understanding of the Hebrew law and oral traditions. They were generally well respected by the general public.[115] Most interactions between Jesus and Pharisees in the New Testament were confrontational with Jesus rebuking hypocritical attitudes and practices. Some Pharisees admired Jesus, however. Jesus often ate with Pharisees. At one point, Pharisees warned Jesus

---

[112]*Ibid.*, 176.

[113]Many Jews had a concept of resurrection at the end of time. However, it was unheard of to imagine a near-term resurrection from death to bodily life as reported by Jesus disciples after his crucifixion. Nicholas Thomas Wright, *The Resurrection of the Son of God*, volume 3 of *Christian Origins and the Question of God* (Minneapolis: Fortress Press, 2003), 205.

[114]Scott, *Jewish Backgrounds*, 207-208.

[115]Ibid., 203.

to leave Jerusalem, informing him of Herod Antipas' plan to kill him (Luke 13:31).

Nicodemus was a Pharisee and also a follower of Jesus. He was a Sanhedrin member, since he was described as a "member of the Jewish ruling council" (John 3:1). He initially visited Jesus secretly at night. Nicodemus' statement to Jesus was telling, "Rabbi, *we know* that you are a teacher who has come from God. For no one could perform the miraculous signs that you do unless God is with him" (John 3:2). In saying "we know," Nicodemus revealed that there was a faction of Pharisees that privately embraced Jesus' teachings.

Only two members of the Sanhedrin are directly named in the New Testament as followers of Jesus, Nicodemus and Joseph of Arimathea (Mark 15:43). Members of the Sanhedrin were unwilling to publicly endorse Jesus for fear of being excommunicated from the Synagogue (John 7:47-50, 12:42). Nicodemus and Joseph of Arimathea at some point lost their shame of affiliating with Jesus. It was Nicodemus who purchased embalming accoutrements and Joseph of Arimathea who purchased a linen shroud for Jesus' body. Together, they took Jesus' body from the cross, wrapped it and placed it in a tomb (John 19:39-40, Luke 23:53, Mark 15:46).

Scribes

As the title indicates, Scribes were originally copyists of the Hebrew law. With the destruction of Solomon's Temple in 586 BC by the Babylonians, practice of the Jewish religion shifted away from priestly ceremonies associated with the Temple to study of ethics and Hebrew law. Scribes assumed a prominent social role since they understood and could interpret the precepts of Hebrew law.[116] Their social and religious prominence persisted in Jesus' time. Scribes were looked to as experts in the law and religious

---

[116]Ibid., 60, 123.

practices.   They ranked alongside priests in terms of religious authority and understanding. In Jesus' time many Scribes were also priests.[117] Jesus frequently found himself in confrontation jointly with both the Scribes and Pharisees (Luke 11:52-54, Mark 7:1-9). Scribes evidently had social prominence separate from the Pharisees but shared similar viewpoints, particularly about Jesus.

Zealots

One of Jesus' disciples was identified as being affiliated with a political faction called *the Zealots*, namely Simon the Zealot (Matt. 3:18). The importance and influence of the Zealots should not be overlooked. The Zealot movement had a wide following. Josephus referred to the Zealots as a *major philosophical school* in first century Judaism.   His reference to Zealots being a *major philosophical school* reflects his Greco-Roman writing style for his intended Roman audience.[118]It also speaks to the prominence and popularity of the Zealot movement within Israel, something Josephus deemed to be historically important. Josephus tied the blame for the 70 AD destruction of Jerusalem to the Zealot movement.

To Roman thinking, Zealots were armed resistance fighters against Rome and therefore thought of as generic criminals.[119] To the Israelis, however, they were extreme religious conservatives. The beginnings of the Zealot faction is commonly traced to 6 AD when Judea became a Roman province and a census was mandated by Quirinius, the legate [Roman Governor] of Syria, for the purpose of determining and mandating tax quotas. Judas of Galilee and a Pharisee named Sadduk organized a rebellion, their sentiment being

[117]Ibid., 166-167.

[118]Josephus referred to four major philosophies in first century Israel; Pharisees, Sadducees, Essences, and the Zealots. Peter Schafer, *History of the Jews in the Greco-Roman world.* (London: Routledge, 2003), 110.

[119]Ibid., 109.

that Israel was a theocracy. In their minds, to pay taxes and submit to the authority of a gentile government was treasonous sacrilege since the King of Israel was God.[120]   Judas of Galilee is the only other Zealot mentioned in the Bible apart from Jesus' disciple Simon the Zealot.   Judas, however, died (presumed at the hands of the Romans) and his following dissipated (Acts 5:37).

The Zealot movement did not cease with the death of Judas, however. Two of his sons were crucified as rebels. Judas' grandson, Eleazar, was a commander at the Jewish fortress of Masada when it was overrun by the Romans.[121] The war with Rome was largely over after the siege of Jerusalem in 70 AD, but finally ended with the fall of Masada in 74 AD.[122]

Zealots were similar to Pharisees in terms of their conservative religious thinking. However, Zealots were unwilling to fold their hands and wait for God to deal with the Romans. They felt it was their divine duty to take matters into their own hands. Josephus referred to the Zealots as *sicarii* (Latin: *men armed with daggers*), literally "armed men" or assassins.[123]

Pontius Pilate traditionally granted a gratuitous annual pardon at every Passover. He offered to release Jesus. However, the crowd demanded a man named Barabbas be released instead. Barabbas was a "revolutionary" (John 18:40). He had been "imprisoned with rebels who had committed murder during an insurrection" (Mark 15:7).[124]The fact that the crowd would call upon Pilate to release Barabbas, apparently a Zealot, speaks to the popularity of the Zealot's resistance movement against Rome.

Judas of Galilee and the 6 AD rebellion against Roman taxation was still within living memory in Jesus' time. It can be assumed

---

[120]F.F. Bruce. *New Testament History* (New York: Doubleday, 1971), 96.

[121]Schafer, *History of the Jews*, 112.

[122]Ibid., 129.

[123]Bruce, *New Testament History*, 99.

[124]It was a custom that the Romans would issue a gratuitous pardon on Passover (Mark 15:6-10).

that tensions over this issue remained high. This provides some insight regarding questions posed to Jesus about paying taxes to Caesar:

Then the Pharisees went out and planned together to entrap him with his own words. They sent to him their disciples along with the Herodians, saying, "Teacher, we know that you are truthful, and teach the way of God in accordance with the truth. You do not court anyone's favor because you show no partiality. Tell us then, what do you think? Is it right to pay taxes to Caesar or not?" But Jesus realized their evil intentions and said, "Hypocrites! Why are you testing me? Show me the coin used for the tax." So they brought him a denarius. Jesus said to them, "Whose image is this, and whose inscription?" They replied, "Caesar's." He said to them, "Then give to Caesar the things that are Caesar's, and to God the things that are God's." Now when they heard this they were stunned, and they left him and went away (Matt. 22:15-22).

The memory of Judas of Galilee and his armed rebellion made their questioning sensitive and politically charged. The Pharisees and Herodians attempted to ignite anger within the crowd by entrapping Jesus. Whatever the answer, "yes" or "no", would have caused the crowd to react. Jesus perceived their trickery, however.

Because of Jesus' rapidly growing popularity and his dynamic leadership, it is easy to understand how members of the Zealot movement would be attracted him. They must have wondered if Jesus might be a leader from God, the Messiah, and the one to ultimately rid Israel of Roman occupation. Zealots would have been expecting the Messiah to be a military leader.

The Messianic Conundrum

How would you know the Messiah if you saw him? The term Messiah ("anointed one") harkens to the ceremonial anointing (pouring oil on the head) of a priest or king. The symbolism was well understood in Hebrew culture. The anointing ceremony signified a special endowment and appointment by God. It was a practice most applied to those in the office of a priest or king. Referring to an individual as "the Messiah" was uncommon, however, since it represented an appointment of profound significance. For example, Cyrus, the king of Persia, was referred to as a Messiah for his decree for the Jews to return to Jerusalem and rebuild the Temple (Isa. 45:1, Ezra 1:1-4, 2 Chron. 36:22-23).

In Jesus' time, there was the hope of a coming leader, *par excellence*, a Messiah divinely gifted by God who would lead Israel and free them from Roman occupation. There were conflicting views of who that might be, however, or even whether there might be more than one person fulfilling the mission of Messiah.[125]

The Sadducees rejected the idea of a Messiah, but many Jews in Jesus' time had the expectation that a divinely appointed leader would come. The Messiah was expected to be a descendent of David, the slayer of Goliath and Israel's most famous historical King. In the Gospels, people often referred to Jesus as the "Son of David", signifying their belief that Jesus was a descendant of King David and the Messiah (Matt. 12:23, Luke 18:37-39). Alternative viewpoints considered a possible Levitical or priestly Messiah.[126] Many thought the Messiah would have the role of a major prophet since Moses foretold that a prophet would come who would have unique and immense theological importance.[127]

John the Baptist was Jesus' cousin. He was the first person to publicly proclaim that Jesus was the Messiah (John 1:29-34). John was imprisoned for openly denouncing the illegitimate marriage of

---

[125]Scott, *Jewish Backgrounds*, 309.

[126]Ibid., 311.

[127]Moses said, "The LORD your God will raise up for you a prophet like me from among you—from your fellow Israelites; you must listen to him." (Deut. 18:15). In fact, some specifically asked John the Baptist if he were the prophet Moses foretold (John 1:21). Others wondered if it was Jesus (John 6:14, 7:40).

Herod Antipas. While in prison, John doubted. He sent messengers to ask Jesus if he truly was the Messiah (Luke 3:19, Luke 7:18-21). The duress of being in prison must have contributed to John's self-doubt about his proclamation that Jesus was the Messiah, but the lack of consensus about the Messianic promise may have added to his doubt. Perhaps John also wondered if Jesus would become a military leader, expel the Romans and become the King of Israel. Jesus responded to John by citing Messianic prophecies from Isaiah, specifically passages stating that the Messiah's public ministry would be dedicated to the poor and associated miraculous signs (Luke 7:22, Isa. 61:1, 35:5-6). Jesus offered John the Baptist spiritual reassurance by affirming that he was fulfilling Isaiah's Messianic prophecies.

The concept that the Messiah would be brutally tortured and killed was not in the thinking of most Jews in Jesus' time. Four passages in the book of Isaiah, collectively referred to as the *Servant Songs*, are widely considered by Christians as prophetic descriptions of Jesus. However, in pre-Christian times there was not a clear consensus as to who Isaiah was referring to.[128] Some considered the Servant Songs as figurative representations of the nation of Israel, while others felt the passages prophetically depicted a specific man. Yet, Isaiah's prophecy of a suffering servant in the Servant Songs seem to refer to one man.[129] However, parsing the nuances of Isaiah's prophecies would have been the domain of theologians of Jesus' day. Thus, a valiant Messiah who would vanquish the Romans must have been the most popular Messianic hope of the common Israeli.

Isaiah's Servant Songs present a strange prophetic dichotomy. They point to a man, a humble servant of God, who is blessed and exalted by God. Yet, he is despised and tortured by men, described

---

[128]The Servant Songs of Isaiah; Isa. 42:1-4, 49:1-7, 50:4-11, and 52:13-53:12.

[129]Isa. 52:13 through 53:12 refers to the suffering of one man through whom the sins of humanity were forgiven.

as a Man of Sorrow acquainted with grief and pain. Ultimately, he was killed for the transgressions of others yet he himself was personally blameless. Through his suffering and death came healing and forgiveness.

Jesus' followers were blind to the concept of a suffering Messiah (Mark 9:31-32). To be sure, Israelis in Jesus' time were hoping for a Messiah and anticipated that he would liberate them from Roman occupation. Actually, the disciples bickered among themselves as to who would have the best appointments when Jesus set up his new government in Israel (Mark 9:34, Matt. 20:20-24). In another example of the disciples lack of insight, Jesus walked and talked with two disciples traveling to the town of Emmaeus later on the day of his resurrection:

Then he [Jesus] said to them, "What are these matters you are discussing so intently as you walk along?" And they stood still, looking sad. Then one of them, named Cleopas, answered him, "Are you the only visitor to Jerusalem who doesn't know the things that have happened there in these days?" He said to them, "What things?" "The things concerning Jesus the Nazarene," they replied, "a man who, with his powerful deeds and words, proved to be a prophet before God and all the people; and how our chief priests and rulers handed him over to be condemned to death, and crucified him. But we had hoped that he was the one who was going to redeem Israel. Not only this, but it is now the third day since these things happened. Furthermore, some women of our group amazed us. They were at the tomb early this morning, and when they did not find his body, they came back and said they had seen a vision of angels, who said he was alive. Then some of those who were with us went to the tomb, and found it just as the women had said, but they did not see him." So he said to them, "You foolish people—how slow of heart to believe all that the prophets have spoken! Wasn't it necessary for the Christ to suffer these things and enter into his glory?" Then beginning with Moses and all the prophets, he interpreted to them the things written about himself in all the scriptures (Luke 24:17-27).

Cleopas stated that he as well as other followers of Jesus "had hoped that he [Jesus] was the one who was going to redeem Israel." They believed Jesus was the Messiah but thought that he would liberate the Jews from Roman domination and reestablish Israel as a theocratic nation state. The concept of a suffering Messiah was unimaginable. It was Jesus himself who taught Cleopas and his companion that the Messiah would suffer torture and death. Cleopas went immediately to tell the other disciples of their meeting with Jesus and what he told them.

The disciples simply could not let go of the expectation that Jesus would establish a theocracy in Israel and free them from the Romans. Moments before Jesus ascended into Heaven the disciples asked, "Lord, is this the time when you are restoring the kingdom to Israel?" (Acts 1:6). Meeting the resurrected Jesus convinced them that he was the Messiah. It must have seemed obvious that the Messiah would now emerge as the military and political leader of Israel. The greater significance of Jesus' role as the Messiah was not yet fully understood.

In Summary

In Jesus' time Israel was a hot bed of political unrest. The political players were many. Jewish rulers walked a tightrope to maintain favor with Rome, quell local unrest, and preserve their positions of power and wealth. Someone like Jesus, a charismatic young leader with a meteoric rise in popularity, could be seen as a threat to the political balance. If Rome came to believe Jesus' popularity represented a threat of insurgency, they would act with swift and overpowering force.

Discontent within the general population fueled hope for a Messianic deliverer and made the political climate potentially volatile. Beliefs about who the Messiah was may have varied, but the unifying expectation was that the Messiah would free Israel from Roman occupation.

A growing public consensus that Jesus could be that Messiah made those in the Israeli religious-political hierarchy nervous. Jesus' popularity was growing at an alarming rate, "...the Pharisees said to one another, 'You see that you can do nothing. Look, the world has run off after him!'" (John 12:19). At one point, Jesus had to escape to nearby mountains to keep the crowds from forcibly crowning him King of Israel (John 6:15). Killing Jesus seemed necessary to preserve the *status quo*. At least, that was the conclusion of the Sanhedrin.

So the chief priests and the Pharisees called the council together and said, "What are we doing? For this man is performing many miraculous signs. If we allow him to go on in this way, everyone will believe in him, and the Romans will come and take away our sanctuary and our nation." Then one of them, Caiaphas, who was high priest that year, said, "You know nothing at all! You do not realize that it is more to your advantage to have one man die for the people than for the whole nation to perish" (John 11:47-50).

So from that day they planned together to kill him (John 11:53).

CHAPTER 4
THE MURDER CONSPIRACY

What motivated a group of Jewish religious leaders to conspire to kill Jesus? Why didn't they kill Jesus themselves instead of involving Roman authorities?

Fear of Insurgency

Jewish court proceedings shortly after Jesus' crucifixion give insight into what Jewish leaders thought about Jesus and his followers. Jesus' disciples Peter and John were arrested and warned by the Sanhedrin to stop preaching that Jesus was the Messiah and that he had risen from the dead. Peter and John refused to stop, however (Acts 4:18). After being released, they again went to the Temple to continue preaching. Peter and John were arrested a second time and again brought before the Sanhedrin:

When they had brought them, they stood them before the council, and the high priest questioned them, saying, "We gave you strict orders not to teach in this name. Look, you have filled Jerusalem with your teaching, and you intend to bring this man's blood on us!" But Peter and the apostles replied, "We must obey God rather than people. The God of our forefathers raised up Jesus, whom you seized and killed by hanging him on a tree. God exalted him to his right hand as Leader and Savior, to give repentance to Israel and forgiveness of sins. And we are witnesses of these events, and so is the Holy Spirit whom God has given to those who obey him." Now when they heard this, they became furious and wanted to execute them. But a Pharisee whose name was Gamaliel, a teacher of the law who was respected by all the people, stood up in the council and ordered the men to be put outside for a short time. Then he said to the council, "Men of Israel, pay close attention to what you are

71

about to do to these men. For some time ago Theudas rose up, claiming to be somebody, and about four hundred men joined him. He was killed, and all who followed him were dispersed and nothing came of it. After him Judas the Galilean arose in the days of the census, and incited people to follow him in revolt. He too was killed, and all who followed him were scattered. So in this case I say to you, stay away from these men and leave them alone, because if this plan or this undertaking originates with people, it will come to nothing, but if it is from God, you will not be able to stop them, or you may even be found fighting against God." He convinced them, and they summoned the apostles and had them beaten. Then they ordered them not to speak in the name of Jesus and released them (Acts 5:27-40).

Gamaliel was a highly revered Pharisee, doctor of the Law, and president of the Sanhedrin.[130] He is mentioned twice in the New Testament, first at the above noted hearing of Peter and John before the Jewish high court, the Sanhedrin. Secondly, the Apostle Paul identified Gamaliel as his mentor when Paul himself was training to become a Pharisee. As a young Pharisee, Paul severely persecuted Christians to the point of death (Acts 9:1-3). Gamaliel may not have shared Paul's prior intense hatred for Christians, but we must assume he had no sympathy for them either.

Gamaliel's comments about Peter and John are telling. To Gamaliel, Jesus and his followers were comparable to two prior political insurgent groups. Judas of Galilee, as noted previously in

---

[130]Gamaliel I, having the title *Rabban Gamliel ha-zaqen*, came from a family of high religious standing in the Hebrew world of his time. There are also historical references to Gamaliel external to the Bible. He was a Pharisee and doctor of the Law. His title *Rabban* (our Rabbi) indicates his renown as a teacher that that he was the president of the Sanhedrin. Solomon Schechter and Wilhelm Bacher, "Gamaliel I", *Jewish Encyclopedia*, http://www.jewishencyclopedia.com/articles/6494-gamaliel-i (accessed January 12, 2017). See also, Risto Santala, "Paul's Childhood Education," *www.RistoSantala.com*.http://www.ristosantala.com/rsla/Paul/paul05.html. (accessed February 2, 2017).

Chapter 3, was a Zealot who led armed resistance against Rome. Little is known about Judas other than he died and his movement dissolved. Gamaliel's comments suggest Judas died at the hands of the Romans. Theudas, according to Gamaliel, also led an uprising but he was killed and his followers dispersed.[131]

The insurgent groups of both Judas of Galilee and Theudas dissipated after the deaths of their leaders. Jesus' religious movement was ostensibly decapitated by his crucifixion. Gamaliel's expectation was that his followers would dissipate and that Jesus' movement would no longer exist. However, he did voice the disclaimer that if perhaps Jesus' movement was from God, there was no point in fighting against it. Gamaliel was thus able to quell the anger of the Sanhedrin members who wanted to kill Peter and John. Gamaliel's words carried a great deal of weight within the Sanhedrin.

Gamaliel gives us historical commentary of what Jewish leaders thought about Jesus and his disciples. Jewish leaders knew the Romans would deal with any perceived insurgent group as they had with others, with lethal force.

We can surmise the Sanhedrin feared that Jesus' growing popularity might look like a rising insurgent movement and invite the wrath of the Roman military. The Sanhedrin's fears of Roman military intervention were relieved by Jesus' crucifixion. They expected killing Jesus would disband his followers and end his religious movement.

---

[131]Josephus refers an individual named Theudas who was a religious charlatan, described as a "magician", that developed a following by claiming to be a prophet. He was beheaded by the Romans and his remains displayed in Jerusalem. The Theudas referred to by Gamaliel, and the person mentioned by Josephus do not match chronologically and are separate individuals if the dates sited by Josephus are accurate. Josephus, *Jewish Antiquities* book 20, chapter 5:1, in *The Works of Josephus*, 531.

Joseph Caiaphas – Chief Antagonist

Caiaphas married the daughter of Annas, the High Priest prior to Caiaphas. He would have been a person of wealth and high social position to be able to do so. Caiaphas was appointed High Priest by Valerius Gratus, the Roman prefect of Judaea before Pontius Pilate. Caiaphas must have been adept at political maneuvering. He was retained as High Priest when Pontius Pilate succeeded Valerius Gratus as prefect of the region and was the longest serving High priest in the first century, from 18-37 AD. He was succeeded by his brother-in-law, Jonathan, a son of Annas. Caiaphas and the family of Annas represented a Jewish religious-political dynasty. As a Sadducee, Caiaphas embraced a largely secular view of his position and aimed to protect a symbiotic relationship with Roman governors.

What the Romans thought of Jesus' growing movement was a major concern to Caiaphas. He worried that Rome would perceive Jesus as the leader of a brewing insurrection and act in a punitive and overpowering way to disband the movement. Caiaphas feared Roman martial law and the loss of the Temple in Jerusalem. Jesus' growing popularity and reports that he was performing miracles were points of discussion within the Sanhedrin:

So the chief priests and the Pharisees called the council together and said, "What are we doing? For this man is performing many miraculous signs. If we allow him to go on in this way, everyone will believe in him, and the Romans will come and take away our sanctuary and our nation." Then one of them, Caiaphas, who was high priest that year, said, "You know nothing at all! You do not realize that it is more to your advantage to have one man die for the people than for the whole nation to perish." (Now he did not say this on his own, but because he was high priest that year, he prophesied that Jesus was going to die for the Jewish nation, and not for the Jewish nation only, but to gather together into one the children of God who are scattered.) So from that day they planned together to kill him (John 11:47-53).

Caiaphas makes a macabre prediction, "You know nothing at all! You do not realize that it is more to your advantage to have one man die for the people than for the whole nation to perish" (John 11:49-50). To Jesus' disciple John, Caiaphas' statement was an unintended double-meaning prophecy having spiritual significance. To John, Caiaphas made an unwitting prophecy that God's forgiveness would come to people of all nations through Jesus' crucifixion. In Caiaphas' mind, however, the death of Jesus would disband his movement. Caiaphas' social position and personal wealth depended on maintaining the political *status quo*. One thing is clear, Caiaphas' intention from that day forward was to have Jesus put to death. Some within the Sanhedrin colluded with him.

Image 13 - *Christ Healing the Blind.* El Greco. Large crowds followed Jesus because of his miraculous cures (Matt. 4:23-25).

Herod's Temple – the Cash Prize

Herod's Temple had a total area of 144,000 square meters, more than the size of twenty six football fields.[132] (Image 4: *Herod's Temple*). A wonder of the ancient world, it was Herod the Great's legacy to himself. More than just the center of Jewish culture and religious life, it was the national financial repository. The wealth of the nation had been stockpiled in the Temple under the auspices of religion. The treasury also served as the national banking system and included the savings of widows and orphans. Tons in precious metal holdings were contained in the Temple and its treasury. A reference in the Dead Sea Scrolls named the precious metal holdings at 4500 talents, possibly equaling as much as 100,000 kilograms.[133] Temple assets would have represented billions of U.S. dollars in modern purchasing power.

The significance of the Temple as a place of worship became eclipsed by the precious metal holdings within the Temple. This angered Jesus. He chided the Pharisees:

Woe to you, blind guides, who say, 'Whoever swears by the temple is bound by nothing. But whoever swears by the gold of the temple is bound by the oath.' Blind fools! Which is greater, the gold or the temple that makes the gold sacred? (Matt. 23:16-17).

In addition to precious metal holdings, transactions occurring in the Temple generated enormous cash flow. The Temple collected tax and served as a depository for monetary collections and religious donations from the general public. There was a money exchange

---

[132]Crandall University Staff, "The Jerusalem Temple and the New Testament, " *www.mycrandall.ca*. Crandall University, November 6, 2014, http://www.mycrandall.ca/courses/ntintro/jerusaltempl4.htm. (accessed January 31, 2017).

[133] Louis Feldman, "Financing the Colosseum" *Biblical Archaeology Review*, 27, no. 4. (2001): 31.

business to convert foreign money to Israeli currency which then enabled purchases from concessions within the Temple itself. Millions of people visited the Temple annually to worship in various rituals and festivals. Hundreds of thousands of animals were sacrificed each year, creating another source of revenue by selling the hides. It can be assumed that graft and corruption were present on many levels. Jesus was aware of the corruption within the Temple (Luke 19:46, Matt. 21:13).

At the head of all this were the chief priests, the Sanhedrin, and most importantly the High Priest as the supreme religious leader. Those in authority benefited from Temple business. Understandably, they would seek to preserve their social position and maintain the tenuous peace between Rome and Israel. To Caiaphas, the death of one man was a small concession in order to protect his personal wealth, political status and avert Roman martial law.

The monetary holdings of the Temple were immense. If Rome impounded Temple assets it would be an enormous blow to Israeli patriotism and irreparable financial injury to the nation. Stakes were high.

Caiaphas' concerns that Rome would seize the Temple were justified. His fears were later realized in 70 AD at the Siege of Jerusalem. The Arch of Titus in Rome depicts a military parade bringing home the spoils of war including treasure from the Temple (Image 8: *Arch of Titus*). Josephus stated that "heaps" of treasure were carried in the parade and that "above all stood out those captured in the Temple in Jerusalem." According to Josephus, gold taken from the Temple glutted the market in Rome to the point that the market price of gold decreased by 50%.[134]

There is archeological evidence that the spoils from the siege of

---

[134]Leen Ritmeyer, "The 'Gold of the Temple' and Financing the Colosseum 1," *thelampstand.com.au*. The Lampstand, 22 no. 4, July 6, 2016, https://thelampstand.com.au/the-gold-of-the-temple-and-financing-the-colosseum1/. (accessed February 7, 2018).

Jerusalem helped finance the construction of the Colosseum in Rome in 72 AD. Originally named *Amphitheatrum Flavium,* the Colosseum is the largest amphitheater ever built and a wonder of the ancient world.[135] (Image 14: *Pollice Verson*).

The original dedication plaque of the Colosseum had bronze letters held in marble by pegs. The letters were later removed and overwritten with a carved inscription, *the Lampadius inscription,* after renovations in the fifth century.[136] Phantom images of the original inscription have been deciphered and reconstructed which read, *Imp. T. Caes. Vespasianus Aug. Amphitheatrum Novum Ex Manubis Fieri Iussit.* Translated, "The Emperor Caesar Vespasian Augustus ordered the new amphitheatre to be made from the (proceeds from the sale of the) booty."[137] This must have referred to the spoils of war commemorated in the adjacent Arch of Titus, loot from the siege of Jerusalem chief among them. (Image 15: *Colosseum Dedication Plaque*).

---

[135] Stefan Anitei, "Colosseum, the Largest Amphitheater," *softpedia.com.* Softpedia News. April 2, 2008. http://news.softpedia.com/news/Colosseum-the-Largest-Amphitheater-82326.shtml. (accessed March 30, 2018).

[136] Leen Ritmeyer, "The 'Gold of the Temple' and Financing the Colosseum 1," *thelampstand.com.au.* The Lampstand, 22 no. 4, July 6, 2016, https://thelampstand.com.au/the-gold-of-the-temple-and-financing-the-colosseum1/. (accessed February 7, 2018). Lampdius was the Roman prefect who completed the renovations of the Colosseum.

[137] Louis Feldman, "Financing the Colosseum," *Biblical Archeology Review,* 27, no. 4 (2001): 20-31, 60-61.

Image 14 – *Pollice Verson* (thumb turned down). Jean-Léon Gérôme, 1872. Colosseum: Initially called *Amphitheatrum Flavium*, the Colosseum seated over 50,000 people and was a major entertainment venue in the center of Rome for over four centuries. Admission was free. Spectacular shows could include trained animals from all over the world. More often, games were characterized by violence and bloodshed. Historic battles were reenacted, plus the floor could be flooded to simulate maritime battles using ships. Games and war time reenactments were not make believe. Thousands died during such performances. Gladiators would fight to the death in groups or man to man, sometimes man versus animals.[138] Crowds determined the fate of a defeated gladiator with a "turn of the thumb."[139] Condemned prisoners and Christians were executed for entertainment. Notably, St. Ignatius of Antioch was fed to lions in the Colosseum on December 20, 107 AD.[140]

---

[138] Durant, *Caesar and Christ*, 383-387.

[139] Juvenal, G.G. Ramsay trans. *Satires of Juvenal* (London: William Heinemann, 1918), 3.34-37. Harhttps://en.wikisource.org/wiki/Juvenal_and_Persius/The_Satires_of_Juvenal/Satire_3. (accessed March 29, 2018).

[140] Alphonsus de Ligouri, "St. Ignatius of Antioch," *Roman Catholic Saints*. Catholic Vitality Publications. http://www.roman-catholic-saints.com/st-ignatius-of-antioch.html. (accessed March 29, 2018).

Image 15 - *Colosseum Dedication Plaque.* The original dedication plaque read, "The Emperor Caesar Vespasian Augustus ordered the new amphitheatre to be made from the (proceeds from the sale of the) booty." Peg holes from the bronze letters of the original inscription are still visible in the marble. Photo by Kathleen Ritmeyer, used with permission.

Jesus Arrested

As much as religious leaders wanted to kill Jesus, they feared backlash from the general public. A cloak and dagger assassination would be difficult if not impossible. It was also important that the plot remained secret. Jesus was so popular that openly arresting him could cause rioting.

Then the chief priests and the elders of the people met together in the palace of the high priest, who was named Caiaphas. They planned to arrest Jesus by stealth and kill him. But they said, "Not during the feast, so that there won't be a riot among the people"(Matt. 26:3-5).

The Chief Priests were happy to bribe Judas Iscariot, one of Jesus' disciples, who agreed to take Temple Guards [the Sanhedrin's police] to a private meeting place frequented by Jesus and his disciples. Jesus could then be arrested without public knowledge.

Now the Feast of Unleavened Bread, which is called the Passover, was approaching. The chief priests and the experts in the law were trying to find some way to execute Jesus, for they were afraid of the people. Then Satan entered Judas, the one called Iscariot, who was one of the twelve. He went away and discussed with the chief priests and officers of the temple guard how he might betray Jesus, handing him over to them. They were delighted and arranged to give him money. So Judas agreed and began looking for an opportunity to betray Jesus when no crowd was present (Luke 22:1-6).

The murder plot was set in motion. The events after Jesus' arrest are described in detail in Chapter 6, *The Execution of Jesus.*

Why didn't the Jews kill Jesus?

The Sanhedrin, the Jewish high court, had lost capital authority by the time Jesus rose to public prominence (John 18:31).[141] Rome seems to have been reluctant to interfere with matters of religious disagreement. For example, Pilate gave the Jews permission to judge Jesus by Hebrew law (John 18:31). Stephen, the first Christian martyr, was slain by an angry mob for his faith without

---

[141]During Roman occupation, Jews were not restricted in adjudicating religious matters leading to excommunication. Additionally, they had authority for corporal punishment, scourging for example, to anyone other than Roman citizens. However, it is thought that the Sanhedrin lost capital authority in 6 AD when Israel became a Roman province, although exactly when Israel lost capital authority not known with certainty. Stewart, "Judicial Procedure in New Testament Times," 95.

record of Roman retribution (Acts 7:58-60).[142] Rome seemed willing to look the other way when it came to religious conflicts among the Jews. Still, Rome maintained final and absolute control over judicial proceedings and capital punishment.

It was problematic for the Jews to execute Jesus. A clear cut conviction of capital crimes didn't seem possible due to a lack of credible witnesses (Matt. 26:59-60). Secondly, they feared public backlash if they killed Jesus. Finally, an unauthorized trial and execution by the Sanhedrin was certain to attract the ire of Roman authorities.[143]

There was not an absolute impasse to the Jews executing Jesus themselves, however. Permission could be granted for the Sanhedrin to try Jesus by Hebrew law and execute him. Such permission was, in fact, granted. Pilate told the Jews, "Take him yourselves and pass judgment on him according to your own law!" (John 18:31). Pilate further stated, "You take him and crucify him! Certainly I find no reason for an accusation against him!"(John 19:6). (Jews did not use crucifixion as a form of execution).[144] Pilate had granted authority to the Jews to try Jesus by Hebrew law and execute him.

Clearing the way for the Sanhedrin to try and execute Jesus under

---

[142]Stephen's hearing before the Sanhedrin degenerated into spontaneous stoning of Stephen by mob action (Acts 7:57). While having the appearance of an unauthorized trial, the stoning of Stephen was spontaneous mob action rather than orderly adjudication and execution by court edict. This could have only been controlled by Roman military presence at the scene. Incidentally, the killing of Stephen marks the beginning of severe persecution of Christians in Jerusalem causing many to flee the city (Acts 8:1).

[143]Josephus records that the High Priest Ananus assembled the Sanhedrin, tried and executed James, the brother of Jesus, without the awareness of Roman authorities. This angered the Roman procurator, Ablinus, leading to Ananus being relieved of his position as High Priest, as well placing him at risk of Roman punishment. Josephus, *Antiquities of the Jews*, Book 20, Chapter 9:1, in *The Works of Josephus*, 539-540.

[144]Jews did not execute criminals by crucifixion. Accepted forms or capital punishment from the Pentateuch were stoning, burning, decapitation, with strangulation later added as an accepted method. Stewart, "Judicial Procedure in New Testament Times," 100. The typical Jewish method of execution for blasphemy was stoning (Lev. 24:13-15).

Hebrew law did not make it any easier for the Sanhedrin. Jesus had a huge following. Thousands would come to listen to him speak. Many felt Jesus was the Messiah, the soon-to-be King of Israel (Luke 19:35-38, John 6:14-15). Inciting mob unrest was an unacceptable risk, particularly during the heightened Roman military presence during the Passover festival.

Furthermore, Roman permission to execute Jesus did not automatically mean Jesus could be executed from the standpoint of Hebrew law. Legal requirements for conviction of a capital crime were well defined in Hebrew law. Testimony was required from a minimum of two, better three, eyewitnesses of the capital offense (Deut. 17:6). Circumstantial evidence or testimony from a single eyewitness was not sufficient. The Sanhedrin had tried to gather testimony for capital charges against Jesus but were unsuccessful.

The chief priests and the whole Sanhedrin were looking for evidence against Jesus so that they could put him to death, but they did not find anything. Many gave false testimony against him, but their testimony did not agree (Mark 14:55-56).

The chief priests and the whole Sanhedrin were trying to find false testimony against Jesus so that they could put him to death. But they did not find anything, though many false witnesses came forward (Matt. 26:59-60).

Legitimate execution of Jesus through the Jewish court system did not seem possible. Even if trumped up charges were possible, railroading Jesus through court proceedings with corrupt witnesses and executing him would cause public outrage. Roman execution of Jesus on charges of sedition was a much better option for Caiaphas and the Sanhedrin members colluding with him.

Engaging the Roman Legal System

Pontius Pilate lived in Caesarea, a coastal harbor. The city was built by Herod the Great and named in honor of Caesar. It was a shipping center for the region, headquarters city for the Roman government and military, and the Roman capital in the province of Judea.[145]Culturally and geographically, Caesarea was a preferred place to live compared to Jerusalem from the Roman point of view.

Passover is the most observed Jewish Holiday. In Jesus' time, an estimated three to five million people came to Jerusalem during Passover.[146]Pilate came to Passover for a show of Roman strength and to openly discourage any thoughts of unrest. Roman presence in Jerusalem during Passover made for opportune timing to bring charges against Jesus before Pontius Pilate.

Jesus and Pilate

Pilate had no interest in Jesus. His attempts to recuse himself from the case were rejected by Jewish religious leaders, however. They were unrelenting in their demand that Pilate try Jesus on charges of sedition, a capital crime.

Jesus had been arrested, interrogated by Caiaphas and beaten by Jewish leaders during the night without public knowledge. He was brought to Pilate early the following morning. The general public was seemingly unaware that Jesus had been arrested. Thus, the crowd assembled before Pilate that morning was biased against Jesus. They had been influenced and "stirred up" by the Chief Priests (Mark 15:11). It may be that those within the crowd were paid operatives planted by the Sanhedrin. Whatever the case, the multitudes that admired Jesus were seemingly unaware of the legal

---

[145]Editors of Encyclopaedia Britannica, "Caesarea: Ancient City, Israel", *www.britannica.com*. February 18, 2015, https://www.britannica.com/place/Caesarea. (accessed January 23, 2017).

[146]Sanders. *Judaism: Practice and Belief,* 126.

proceedings against him and his impending execution.

Pilate was amazed that Jesus refused to answer the false allegations from the Chief Priests (Matt. 27:12-14). He knew that the charges were motivated by envy among the Chief Priests (Matt. 27:18). In spite of this, Pilate still interrogated Jesus as to whether he had intentions of insurrection.

So Pilate went back into the governor's residence, summoned Jesus, and asked him, "Are you the king of the Jews?" Jesus replied, "Are you saying this on your own initiative, or have others told you about me?" Pilate answered, "I am not a Jew, am I? Your own people and your chief priests handed you over to me. What have you done?" Jesus replied, "My kingdom is not from this world. If my kingdom were from this world, my servants would be fighting to keep me from being handed over to the Jewish authorities. But as it is, my kingdom is not from here." Then Pilate said, "So you are a king!" Jesus replied, "You say that I am a king. For this reason I was born, and for this reason I came into the world—to testify to the truth. Everyone who belongs to the truth listens to my voice." Pilate asked, "What is truth?" When he had said this he went back outside to the Jewish leaders and announced, "I find no basis for an accusation against him..." (John 18:33-38).

Jesus expressly stated to Pilate that he was a King but in an *otherworldly* sense. Romans were superstitious and intensely religious. Pilate would have understood their conversation from a religious and philosophical perspective. He even responded to Jesus in rhetorical language ending their conversation by saying, "What is truth?" (Image 16: *Quod Est Veritas?*). He then announced to the crowd, "I find no basis for an accusation against him."

Pilate's wife had nightmares about Pilate's dealings with Jesus and asked him to recuse himself from the case (Matt. 27:19). Whether Pilate was motivated by superstition or desires for ethical adjudication, he sought to release Jesus. Even though he knew Jesus was innocent, Pilate was a shrewd and practical politician whose actions were calculated. Political expediency would ultimately rule the day.

It is noteworthy that neither Pilate, Caiaphas nor the Sanhedrin dealt with Jesus as if he were a lunatic. To Caiaphas and the Chief Priests, Jesus represented a threat to their way of life. They also envied his popularity. Pilate recognized Jesus was an innocent man and that Jewish leaders were motivated by jealousy.

Image 16 - *Quod Est Veritas?* (What is truth?). Nikolai Ge.

Pilate talks to the Crowd

The voices in the crowd repeated charges that Jesus was a political insurgent. Furthermore, they threatened Pilate that releasing Jesus would be an act of disloyalty to Caesar. "Pilate tried to release him. But the Jewish leaders shouted out, "If you release this man, you are no friend of Caesar! Everyone who claims to be a king opposes Caesar!"(John 19:12). Pilate was unwilling to risk potential allegations of disloyalty to Caesar. He was cornered.

Pilate Washes His Hands

A macabre dialogue then takes place between Pilate and those in the crowd.

Pilate said to them, "Then what should I do with Jesus who is called the Christ?" They all said, "Crucify him!" He asked, "Why? What wrong has he done?" But they shouted more insistently, "Crucify him!" When Pilate saw that he could do nothing, but that instead a riot was starting, he took some water, washed his hands before the crowd and said, "I am innocent of this man's blood. You take care of it yourselves!" In reply all the people said, "Let his blood be on us and on our children!" (Matt. 27:22-25).

Washing of hands to signify relinquishing responsibility was not a Roman custom. The symbolism harkens to Jewish law with implications clearly understood by the crowd driving the agenda that morning.

In Jewish law, when an unsolved murder occurred an animal sacrifice and prayer of atonement had to be made. The elders of the closest nearby city would perform the ceremony which included killing a heifer by breaking its neck. The elders of the city then washed their hands over the sacrificial animal. A pronouncement of innocence and plea for forgiveness completed the ceremony.

... and all the elders of that city nearest the corpse must wash their hands over the heifer whose neck was [sacrificially] broken in the valley. Then they must proclaim, "Our hands have not spilled this blood, nor have we witnessed the crime. Do not blame your people Israel whom you redeemed, O Lord, and do not hold them accountable for the bloodshed of an innocent person." Then atonement will be made for the bloodshed. In this manner you will purge out the guilt of innocent blood from among you, for you must do what is right before the Lord (Deut. 21:6-9).

By washing his hands Pilate indicted the crowd for the murder of Jesus (Image 17: *Pilate se lave les mains*). Pilate reiterated this directly by stating, "I am innocent of this man's blood" (Matt. 27:24). Pilate's reference to Hebrew law was fully understood by the Jewish audience. The response from the crowd can be understood in a legal context. They accepted Pilate's statement of innocence and accepted upon themselves the responsibility, or *the blood guilt*, for Jesus' death. "In reply all the people said, "Let his blood be on us and on our children!" (Matt. 27:25).

The Titulus Crucis

Every person crucified had a plaque, the *titulus crucis* ("title of the cross"), affixed to the cross stating the crimes for which they were being executed (Image 19: *Cross Construction*). Pilate ordered that the plaque state Jesus' crime was being, "The King of the Jews" written in Latin, Greek, and Hebrew.[147]

Pilate also had a notice written and fastened to the cross, which read: "Jesus the Nazarene, the king of the Jews." Thus many of the

---

[147]The use of multiple languages on the *titulus crucis* was probably routine. Latin was the official administrative language of Rome, Greek the language of international trade and culture, and Hebrew the local language. Frederick T. Zugibe, *The Crucifixion of Jesus: A Forensic Inquiry* (New York: M. Evans and Co., 2005), 44.

Jewish residents of Jerusalem read this notice, because the place where Jesus was crucified was near the city, and the notice was written in Aramaic, Latin, and Greek. Then the chief priests of the Jews said to Pilate, "Do not write, 'The king of the Jews,' but rather, 'This man said, I am king of the Jews.'" Pilate answered, "What I have written, I have written" (John 19:19-22).

Pilate's anger was palpable. The *titulus crucis* was Pilate's final snub to the Sanhedrin.

Image 17 - *Pilate se lave les mains (Pilate Washes His Hands).* James Tissot.

In Summary

Jesus' crucifixion was the culmination of a murder plot devised by Caiaphas and the Chief Priests of the Sanhedrin. It was driven by jealousy and the perceived threat that Jesus' popularity could incite a Roman police state and undo their way of life. If the Romans implemented martial law, they might also seize Herod's Temple. Seizure of the Temple would be a national financial catastrophe. Unwilling to kill Jesus themselves for fear of public outrage, Jewish leaders were able to successfully entangle Pontius Pilate in their murder plot and manipulate him into executing Jesus on trumped up charges of sedition against Rome.

CHAPTER 5
ROMAN CRUCIFIXION

Six thousand rebel prisoners were crucified along the Appian Way, a major Roman road, when the Roman army crushed the Spartacus Rebellion in 70 BC.[148] During the siege of Jerusalem in 70 AD, Roman soldiers crucified up to five hundred people per day. According to Josephus, the number was so great, "...there was not enough room for the crosses and not enough crosses for the bodies."[149] The Roman government had strong belief in capital punishment as a deterrent and utilized crucifixion liberally. Crucifixion was the expected form of execution for political insurgents.

Stringing up hated or convicted people on a stake or tree has been practiced in many cultures dating back to ancient times.[150] Crucifixion, however, was considered a particularly cruel form of execution to the point of obscenity.[151] The Romans are thought to have adopted the practice from the Carthaginians in the third century BC.[152] Roman crucifixion was the "supreme penalty," *summa supplica*, followed in order of severity by the less severe forms of execution of being burned alive and decapitation.[153]Rome used crucifixion as a form of capital punishment for six centuries until it was eliminated from the Roman judicial system by the Emperor Constantine. Constantine's written decree abolishing crucifixion

---

[148]Barbet, *Doctor at Calvary*, 44.

[149]Hengel, *Crucifixion*, 26.

[150]Hanging on a tree was also practiced in Hebrew culture. After the military conquest of the city of Ai, Joshua hung the king on a tree until sundown (Josh. 8:29). Hanging an executed man on a tree indicated the man was cursed by God. The body was to be taken down by evening and buried according to Hebrew law (Deut. 21:22-23).

[151]Hengel, *Crucifixion*, 22-23.

[152]Barbet, *Doctor at Calvary*, 41.

[153]Hengel, *Crucifixion*, 33.

has not survived and its exact date is unknown.[154] When crucifixion finally ceased in the Roman Empire is not precisely known but it apparently did not persist beyond Constantine's reign.[155]

Being Crucified

The condemned prisoner (*crucarius*) was placed in the custody of an execution team of Roman soldiers. The executioners were supervised by a centurion. To begin with, the naked victim was tied to a post and scourged over the whole body. The scourging whip, called *flagrum* or *flagellum*, consisted of leather strips with dumbbell shaped pieces of lead tied to the ends of the strips (Image 18: *Roman Scourging*). In Hebrew law scourging beyond forty lashes was not permitted. Romans had no lash limit. Only the victim should not be beaten to death prior to crucifixion. Multiple soldiers participated in scourging each victim.[156]

Scourging and torture prior to crucifixion was grisly and brought the condemned victim close to death. It is easily conceivable that the lashes would cut deeply through the flesh. The fourth century church historian, Eusebius, described scourging practices prior to crucifixion, "…. bystanders were struck with amazement when they saw them lacerated with scourges even to the innermost veins and arteries, so that the hidden inward parts of the body, both their bowels and their members, were exposed to

---

[154]Roger Pearse, "Constantine banned crucifixion – sources," *www.roger-pearse.com.* Roger Pearse blog, February 16, 2015,http://www.roger-pearse.com/weblog/2015/02/26/constantine-banned-crucifixion-sources/. (accessed June 21, 2016).

The banning of crucifixion appears to have coincided with Constantine making Christianity the revered and official religion of the empire. Sozomen, *Ecclesiastical History*, trans. Edward Walford, (London: H. Bohn Pub., 1855), 19.

[155]John Granger Cook, *Crucifixion in the Mediterranean World* (Tubingen: Mohr Siebeck, 2014), 398.

[156]Barbet, *Doctor at Calvary*, 47-48.

view."[157] The first century Roman philosopher, Seneca, noted that the crucifixion victim "would have many excuses for dying even before mounting the cross."[158]

After scourging, the arms of the condemned prisoner were outstretched and tied to a single straight plank of wood called the *patibulum*.[159] The *patibulum* had an estimated weight of 60 pounds (27 kilograms) and would become the horizontal piece of the cross. The condemned prisoner was then forced to parade through town naked carrying the *patibulum* and a sign (*titulus crucis*) stating the capital offenses for which they were being executed.[160] (Image 19: *Cross Construction*). [Jesus appears to have been spared the humiliation of walking naked to the crucifixion site. However, his clothes were taken from him prior to crucifixion (Matt. 27:31,35)]. The condemned prisoner with arms nailed to the *patibulum* was then lifted and placed on the *stipes*, the vertical section of the cross which was in a fixed location and stationary. The *titulus crucis* was fastened to the cross as a public notice of the convicted crimes. The crucifixion site was conspicuously located near the city. Crucifixion was a public spectacle intended to instill fear.

To be *lifted onto the cross* is a literary expression found in both ancient Greek and Latin.[161] Jesus himself used this expression when

---

[157]Eusebius, *Ecclesiastical History*, Book IV, chapter 15:4, in Arthur Cushman McGiffert, *Nicene and Post-Nicene Fathers, Second Series*, Vol. 1. Philip Schaff and Henry Wace, eds., (Buffalo: Christian Literature Publishing Co., 1890) *www.newadvent.org*. http://www.newadvent.org/fathers/250104.htm. (accessed December 15, 2017).

[158]Hengel, *Crucifixion*, 31.

[159]Initially, the patibulum was most likely the wooden plank used to bar a door (from *patere*, Latin to open). Barbet, *Doctor at Calvary*, 44.

[160]Zugibe, *The Crucifixion of Jesus*, 43, 46. See also, Dionysius of Halicarnassus, (60 BC to 7 BC) apparent description of beating prior to Roman crucifixion, the condemned "having stretched out both his arms and fastened them to a piece of wood which extended across his breasts and shoulders as far as his wrists"...was scourged "tearing his naked body with whips." Dionysius of Halicarnassus. "Roman Antiquities." VII, 69:1-2, *uchicago.edu*. Bill Thayer, University of Chicago. http://penelope.uchicago.edu/Thayer/E/Roman/Texts/Dionysius_of_Halicarnassus/7C*.html. (accessed September 23, 2017).

[161]Barbet, *Doctor at Calvary*, 50.

he foretold his crucifixion, "when I am lifted up from the earth, will draw all people to myself." (Now he said this to indicate clearly what kind of death he was going to die.)" (John 12:32-33). Jesus again made reference to arms being fastened to a *patibulum* prior to crucifixion when he foretold how Peter would die.

"I tell you the solemn truth, [Jesus speaking to Peter] when you were young, you tied your clothes around you and went wherever you wanted, but when you are old, you will stretch out your hands, and others will tie you up and bring you where you do not want to go." (Now Jesus said this to indicate clearly by what kind of death Peter was going to glorify God.)" (John 21:18-19).

It is traditionally understood that Peter was crucified upside down, preaching to his executioners until he died.[162]

Positioning of victims on the cross could vary depending on the sadistic mood of the executioners. The Roman philosopher, Seneca, noted that "…some hang a man head downwards, some force a stick upwards through his groin, some stretch out his arms on a forked gibbet (*patibulum*)."[163] When Roman soldiers crucified hundreds of people per day during the siege of Jerusalem in 70 AD, Josephus reported that victims were placed on crosses in various postures "by way of jest" after they had been "tortured with all sorts of tortures."[164]

---

[162]M.R. James, "The Acts of Peter", in *The Apocryphal New Testament* (Oxford: Clarendon Press, 1924), *www.earlychristian writings.com*. http://www.earlychristianwritings.com/text/actspeter.html. (accessed March 1, 2017).

[163]Hengel, *Crucifixion*, 25.

Wikisource contributors, Annaeus Seneca, "Of Consolation: To Marcia," XX. *Wikisource*, https://en.wikisource.org/w/index.php?title=Of_Consolation:_To_Marcia&oldid=79227 87. (accessed January 11, 2018)

[164]Hengel, *Crucifixion*, 26.

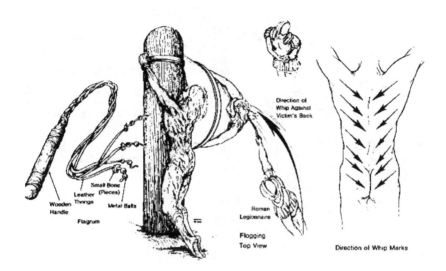

Image 18 - *Roman Scourging*. Soldiers on the execution team scourged condemned prisoners over their entire body prior to walking to the crucifixion site. The flagrum (whip) had metal balls sown into the ends of leather strips. Image used with permission.

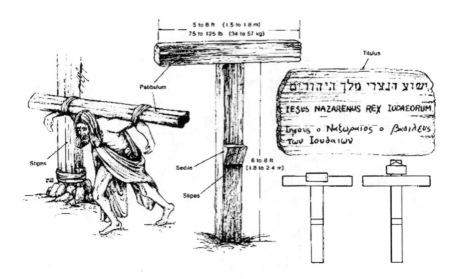

Image 19 - *Cross Construction*. The prisoner carried the horizontal section of the cross (patibulum) to the execution site. In constructing the crux commissa, or Tau Cross, the patibulum was lifted with the victim's arms already attached by nails and placed on top of the stipes (the vertical section of the cross). The stipes was fixed in the ground and stationary. The patibulum was held on top of the stipes by a mortis and tenon joint. The Titulus Crucis (a plaque stating the convicted crimes) was carried by the prisoner to the execution site then attached to the cross. A sedile (seat) depicted in this illustration may have been used on rare occasion but is unlikely to have been part of usual cross construction.[165] Image used with permission.

---

[165] William Edwards, Wesley Gabel, and Floyd Hosmer, *On the Physical Death of Jesus Christ*, JAMA Vol 255, No. 11, 1458.

The Nails

Arms and legs were typically fastened with nails, but ropes might be used if nails were in short supply.[166] A nail through the mid-palm could potentially be unstable and pull through the flesh between the fingers from the force of the victim's body weight, but a nail placed through the wrist bones (carpal bones) or above the wrist would be stable and hold the victim on the cross.

The French surgeon, Pierre Barbet, experimented by hammering a large nail through wrists that had been freshly amputated. He found that a 100 lb. force would pull the nail out through between the fingers if nailed in the mid-palm. Barbet felt the nail needed to be stable to at least 240 lbs. of force. He found that hammering the nail through the wrist separated the wrist bones (carpals) and the nail passed through Destot's Space (the area bounded by the hamate, capitate, triquetral and lunate bones) without fracturing the wrist bones. He did this over a dozen times and found nail placement with each to be consistent. When dissecting the wrists after his nail experiment, Barbet found that the median nerve had been macerated and fragmented. (This kind of injury to the median nerve in the wrist would cause intense pain in the hand and up the arm). Thus, Barbet found that nails could be consistently driven through the wrist bones at Destot's Space and were able to hold the weight of the victim hanging on the cross.[167] (Image 20: *Wrist X-rays with Crucifixion Nail*).

It has been commonly assumed that nails were driven through the top of the victim's feet. Artists typically portray Jesus' feet nailed to a small block of wood (*suppedaneum*) fastened to the front of the vertical section of the cross, the *stipes* (Image 21: *Suppedaneum*). The *suppedaneum* is the product of artistic

---

[166] Crucifixion nails were collected for other uses. They were used in magic and also made into amulets thought to have curative powers. Cook, *Crucifixion in the Mediterranean World*, 294.

[167] Barbet, *Doctor at Calvary*, 98-105.

imagination, however, and was not part of Roman crucifixion practice.[168] Nails piercing the top of Jesus' feet may also be an artistic invention. Archaeological evidence suggests it may actually have been common practice to hammer a nail through the heel.

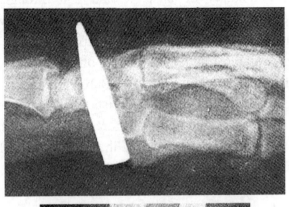

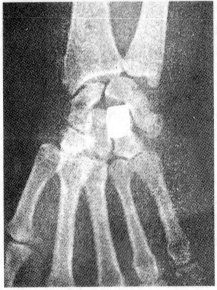

Image 20 - *Wrist X-rays with Crucifixion Nail.* Above are X-rays from Pierre Barbet's experiment showing a nail in the wrist bones of a freshly amputated hand. No bones were fractured. Image used with permission. Courtesy of Roman Catholic Books, P.O. Box 2286, Fort Collins, Colorado, 80522.

---

[168]Barbet, *Doctor at Calvary*, 61-62. Zugibe, *The Crucifixion of Jesus*, 58.

Image 21 – *Suppedaneum*. The suppedaneum, a block of wood attached to the front of the cross supporting the feet, is considered an artistic invention. It was not used in first century Roman cross construction. *Crucifixion, by Thomas Eakins, 1880. (adapted)*

How many people were crucified by the Romans is unknown but must have numbered in the hundreds of thousands. Yet, archaeologists have found the remains of only two crucifixion victims.

In 1968 bones showing clear evidence of crucifixion were found by archeologists in the Giv'at ha-Mitvar area of Jerusalem. The victim is thought to have died in the early part of the first century.[169]

Both heel bones (calcanei) were found in an ossuary immersed in a syrupy liquid, stuck together and covered with a thick calciferous crust. The right calcaneus (heel bone) had a large iron nail still in place. The tip of the nail was bent, making it impossible to remove (Image 22: *Heel Bones*). Removing the body from the cross would have been problematic with the right foot secured in place by the bent nail. A horizontal cut mark on the right talus (part

---

[169]V. Tzaferis, Jewish Tombs at and near Giv'at ha-Mitvar, Jerusalem," *Israel Exploration Journal*, 20, no. 1/2 (1970): 31.

of the ankle joint) is thought to indicate that the right foot was amputated (with an axe or hatchet) in order to remove the body from the cross and then pry the foot and bent nail from the *stipes*. A nail had also been driven through the left calcaneus also but had been removed (Image 23: *Left Calcaneus*). An indentation on the right radius (the large bone in the forearm) is thought to be evidence that a nail had been driven between the forearm bones (radius and ulna) just above the wrist (Image 24: *Nail through the Forearm*). There were no signs of injury to bones within the wrists or hands. The bones in both legs were fractured, consistent with the practice of *crurifragium*, i.e. fracturing the legs during crucifixion (Image 25: *Crurifragium*).

Remnants of olive wood were still present between the right heel and the head of the nail, indicating that the feet were held in place with a plaque of wood. A nail was then driven through the wood and heel bones into the vertical section of the cross, the *stipes*. Fragments of wood were also present on the bent tip of the nail.[170] (Image 26: *Anatomy of the Heel Bones*).

The only other archeological find of a crucifixion victim was discovered in 2007 in the Gavello region of northern Italy. The body had been buried directly in the earth without a coffin. Similar to the Jerusalem find, there is a hole through the right calcaneus (heel bone), apparently a puncture wound from a nail. The nail had been driven into the calcaneus medially to laterally, from the inside of the heel to the outside (Image 27: *The Right Calcaneus*). The nail had been removed and was not found with the remains. The left calcaneus was not found. None of the other skeletal remains had

---

[170]N. Haas, "Anthropological Observations on the Skeletal Remains from Giv'at ha-Mitvar," *Israel Exploration Journal,* 20, no. 1/2 (1970): 49-59. Haas felt the wood near the head of the nail was Acacia or Pistacia and that olive wood was found on the nail tip. However at later analysis, Zias and Sekeles confirmed that the wood near the nail head was olive and that the wood fragments on the tip of the nail were too minute to identify the type of wood. Zias and Sekeles also question Haas' interpretation of the marks on the distal radius. Joseph Zias and Eliezer Sekeles, "The Crucified Man from Giv'at ha-mivtar: A Reappraisal" Israel Exploration Journal, 35. No. 1 (1985): 24.

traumatic markings. The victim was a male, confirmed by DNA testing, with an estimated age in his early 30's. The skeletal remains dates to the Roman Era, but carbon dating was not possible due to the poor condition of the bones.[171]

The heel bones from the remains at Giv'at ha-Mitvar, suggest that the victim's feet were nailed to the front of the cross with the legs adjacent and rotated to the victim's right. The feet of the Gavello victim may have been nailed to the cross in the same way, or possibly in a "frog-leg" or open position (Image 28: *Position on the Cross*).

While there is no direct evidence, it is possible that nails were driven through the top of the feet of crucifixion victims. However, from a utilitarian standpoint it may have been easier to drive the nail through the side of the heel. This would create stable fixation of the foot against the cross. A piece of wood between the foot and head of the nail would in effect enlarge the head of the nail, making it essentially impossible to pry the foot loose. It may also have been easier to place a nail through the heel rather than through the top of the foot of a condemned prisoner protesting and kicking.

It may seem peculiar that remains of crucifixion victims are so rare, but their bodies were seldom buried. After death, corpses were left hanging on the cross to be devoured by scavenging animals.[172] The low height of the typical *Tau* cross made dead bodies easily accessible to scavengers.[173] No doubt, decaying bodies being eaten by animals added to the public fear and intimidation intended by the Romans.

---

[171] Emamuela Gualdi-Russo, et al., "A multidisciplinary study of calcaneal trauma in Roman Italy: a possible case of crucifixion?" Archaeological and Anthropological Sciences, (April 2018): DOI: 10.1007/s12520-018-0631-9

[172] Barbet, *Doctor at Calvary*, 51. Hengel, *Crucifixion*, 9.

[173] Victims crucified in an arena would have animals set loose to devour them for public entertainment. Pierre Barbet, *Doctor at Calvary*, 43. Nero reportedly had crucifixion victims burned to serve as lamps in the evening, Hengel, *Crucifixion*, 26.

Skeletal Remains found at Giv'at ha-Mitvar, Jerusalem

Image 22 - *Heel Bones*. The left and right calcaneus bones were found in an ossuary immersed in fluid and had a heavy calcified crust as shown. The left and right calcaneus bones were stuck together with the nail *in situ* in the right calcaneus. Haas, "Skeletal Remains from Giv'at ha-Mitvar," Plate 19, C. Used with permission, Israel Exploration Society.

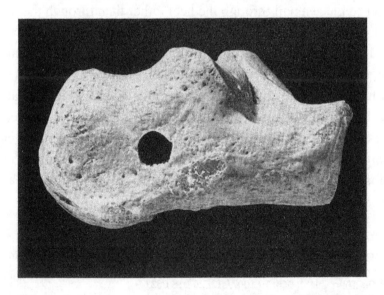

Image 23 - *Left Calcaneus*. The left calcaneus (heel bone) had been punctured by a nail which was later removed by the executioners. Haas, "Skeletal Remains from Giv'at ha-Mitvar," Plate 21, A. Used with permission, Israel Exploration Society.

Image 24 - *Nail through the forearm*. An indentation on the radius (the large bone in the forearm) is thought to be evidence that a nail had passed between the forearm bones (radius and ulna) just above the wrist. Haas, "Skeletal Remains from Giv'at ha-Mitvar," Plate 22, A. Used with permission, Israel Exploration Society.

Image 25 – *Crurifragium (the practice of fracturing the legs)*. The bones in both legs had been fractured. Left tibia and fibula are shown above. Haas, "Skeletal Remains from Giv'at ha-Mitvar," Plate 23, A. Used with permission, Israel Exploration Society.

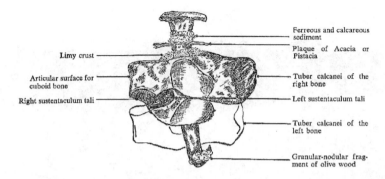

Image 26 - *Anatomy of the Heel Bones*. This illustration shows the anatomy of the heel bones (calcanei), nail placement and wood fragment findings. Since the left and right heel bones were stuck together, it is suspected that both feet were held together in parallel and fastened to the front of the cross with nails. Haas, "Skeletal Remains from Giv'at ha-Mitvar," 56. Used with permission, Israel Exploration Society.

Skeletal Remains found at Gavello, Italy

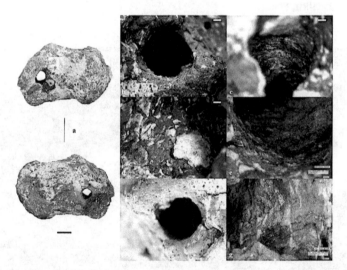

Image 27 - *The Right Calcaneus*. A single perforation passes through the bone under the sustentaculum (a). An ellipisoidal depressed fracture (b, c) on the mesial side is documented, showing break-through in the impact area (d). The round section of the hole is clearly visible (c,e). In the lateral side, the edges of the grove are not well preserved and they do not bear any impact damage, suggesting the exit point (g. round section in proximity of the exit point). a (bar scale 1 cm); b, c, d, f (bar scale 1 mm: images at stereomicroscope LEICA SD6 lab Acheozoology). (e, g 3D images Hirox University of Siena). Images used with permission.

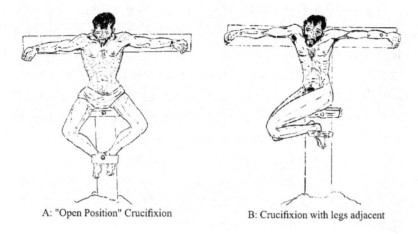

A: "Open Position" Crucifixion   B: Crucifixion with legs adjacent

Image 28 - *Position on the Cross based on Archeological Evidence.* The skeletal remains found in Jerusalem suggest both feet were nailed to the front of the cross with the legs adjacent and rotated to the victim's right (B). The feet of the crucifixion victim of Gavello, Italy may have been nailed the same way or possibly with the legs in an open or frog-leg position (A). Haas, "Skeletal Remains from Giv'at ha-Mitvar," Plate 24. Image used with permission, Israel Exploration Society.

Shape of the Cross

Romans executed prisoners by suspending them in a variety of positions. A simple upright stake or pole has been called the *crux simplex*. Based on a description from Seneca, a first century Roman philosopher, a simple stake (*crux simplex*) was used to impale victims. Seneca stated, "I see before me crosses not all alike, but differently made by different peoples: some hang a man head downwards, *some force a stick upwards through his groin*, some stretch out his arms on a forked gibbet."[174] According to tradition, St. Andrew, one of Jesus' original twelve disciples, is thought to

---

[174]Wikisource contributors, Annaeus Seneca, "Of Consolation: To Marcia," XX. *Wikisource,* https://en.wikisource.org/w/index.php?title=Of_Consolation:_To_Marcia&oldid=7922787. (accessed January 11, 2018

have been executed on a *crux decussata*, an X-shaped frame that has become known as the "St. Andrew's Cross." Documents stating St. Andrew was executed on a *crux decussata* (**X**) do not appear until the tenth century, however. Some historians doubt that this was used in the first century.[175] Historical and literary evidence seem to be clear that the predominant method of Roman crucifixion was with the prisoners' arms outstretched on a cruciform structure.

The Greek word translated "cross" in the Gospels is *stauros,* (σταυρός). In ancient Classical Greek this had the specific meaning of an *upright stake* in the ground. This has caused some disagreement regarding the shape of the cross used for Jesus.[176] The conundrum arises from a misunderstanding of New Testament language. The New Testament was written in *Koine* (common dialect) Greek, a post-classical from of Greek that was the *lingua franca* of the first century Mediterranean world. Koine Greek transcended national boundaries and had variations in form as well as spoken vernacular.[177] Translating Koine Greek as if it were Classical Greek would introduce error in the translated text. *Stauros* in the New Testament is translated as "cross" and in general terms means the instrument of death used by Romans for crucifixion. However, it is also used with the specific meaning of *the horizontal section of the cross carried by the prisoner to the execution site,* namely the *patibulum*.[178] (Image 19: *Cross Construction*). For example, *Stauros* means *patibulum* when Jesus said to his followers,

---

[175]Zugibe, *The Crucifixion of Jesus*, 41.

[176]J. Warner Wallace, "What Was the Shape of Jesus' Cross?," *coldcasechristianity.com*. Cold-Case Christianity, January 8, 2018, http://coldcasechristianity.com/2018/what-was-the-shape-of-jesus-cross/?utm_source=feedburner&utm_medium=email&utm_campaign=Feed%3A+ColdCaseChristianity+%28Cold+Case+Christianity%29. (accessed January 11, 2018).

[177]Wikipedia contributors, "Koine Greek," *Wikipedia, The Free Encyclopedia,*https://en.wikipedia.org/w/index.php?title=Koine_Greek&oldid=819246217 (accessed January 11, 2018).

[178]Strong's Concordance, 4716, "stauros", biblehub.com. Bible Hub, http://biblehub.com/greek/4716.htm. (accessed January 11, 2018).

"whoever does not take up his cross *(stauros)* and follow me is not worthy of me." (Matt. 10:38).

Most artistic depictions of Jesus on a cross show him on a *crux immissa*, with the vertical part of the cross extending above the horizontal beam (✝). However, this is an artistic interpretation and appears to be erroneous. Literary references to crucifixion, including those external to the Bible, indicate the T-shaped *Tau* cross (named for the Greek letter *Tau*: **T**) was the typical shape of cross construction.

The cross was an implement of torture and death. For this reason, images of Jesus on the cross are not found in early Christian iconography. What may be the earliest known depiction of Jesus on a cross is actually sacrilegious graffiti mocking the faith of a Christian named Alexamenos. The *graffito blasfemo* ("blasphemous graffiti") is thought to date to the early third century, around 200 AD. It was etched in plaster and depicts Alexamenos worshiping a figure on a cross having a human body with a donkey's head.[179] (Image 29: *graffito blasfemo*). Interestingly, Tertullian (160 AD – 220 AD) noted that it had become popular in Rome to ridicule the Christian God as a human having features of an ass.[180] It is noteworthy that the *graffito blasfemo* depicts a *Tau* cross (**T**).

---

[179]James Grout, "Alexamenos Graffito" in Encyclopaedia Romana, University of Chicago, Penelope.uchicago.edu., April 1, 2017, http://penelope.uchicago.edu/~grout/encyclopaedia_romana/gladiators/graffito.html. (accessed January 11, 2018).

[180]Orazio Marucchi, "Archeology of the Cross and Crucifix", in *The Catholic Encyclopedia*, vol. 4 (New York: Robert Appleton Co. 1908). http://www.newadvent.org/cathen/04517a.htm. (accessed December 13, 2016). Additionally, Tertullian noted that a gladiator had published a caricature mocking the Christian God as a figure with both human and donkey characteristics. Tertullian indicated that it had become popular among Romans to ridicule Christian faith in this way. Tertullian, *The Apology of Tertullian*, W.M. Reeve translator, (London: Griffith Farran, 1889) 53. http://www.tertullian.org/articles/reeve_apology.htm. (accessed December 21, 2016).

Image 29 - *Graffito Blasfemo*: The inscription states, "Alexamenos adores [his] God." Note: A Tau cross (crux commissa) (T) is depicted in the caricature.

By the second century it had become common practice among Christians to make the sign of the cross on their foreheads. The symbol used was the *Tau* (**T**), identical to the English capital "T" shape.[181] Crucifixes were not utilized in Christian faith and practice until the sixth century, three centuries after Roman crucifixion had been abolished.[182] Artists making crucifixes and medieval paintings had never seen crucifixion.

The awkward carpentry of the *crux immissa* (✝) made it impractical for routine use. Also, it would be essentially impossible for a condemned prisoner to singlehandedly carry the weight of an entire assembled cross to the crucifixion site. [The weight of an entire cross would likely exceed 300 lbs. (136 kilograms)].[183] From a practical standpoint, a short *crux commissa*, T-shaped cross, made

---

[181]Barbet, *Doctor at Calvary*, 57. See also, "Archeology of the Cross and Crucifix", Catholic Encyclopedia, online. http://www.newadvent.org/cathen/04517a.htm (accessed December 22, 2016).

[182]*John Stott, The Cross of Christ (Downers Grove: InterVarsity Press, 2006) 27.*

[183]Edwards, "On the Physical Death of Jesus Christ," 1459.

more sense and is most consistent with known Roman crucifixion practices.

Lucian of Samosata (c. 125 to 180 AD) provides further non-Christian literary evidence for the cross shape. Lucian uses the Greek alphabet in his satirical play, "Trial in the Court of the Vowels." Lucian writes "Men weep, and bewail their lot, and curse Cadmus [Greek god credited with introducing the Greek alphabet] with many curses for introducing *Tau* (**T**) into the family of letters; they say it was his body that tyrants took for a model, his shape that they imitated, when they set up the erections on which men are crucified."[184] Lucian clearly stated that the shape of the cross was the Greek letter *Tau* (**T**).

With reasonable certainty, Jesus was crucified on a *crux commissa*, a T-shaped Cross, having a height of six to eight feet. Jesus would have been eye to eye with his executioners while hanging on the cross.

Construction of the Cross

The long vertical piece of the cross, the *stipes*, was permanently fixed in the ground.[185] The shorter horizontal section of the cross, the *patibulum*, was carried by the condemned prisoner to the crucifixion site. The arms were then nailed to the *patibulum*. Soldiers lifted the *patibulum* with the attached victim up onto the *stipes*. The *patibulum* was held in place on top of the *stipes* by a mortise and tenon joint. The feet were then nailed to the *stipes*. This type of construction created an easily assembled T-shaped *Tau* cross (*crux commissa*) having a height of six to eight feet (1.8 to 2.5 meters).[186]

---

[184]Lucian of Samosata, "Trial in the Court of Vowels", *Sacred-texts.com*. http://www.sacred-texts.com/cla/luc/wl1/wl110.htm. (accessed January 10, 2018). Public domain.

[185]Barbet, *Doctor at Calvary*, 45. *Stipes* can be translated as stake or trunk, Ibid., 43.

[186]Edwards, *the Physical Death of Jesus Christ*, 1458.

The height of the *stipes* needed to be within arms' reach so that soldiers could lift the *patibulum* and place it on top. Crosses needed to be easily assembled with the victim's arms already nailed to the *patibulum*. Ease of construction would be particularly important if soldiers were tasked with multiple executions. It should not be overlooked that Roman crucifixion was a centuries old practice and well perfected by Jesus' time. Julius Firmicus Maternus was a Roman writer, astrologer, and Christian apologist who lived in the early fourth century during Constantine's reign. He would have had first-hand knowledge of Roman crucifixion practices. Firmicus Maternus' description of crucifixion confirms the practice of lifting the victim onto the cross with arms already attached to the patibulum, noting "...[the condemned man] having been nailed to the patibulum is raised up on to the cross."[187]

Tall crosses, referred to as the *crux sublimus*, could be used on rare occasions for famous or politically important prisoners.[188] Complex carpentry made tall crosses impractical for routine use, however. Therefore, the shorter version of the Tau cross, *crux commissa*, was used routinely. It can be assumed that the shorter cross version would have been used for Jesus since he was insignificant from the Roman point of view.

There are some literary references to a *sedile* (seat) perhaps half-way down from the top of the cross. This was not intended to provide comfort, rather the *sedile* would have the shape of a horn with the intent of increased torture. Crucifixion was a routine form of Roman execution. The carpentry demands of adding seats to crosses when it served no real purpose makes it unlikely that this was routinely done.[189]

---

[187]Barbet, *Doctor at Calvary*, 50.

[188]Hengel, *Crucifixion*, 40.

[189]Pierre Barbet, *Doctor at Calvary*, 45. Cook, *Crucifixion in the Mediterranean World*, 7.

Certainty of Death

The soldiers' task was to see that prisoners were successfully executed. Crucifixion teams were made up of professional soldiers who knew their job. They were trained in how to deliver a death blow. A sword or spear impaling the chest in the direction of the heart, as described in Jesus' case, would be the most straightforward way to deliver a *coup de gras*. This would collapse the lung and rupture the heart. Impaling the chest with a sword or spear may have been common practice in Roman crucifixion.

Discipline within the Roman military was austere, if not inhumane. A guard who was caught nodding off and falling asleep during his watch was beaten to death, for example.[190] Crucifixion teams were professional soldiers and experienced in executing prisoners. It can be safely assumed that soldiers on an execution team were credibly able to pronounce death. It was their job to assure that each condemned prisoner die.[191] If a criminal convicted of a capital offense escaped crucifixion, it would mean certain death for the centurion and his soldiers.[192] With reasonable certainty Jesus died by crucifixion. A spear through the center of Jesus' chest finished the job and reassured the soldiers that he was irrefutably dead.

---

[190]"Grisly Roman Army Discipline", Great Names in History, August 28, 2008. https://100falcons.wordpress.com/2008/08/28/grisly-roman-army-discipline/. (accessed November 11, 2016).

[191] Josephus requested a stay of execution from Emperor Titus when he saw three friends being crucified. In spite of care by physicians, two of them died and one survived. See, Chapter 8, fn 282. To the author's knowledge, there is no other historical record of anyone surviving crucifixion.

[192]Peter Kreeft and Fr. Ronald Tacelli, *Handbook of Catholic Apologetics: Reasoned Answers to Questions of Faith* (Downers Grove: InterVarsity Press, 2009), 193. Also, Acts 16:26-28 appears to verify the cruel reputation of Roman military discipline. The guard in the Philippian jail intended to kill himself when he believed the prisoners under his watch had escaped.

CHAPTER 6
THE EXECUTION OF JESUS

The Passion of Jesus Christ

Christians often refer to the events leading to Jesus' crucifixion as the *Passion of Jesus Christ*. In modern parlance *passion* has come to mean feelings of strong emotion. The term "passion" comes from the Greek word "to suffer" (paskho, πασχω), an obsolete meaning in modern English. The *Passion of Jesus Christ* refers to his suffering and death.

Each of the Gospels describes Jesus' crucifixion and the events leading to it. There are minor variations in the detail among them. However, they all tell the same overarching story of what occurred that day. Some variation in detail can be expected in eyewitness accounts separately recorded, as mentioned previously.[193] The most detailed Gospel passages have been selected and conjoined for the narrative below. A medical commentary follows.

Jesus ate his Last Supper with his disciples on the first day of the Feast of Unleavened Bread (Mark 14:12). [Passover was a one-day religious holiday which marked the beginning of the week-long Feast of Unleavened Bread. Passover plus the Feast of Unleavened Bread could also be collectively referred to as *the Passover* (Exek.45:21, Luke 22:1)]. The Gospels are clear in stating Jesus' Last Supper was a Passover Seder (Matt. 26:18, Mark 14:14, Luke 22:15).

Jesus used the context of Passover to teach his disciples the significance of his death. Additionally, he expanded the meaning of Passover and instituted a new celebratory meal which Christians

---

[193]Wallace, *Cold-Case Christianity*, 76-80.

celebrate as the Eucharist or Holy Communion.[194 and 195]

The crucifixion of Jesus was on a Friday since it occurred on the Day of Preparation for the Sabbath. Sabbath is observed on Saturday each week. In John's Gospel, he stated "that Sabbath was an especially important one" indicating that this particular Sabbath occurred during a religious festival (John 19:31).

The exact date of Jesus' crucifixion has been the subject of debate for centuries. The most accepted options fulfilling the day-to-day sequence described in the Bible are either April 7, AD 30 and April 3, AD 33. Friday, April 7, AD 30 is considered by many to be the most favored date of Jesus' execution.[196]

The Gospel Narrative of Jesus' Execution

About 7:00 PM

Jesus' Last Supper with his Disciples (Mark 14:17-26):

Then, when it was evening, he came to the house with the twelve. While they were at the table eating, Jesus said, "I tell you the truth, one of you eating with me will betray me." They were distressed,

---

[194]Robin Routledge, "Passover and Last Supper," *Tyndale Bulletin*, 53, no.2 (2002): 204-206.

[195]John 18:28 states that Caiaphas did not enter the Roman governor's residence during Jesus' trial so as not to ceremonially defile himself so he "could eat the Passover meal." This begs the question of whether Jesus' Last Supper was actually on Passover. To consider reconciliation of this passage with the synoptic Gospels, some have suggested the Last Supper was some other ceremonial meal, or perhaps Jesus celebrated Passover a day early. Perhaps Jesus and the Chief Priests used slightly different calendars. Perhaps Caiaphas was celebrating a separate feast also during that week and intended to observe it as a Passover Seder. A clear consensus has not emerged among theologians, however. Jesus was clear in his use of Passover imagery to signify that his death was sacrificial. The significance of John's statement in John 18:28 remains unclear. Wayne Jackson, "Did Jesus Eat the Passover Supper?" *Christiancourier.com*, Christian Courier Publications. https://www.christiancourier.com/articles/390-did-jesus-eat-the-passover-supper. (accessed April 5, 2018).

[196]Craig L. Blomberg, *The Historical Reliability of the Gospels*, (Downers Grove: Intervarsity Press, 2007), 225.

and one by one said to him, "Surely not I?" He said to them, "It is one of the twelve, one who dips his hand with me into the bowl. For the Son of Man will go as it is written about him, but woe to that man by whom the Son of Man is betrayed! It would be better for him if he had never been born." While they were eating, he took bread, and after giving thanks he broke it, gave it to them, and said, "Take it. This is my body." And after taking the cup and giving thanks, he gave it to them, and they all drank from it. He said to them, "This is my blood, the blood of the covenant, that is poured out for many. I tell you the truth, I will no longer drink of the fruit of the vine until that day when I drink it new in the kingdom of God." After singing a hymn, they went out to the Mount of Olives.[197]

Peter's Denial Foretold (Mark 14:27-31):

Then Jesus said to them, "You will all fall away, for it is written, 'I will strike the shepherd, and the sheep will be scattered.' But after I am raised, I will go ahead of you into Galilee." Peter said to him, "Even if they all fall away, I will not!" Jesus said to him, "I tell you the truth, today—this very night—before a rooster crows twice, you will deny me three times." But Peter insisted emphatically, "Even if I must die with you, I will never deny you." And all of them said the same thing.

About 9:00 pm

The Prayer on the Mount of Olives (Luke 22:39-46):

Then Jesus went out and made his way, as he customarily did, to the Mount of Olives, and the disciples followed him. When he came

---

[197] Jews typically recite *Hallel*, Ps. 113-118, at Passover as well as at other religious holidays. Rabbi Isaiah Wohlgemuth, "Hallel," *myjewishlearning.com*. My Jewish Learning, https://www.myjewishlearning.com/article/hallel/. (accessed January 23, 2018).

to the place, he said to them, "Pray that you will not fall into temptation." He went away from them about a stone's throw, knelt down, and prayed, "Father, if you are willing, take this cup away from me. Yet not my will but yours be done." [Then an angel from heaven appeared to him and strengthened him. And in his anguish he prayed more earnestly, and his sweat was like drops of blood falling to the ground.] When he got up from prayer, he came to the disciples and found them sleeping, exhausted from grief. So he said to them, "Why are you sleeping? Get up and pray that you will not fall into temptation!"

Image 30 - *On the Mount of Olives.* Nikolai Ge.

About Midnight

The Betrayal and Arrest of Jesus (John 18:1-11):

There was an orchard there, and he and his disciples went into it. (Now Judas, the one who betrayed him, knew the place too, because Jesus had met there many times with his disciples.) So Judas obtained a squad of soldiers and some officers of the chief priests and Pharisees. They came to the orchard with lanterns and torches and weapons.

Then Jesus, because he knew everything that was going to happen to him, came and asked them, "Who are you looking for?" They replied, "Jesus the Nazarene." He told them, "I am he." (Now Judas, the one who betrayed him, was standing there with them.) So when Jesus said to them, "I am he," they retreated and fell to the ground. Then Jesus asked them again, "Who are you looking for?" And they said, "Jesus the Nazarene." Jesus replied, "I told you that I am he. If you are looking for me, let these men go." He said this to fulfill the word he had spoken, "I have not lost a single one of those whom you gave me."

Then Simon Peter, who had a sword, pulled it out and struck the high priest's slave, cutting off his right ear. (Now the slave's name was Malchus.) But Jesus said to Peter, "Put your sword back into its sheath! Am I not to drink the cup that the Father has given me?"

Jesus Before the High Priest and Sanhedrin (Mark 14:53-65):

Then they led Jesus to the high priest, and all the chief priests and elders and experts in the law came together. And Peter had followed him from a distance, up to the high priest's courtyard. He was sitting with the guards and warming himself by the fire. The chief priests and the whole Sanhedrin were looking for evidence against Jesus so that they could put him to death, but they did not find anything. Many gave false testimony against him, but their testimony did not agree. Some stood up and gave this false testimony against him: "We heard him say, 'I will destroy this temple made with hands and in three days build another not made with hands.'" Yet even on this point their testimony did not agree. Then the high priest stood up before them and asked Jesus, "Have you no answer? What is this that they are testifying against you?" But he was silent and did not answer. Again the high priest questioned him, "Are you the Christ, the Son of the Blessed One?" "I am," said Jesus, "and you will see the Son of Man sitting at the right hand of the Power and coming with the clouds of heaven." Then the high priest tore his clothes and said, "Why do we still need witnesses? You have heard the blasphemy! What is your verdict?" They all condemned him as deserving death. Then some began to spit on him, and to blindfold him, and to strike him with their fists, saying, "Prophesy!" The guards also took him and beat him.

Peter's Denial of Jesus (Mark 14:66-72):

Now while Peter was below in the courtyard, one of the high priest's slave girls came by. When she saw Peter warming himself, she looked directly at him and said, "You also were with that Nazarene, Jesus." But he denied it: "I don't even understand what you're talking about!" Then he went out to the gateway, and a rooster crowed. When the slave girl saw him, she began again to say to the bystanders, "This man is one of them." But he denied it again. A short time later the bystanders again said to Peter, "You must be one of them, because you are also a Galilean." Then he began to curse, and he swore with an oath, "I do not know this man you are talking about!" Immediately a rooster crowed a second time. Then Peter remembered what Jesus had said to him: "Before a rooster crows twice, you will deny me three times." And he broke down and wept.

6:30 AM

Jesus Before Pilate (Mark 15:1-5):

Early in the morning, after forming a plan, the chief priests with the elders and the experts in the law and the whole Sanhedrin tied Jesus up, led him away, and handed him over to Pilate.[198] So Pilate asked him, "Are you the king of the Jews?" He replied, "You say so." Then the chief priests began to accuse him repeatedly. So Pilate asked him again, "Have you nothing to say? See how many charges they are bringing against you!" But Jesus made no further reply, so that Pilate was amazed.

Jesus Before Herod Antipas (Luke 23:5-12):

But they persisted in saying, "He incites the people by teaching throughout all Judea. It started in Galilee and ended up here!" Now when Pilate heard this, he asked whether the man was a Galilean. When he learned that he was from Herod's jurisdiction, he sent him over to Herod, who also happened to be in Jerusalem at that time. When Herod saw Jesus, he was very glad, for he had long desired to see him, because he had heard about him and was hoping to see him perform some miraculous sign. So Herod questioned him at considerable length; Jesus gave him no answer. The chief priests and the experts in the law were there, vehemently accusing him. Even Herod with his soldiers treated him with contempt and mocked him. Then, dressing him in elegant clothes, Herod sent him back to Pilate. That very day Herod and Pilate became friends with each other, for prior to this they had been enemies.

---

[198] Sunrise in Jerusalem occurs at 6:20 AM on April 7. Staff writer, "April 2018 – Sun in Jerusalem." *TimeandDate.com*, https://www.timeanddate.com/sun/israel/jerusalem?month=4. (accessed January 23, 2018).

The Death of Judas (Matt. 27:3-10):

Now when Judas, who had betrayed him, saw that Jesus had been condemned, he regretted what he had done and returned the thirty silver coins to the chief priests and the elders, saying, "I have sinned by betraying innocent blood!" But they said, "What is that to us? You take care of it yourself!" So Judas threw the silver coins into the temple and left. Then he went out and hanged himself. The chief priests took the silver and said, "It is not lawful to put this into the temple treasury, since it is blood money." After consulting together they bought the Potter's Field with it, as a burial place for foreigners. For this reason that field has been called the "Field of Blood" to this day. Then what was spoken by Jeremiah the prophet was fulfilled: "They took the thirty silver coins, the price of the one whose price had been set by the people of Israel, and they gave them for the potter's field, as the Lord commanded me."

Jesus Again Before Pilate (John 18:28-38):

So Pilate came outside to them and said, "What accusation do you bring against this man?" They replied, "If this man were not a criminal, we would not have handed him over to you."

Pilate told them, "Take him yourselves and pass judgment on him according to your own law!" The Jewish leaders replied, "We cannot legally put anyone to death." (This happened to fulfill the word Jesus had spoken when he indicated what kind of death he was going to die.)

Pilate Questions Jesus:

So Pilate went back into the governor's residence, summoned Jesus, and asked him, "Are you the king of the Jews?" Jesus replied, "Are you saying this on your own initiative, or have others told you about me?" Pilate answered, "I am not a Jew, am I? Your own people and your chief priests handed you over to me. What have you done?"

Jesus replied, "My kingdom is not from this world. If my kingdom were from this world, my servants would be fighting to keep me from being handed over to the Jewish authorities. But as it is, my kingdom is not from here." Then Pilate said, "So you are a king!" Jesus replied, "You say that I am a king. For this reason I was born, and for this reason I came into the world—to testify to the truth. Everyone who belongs to the truth listens to my voice." Pilate asked, "What is truth?"

When he had said this he went back outside to the Jewish leaders and announced, "I find no basis for an accusation against him."

Image 31 - *Ecce Homo* (Behold the Man), John 19:5. Antonio Ciseri.

Jesus Sentenced to Death (Mathew 27:15-23):

During the feast the governor was accustomed to release one prisoner to the crowd, whomever they wanted. At that time they had in custody a notorious prisoner named Jesus Barabbas. So after they had assembled, Pilate said to them, "Whom do you want me to release for you, Jesus Barabbas or Jesus who is called the Christ?" (For he knew that they had handed him over because of envy.) As he was sitting on the judgment seat, his wife sent a message to him: "Have nothing to do with that innocent man; I have suffered greatly as a result of a dream about him today." But the chief priests and the elders persuaded the crowds to ask for Barabbas and to have Jesus killed. The governor asked them, "Which of the two do you want me to release for you?" And they said, "Barabbas!" Pilate said to them, "Then what should I do with Jesus who is called the Christ?" They all said, "Crucify him!" He asked, "Why? What wrong has he done?" But they shouted more insistently, "Crucify him!"

Jesus is Condemned and Mocked (Matt. 27:24-31):

When Pilate saw that he could do nothing, but that instead a riot was starting, he took some water, washed his hands before the crowd and said, "I am innocent of this man's blood. You take care of it yourselves!" In reply all the people said, "Let his blood be on us and on our children!" Then he released Barabbas for them. But after he had Jesus flogged, he handed him over to be crucified. Then the governor's soldiers took Jesus into the governor's residence and gathered the whole cohort around him. They stripped him and put a scarlet robe around him, and after braiding a crown of thorns, they put it on his head[199]. They put a staff in his right hand, and kneeling down before him, they mocked him: "Hail, king of the Jews!" They spat on him and took the staff and struck him repeatedly on the head. When they had mocked him, they stripped him of the robe and put his own clothes back on him. Then they led him away to crucify him.

Walking to the Crucifixion site (Luke 23:26-27):

As they led him away, they seized Simon of Cyrene, who was coming in from the country. They placed the cross on his back and made him carry it behind Jesus. A great number of the people followed him, among them women who were mourning and wailing for him.

---

[199]The Crown of Thorns made by Roman soldiers may have been a mock Crown of Grass. According to Pliny the Elder (AD 23-79), the Crown of Grass (*corona graminea*) was the rarest and most revered crown awarded by the Roman army. It was only conferred after a desperate military crisis to the leader credited with averting disaster and vanquishing the enemy. The Crown of Grass was awarded by unanimous acclamation of the whole army rather than by a general or Caesar. It was also called the obsidional crown (Latin: *obsidio*, siege or blockade) and was made of grass or shrubs of the conquered region. Romans awarded crowns of various types to citizens who demonstrated valor, some with precious metals and gems, but none was so revered as the Crown of Grass. Pliny the Elder, *The Natural History*, 22: 4, trans. John Bostock and H.T. Riley (London: Taylor and Francis, 1855). *www.perseus.tufts.edu*. Perseus Digital Library, Tufts University, http://www.perseus.tufts.edu/hopper/text?doc=Perseus:text:1999.02.0137:book=22:chapter=4. (accessed February 20, 2018).

Image 32 - *The Scourging on the Back*. James Tissot.

9:00 AM

The Crucifixion (John 19:16-27):

Then Pilate handed him over to them to be crucified.[200]
So they took Jesus, and carrying his own cross he went out to the place called "The Place of the Skull" (called in Aramaic Golgotha). There they crucified him along with two others, one on each side, with Jesus in the middle. [19] Pilate also had a notice written and fastened to the cross, which read: "Jesus the Nazarene, the king of the Jews." Thus many of the Jewish residents of Jerusalem read this notice, because the place where Jesus was crucified was near the city, and the notice was written in Aramaic, Latin, and Greek. Then the chief priests of the Jews said to Pilate, "Do not write, 'The king of the Jews,' but rather, 'This man said, I am king of the Jews.'" Pilate answered, "What I have written, I have written."

*Now when the soldiers crucified Jesus, they took his clothes and made four shares, one for each soldier, and the tunic remained. (Now the tunic was seamless, woven from top to bottom as a single piece.) So the soldiers said to one another, "Let's not tear it, but throw dice to see who will get it." This took place to fulfill the scripture that says, "**They divided my garments among them, and for my clothing they threw dice.**"[201] So the soldiers did these things.*

Now standing beside Jesus' cross were his mother, his mother's sister, Mary the wife of Clopas, and Mary Magdalene. So when Jesus saw his mother and the disciple whom he loved standing there, he said to his mother, "Woman, look, here is your son!" He then said to his disciple, "Look, here is your mother!" From that very time the disciple took her into his own home.

---

[200]Mark's Gospel states the time of Jesus' crucifixion was 9:00 am (Mark 15:25) while John's Gospel states it was "about noon" (John 19:14). Matthew and Luke do not state the time of crucifixion. Matthew, Mark and Luke place Jesus' time of death at 3:00 pm (Matt. 27:45-50, Mark 15:33-37, Luke 23:44-46). John does not state the time of death.
[201]Ps. 22:18

Noon

The Darkness (Luke 23:44):

It was now about noon, and darkness came over the whole land until three in the afternoon, because the sun's light failed.

Image 33 – *Crucifixion*. Nikolay Ge.

3:00 PM

Death of Jesus (Mark 15:33-4):

*Around three o'clock Jesus cried out with a loud voice, "Eloi, Eloi, lama sabachthani?" which means, "**My God, my God, why have you forsaken me?**" When some of the bystanders heard it they said, "Listen, he is calling for Elijah!" Then someone ran, filled a sponge with sour wine, put it on a stick, and gave it to him to drink, saying, "Leave him alone! Let's see if Elijah will come to take him down!"*

But Jesus cried out with a loud voice and breathed his last. And the temple curtain was torn in two, from top to bottom. Now when the centurion, who stood in front of him, saw how he died, he said, "Truly this man was God's Son!"

The Piercing of Jesus' Side (John 19:31-37):

*Then, because it was the day of preparation, so that the bodies should not stay on the crosses on the Sabbath (for that Sabbath was an especially important one), the Jewish leaders asked Pilate to have the victims' legs broken and the bodies taken down. So the soldiers came and broke the legs of the two men who had been crucified with Jesus, first the one and then the other. But when they came to Jesus and saw that he was already dead, they did not break his legs. But one of the soldiers pierced his side with a spear, and blood and water flowed out immediately. And the person who saw it has testified (and his testimony is true, and he knows that he is telling the truth), so that you also may believe. For these things happened so that the scripture would be fulfilled, "**Not a bone of his will be broken**."[202] And again another scripture says, "**They will look on the one whom they have pierced**."[203]*

---

[202]Ps. 34:20
[203]Zech. 12:10

Medical Commentary

Sweating Blood

Sweating blood, called *hematidrosis* in medical terminology, is a rarely observed phenomenon. It is the spontaneous discharge of blood through the skin, *sweating blood*. Descriptions and symptoms vary. In some people, the skin can become sensitive and blood expressible from the skin. Others experience less pronounced manifestations, for example blood tinged sweat.[204] A handful of cases have been evaluated with modern medical technology but the etiology, or exact medical cause, remains unknown. Thus, the pathophysiology of hematidrosisis still a medical mystery.

Case reports in medical literature are of patients with recurrent episodes of hematidrosis, making them somewhat unlike Jesus who experienced only one episode prior to his execution. Anxiety or fear appear to be triggering factors. For example, a ten year old girl in India developed hematidrosis after seeing her elder sister being abducted.[205] Recurrent hematidrosis typically subsides when patients are treated with medications for anxiety.[206]

A fourteen year old Thai girl was hospitalized for recurrent hematidrosis. She had frequent episodes of bleeding from the scalp, palms, trunk and legs. She underwent thorough medical evaluation. Extensive laboratory testing was normal. Biopsy showed that blood cells collected in vacuoles in the dermis, an under-layer of the skin, or in hair follicles. How these spaces became filled with blood remained unclear, however, since there were no adjacent blood vessels. Electron microscopy was without evidence of vasculitis (i.e. inflammation of the blood vessels) or alteration in blood vessel

---

[204] J.E. Holoubek and A.B. Holoubek, "Blood, sweat and fear. A classification of hematidrosis," *Journal of Medicine*, 2, no. 3-4 (1996):115-33.

[205] B.K. Praveen and Johny Vincent. "Hematridosis and hemolacria: A Case Report." *Indian Journal of Pediatrics*. 79. (2012):109-111.

[206] Ibid.

structure. Blood extruded from the vacuoles directly through the skin or through hair follicles but not through sweat glands (Image 34: *Hematidrosis Skin Biopsy*). This caused the appearance of sweating blood but sweat glands were not involved. After the hematidrosis stopped, the empty vacuoles collapsed without leaving scars.[207]

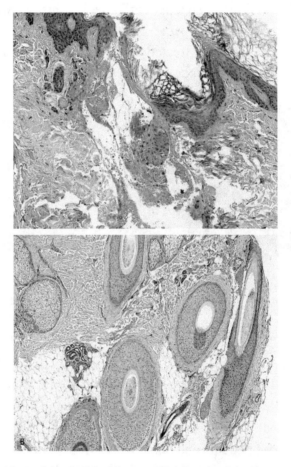

Image 34 - *Hematidrosis Skin Biopsy*. The upper slide shows vacuoles of blood cells within the skin being extruded directly through the skin surface. The slide below shows blood cells collected around hair follicles. (Both images magnified x 4). Image used with permission.

---

[207]Jane Manonukul, et al. "Hematidrosis: a pathological process of stigmata. A case report with comprehensive histopathological and immunoperoxidase studies," *American Journal of Dermatopathology* 2. (2008): 135-139

In a similar case, a 21 year old woman was hospitalized for repetitive episodes of hematidrosis. There was no apparent cause for the bleeding episodes. Laboratory testing was normal, specifically without any evidence of a bleeding disorder. Unlike the prior case, skin biopsies in this patient were normal (Image 35: *Hematidrosis Patient*). A physiological source for her hematidrosis could not be identified. This patient's medical history was notable for major depression and panic disorder. Hematidrosis episodes subsided when she was treated with propanalol, a medication sometimes used to treat anxiety.[208]

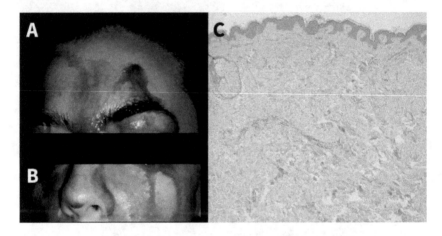

Image 35 - *Hematidrosis Patient*. A 21 year old woman is pictured who had unexplained recurrent bleeding discharges through her skin (A,B). Skin biopsy (C) of a bleeding area was normal, without any hisopathologic changes(hematoxylin-eosin stain, magnification x 20). Image used with permission.

Both of these patients had been hospitalized for observation and testing. There was no evidence of self-inflicted wounds; had self-inflicted causes for bleeding been present it would have been evident on biopsy. Thorough medical evaluation was performed.

[208]Roberto Maglie and MarziaCaprioni, "A case of blood sweating: hematohydrosis syndrome" *Canadian Medical Association Journal*, 189, no. 42 (2017): E1314. doi: 10.1503/cmaj.161298.

Laboratory testing was normal for both, specifically without evidence of any bleeding disorder. In spite of thorough medical evaluation, the pathophysiology of their hematidrosis could not be identified. However, anxiety appears to have been a contributing triggering factor in each case.

Jesus experienced extreme emotional distress the night before his execution. He had premonition of his crucifixion and had warned his disciples about his impending execution but they didn't seem to understand (Matt. 20:17-19, Mark 10:33-34, Luke 9:22). Jesus' disciples couldn't fathom the idea that the man they believed to be the Messiah could suffer such an ignominious death. Jesus had seen people crucified. He understood the extreme torture he was about to experience.

The rarest form of hematidrosis is *Single-episode* psychogenic hematidrosis and is associated with the fear of death prior to execution. There are only a handful of reported cases of this kind.[209] That Jesus sweat blood indicates he had clear understanding of the horror he was about to experience. It is interesting that only Luke, a physician, wrote about Jesus sweating blood. He must have considered it a significant detail.

Fluid Deprivation

During times of emotional distress, sweating is increased due to increased elevated circulating catecholamines (hormones made by the adrenal gland) in the blood. This is caused by sympathetic nervous system activation and commonly called a "fight or flight" response or an "adrenaline rush."[210] A high state of anxiety and

---

[209]Holoubek and Holoubek. "Blood, sweat and fear," 120.

[210]The Sympathetic Nervous System is part of the Autonomic Nervous System. The Autonomic Nervous System is the part of the nervous system that controls visceral functions. Effects from sympathetic nervous system activation can be rapid and profound. Sweating and dramatic elevations in heart rate can occur within seconds for example. Guyton and Hall, *Medical Physiology*. p. 729.

sweating would contribute to dehydration. Jesus would have been without food or water for at least twelve hours prior to being placed on the cross. We can safely assume that Jesus would have been deprived of anything to eat or drink after his arrest. Symptoms of dehydration could include thirst, dry mouth, headache, dizziness, confusion, muscle cramps and heart palpitations.

Severity of Jesus' Beating

Jesus' beatings were particularly severe, beyond what a condemned prisoner would ordinarily experience. Jesus was beaten by Jewish Temple Guard soldiers prior to being placed into Roman custody. He was then again beaten and scourged by Roman soldiers. The "whole cohort" of Roman soldiers participated in mocking and severely beating him. He was severely flogged, spit on, blindfolded and hit with a rod used as a mock royal scepter (Matt. 27:27-31, John 19:1-3).

The severity of Jesus' initial beatings while in Jewish custody should not be overlooked. Thomas McGovern, M.D., makes an interesting observation about Luke's description of Jesus' first beating while in Jewish custody. "Now the men who were holding Jesus under guard began to mock him and beat him." (Luke 22:63). Luke uses the Greek verb *derontes* (δέροντες) for the phrase "and *beat* him." The Greek root of this word is the same for skin, *derma* (δέρμα), and carries the primary meaning of "to flay the skin." "To beat" is a secondary meaning. When the word is used to describe a beating or whipping, it implies a heightened severity of thrashing and cudgeling.[211] Luke as a physician seems to use specific language to precisely describe the severity of Jesus' beating.

Since the Sanhedrin would have executed Jesus if they had

---

[211]Thomas McGovern, Lesson 2 in online course "Another Doctor at Calvary," *Catholic Distance University*. https://cdu.catalog.instructure.com/browse/cma/courses/another-doctor-at-calvary. (accessed May 3, 2016).

opportunity to do so, it seems likely that his beating from the Temple Guard would have been particularly severe. The maximum penalty short of death by Jewish law was forty stripes (Deut. 25:3). Jewish courts had autonomy in corporal punishment and could lash offenders at their discretion without Roman interference.[212] Roman soldiers were free to beat condemned prisoners without restriction, the only stipulation being that the prisoner should not be beaten to death prior to crucifixion.

Accordingly, it is traditionally held that Jesus was scourged twice. The first beating was in the home of Caiaphas the High Priest, the second by Roman Soldiers under order of Pontius Pilate. The scourging pillar from the home of Caiaphas is said be in the *Chapel of the Apparition of Jesus to His Mother* in the Church of the Holy Sepulchre in Jerusalem (Image 36: *Column of Flagellation*). The scourging pillar used by Pilate's soldiers is believed to be in the Church of Santa Prassede in Rome.[213] (Image 37: *Colonna della flagellazione di Cristo*).

---

[212]The Jews were free to implement corporal punishment unless the offender was also a Roman citizen. Roy A. Stewart, "Judicial Procedure in New Testament Times." *Evangelical Quarterly*. 1975. 94-109

[213]Thomas McGovern, Lesson 2 in "Another Doctor at Calvary," *Catholic Distance University*. https://cdu.catalog.instructure.com/browse/cma/courses/another-doctor-at-calvary. (accessed May 3, 2016)

Image 36 - *Column of Flagellation,* thought to be the scourging pillar used by Caiaphas, can be seen at the Chapel of the Apparition of Jesus to His Mother in the Church of the Holy Sepulchre in Jerusalem, Israel. Used with permission, courtesy of Associazione pro Terra Sancta, www.proterrasancta.org.

Image 37 - Colonna della flagellazione di Cristo. Church of Santa Prassede in Rome. The pillar is thought to be the scourging post used by the Roman soldiers to scourge Jesus.

Roman Scourging

Roman soldiers scourged all condemned prisoners prior to execution. Jesus' scourging was more severe than usual due to the particular disdain exhibited by the Roman soldiers. Romans were known to have anti-Semitic sentiments which would have been heightened by thinking of Jesus as a political insurgent.[214]

The obvious immediate effect of scourging would be intense and diffuse pain. This would have caused further sweating, rapid breathing and heartbeat from the "fight or flight" physiologic response to pain. Roman scourging caused blunt trauma, contusions, and lacerations all over the body. This would have caused significant blood loss from the cuts and tears in his flesh as well as bruising from blunt trauma.(See Chapter 5 for discussion of Roman crucifixion practices).

Lung Injury

Scourging and blunt trauma to the chest wall can cause injury to the lungs. This can include several possible types of injury. The lungs themselves can become bruised (pulmonary contusion) with blood and fluid collecting within the lung tissue, sometimes called a "traumatic wet lung." The lung can also collapse, called "pneumothorax." Fluid can collect around the lungs, called a "pleural effusion." Fluid around the lungs is typically clear, but could have a bloody appearance if bleeding occurred or if there was a penetrating wound to the chest.

Dr. Frederick Zugibe describes the autopsy of a murder victim beaten to death with a belt and an electric cord. The victim had a collapsed lung (pneumothorax), as well as bruising and bleeding

---

[214]Hynek RW. *Science and the holy shroud, an examination into the sacred passion and the direct cause of Christ's death* (Chicago: Benedictine Press; 1936), 52. Also, Josephus F In: Whiston W, editor. *The works of Josephus: new updated edition.* In "The Wars of the Jews", 5. Peabody: Hendrickson Pub Inc.; 1987. p. 11. 1. p 720

within the lungs.[215] Scourging prior to crucifixion would be equally, if not more severe.

Water and Blood from the Chest Wound

The description of water and blood flowing from Jesus' side has been a point of controversy. Early theologians struggled with possible figurative or spiritual meanings.[216]Origen, a third century theologian and Church Father, believed that blood would clot in a dead body and therefore concluded the water and blood emanating from Jesus' chest wound was a miraculous sign.[217] We now understand that the literal description of water and blood coming from Jesus' chest wound can be readily explained medically.

Roman soldiers knew how to deliver a death blow. In the Greek text, John used the word pleura (πλευρα, rib) to indicate the location of the spear wound (translated "side", John 19:34). The spear would have entered Jesus' chest wall between the ribs. John does not say which side of the chest the spear entered, but it is considered to have been the right side since the right side of the heart would be more likely to have a reservoir of blood at the moment of death.[218]Pleural effusion (fluid around the lung) generally has a clear appearance and would be described as "water" by someone in the ancient world. When the spear ruptured the heart, blood would mix with fluid in the chest and give the appearance of blood emanating from the chest

---

[215]Zugibe, *The Crucifixion of Jesus*, 21-23.

[216]Wallace, J. Warner, "Was John Describing Something He saw, or Was He trying to Make a Point?" *ColdCaseChristianity.com*. Cold Case Christianity, August 17, 2016. http://coldcasechristianity.com/2016/was-john-describing-something-he-saw-or-was-he-trying-to-make-a-point/?utm_source=feedburner&utm_medium=email&utm_campaign=Feed%3A+ColdCaseChristianity+%28Cold+Case+Christianity%29.(accessed June 1, 2017).

[217]RC Foster, *Studies in the Life of Christ: introduction, the Early Period, and middle Period, the Final Week*. College Press Pub Co, 1995. p. 1287. See also, Origen, *Contra Celsum*, Book II, Ch 36, trans. Henry Chadwick (Cambridge: Cambridge University Press, 1953) 96.

[218] Edwards, *the Physical Death of Jesus Christ*, 1462.

wound (Image 38: *Chest Wound*).

Seeing water and blood come from Jesus' chest seemed peculiar to those who watched him die. However, no miracle is necessary to explain the appearance of water and blood emanating from Jesus' chest wound. The biblical description of a spear impaling Jesus' chest is taken to be accurate from a medical perspective.

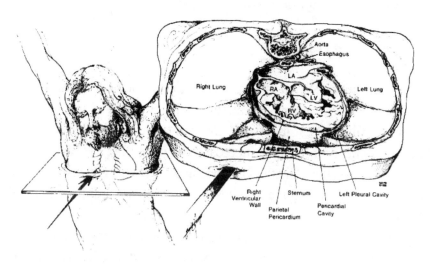

Image 38 - *Chest Wound*. A spear entering Jesus' chest would first tap clear fluid around the lungs. Blood would mix with the fluid when the spear ruptured the heart. This would cause the appearance of water and blood separately. Image used with permission.

Early Signs of Shock

Shock occurs because of decreased blood perfusion to the organs and tissues of the body. In Traumatic Hemorrhagic Shock, seemingly the case with Jesus, shock occurs from decreased circulating blood volume due to injury and bleeding. Symptoms can include confusion, light-headedness, feeling cold and clammy, weakness, and extreme thirst. Jesus was unable to carry the short horizontal section of the cross, the *patibulum* (about 60 lbs.), to the execution site, something that would have been expected of him. Since no Roman would be willing to carry the *patibulum*, Simon of Cyrene, an innocent bystander was recruited to carry it for him (Matt. 27:32).

Jesus was in a weakened condition from the effects of multiple beatings, fluid deprivation and blood loss. More likely than not, he was in early stages of shock prior to being lifted onto the cross (see Chapter 7 for further discussion about shock).

Pronounced Dead

It is an unwelcomed task for those in the medical profession to pronounce the death of a patient. There are certifications and statutory filings required with the cessation of human life that require some training and medical understanding. However, the determination that death has occurred is straightforward and obvious. Recognizing that life has ceased does not require a medical degree.

It can be assumed that the Roman soldiers overseeing Jesus' execution would have credible expertise and experience in the pronouncement of death. To err and allow a capital criminal to escape the death sentence would have dire consequences for the Centurion and his soldiers. It was the Centurion's job to verify the death of each prisoner. Verification of Jesus' death was provided to Pontius Pilate prior to release of his remains for burial, for example (Mark 15:43-46).

It can be reasonably concluded that Jesus was dead prior to the stab wound. However, a spear plunged through his chest gave the Roman soldiers further assurance that Jesus was unquestionably dead.

Jesus' cause of death has been a topic of speculation for centuries. *Cause of death* in general terms refers to the events or conditions leading to the cessation of life. Jesus' cause of death was crucifixion. However, exactly what physiological process led to his death has perplexed physicians. In medical parlance, the physiological process leading to death is more precisely termed the *mechanism of death.*

Death from crucifixion resulted from the physiological effects of prolonged torture rather than from a specific mortal wound. The mechanism of death in crucifixion is not obvious compared to a gunshot wound from a firing squad, for example. Rather, crucifixion was designed to delay death by sparing vital organs from direct injury. Medical writers as well as clergy have speculated as to what may have ultimately led to Jesus' death, but a clear consensus has been elusive. This is understandable since the physiological mechanism leading to Jesus' death is not self-evident and cannot be known with absolute certainty. Since Jesus did not die in a hospital, there are no medical records or autopsy reports to review. However, medical analysis of the biblical descriptions of Jesus' death provide clues to the physiological processes that were most likely occurring in Jesus' body.

The most well-known potential explanations for the mechanism of Jesus' death have been cardiac rupture, fatal chest wound, suffocation, and shock.[219] Each of these physiologic mechanisms is very different medically. The logical merit of each requires examination.

---

[219]Other lesser known hypotheses for Jesus' death have been proposed, including suspension trauma and deep venous thrombosis. These have limited logical merit and have not found popular favor or medical consensus. For further discussion, the reader is referred to Bergeron, "The Crucifixion of Jesus," 113–116.

A Broken Heart

The first literary reference to Jesus dying from a ruptured heart is from the fourteenth century by St. Bridget of Sweden, "When his death drew near, his heart burst because of the violence of the pain."[220]The idea that Jesus died of a "broken heart" has some sentimental appeal. In orthodox Christian faith, Jesus' crucifixion was the sacrificial atonement for the sins of all humanity (1 John 2:2). It stands to reason that some Christian faithful might assume the emotional duress and physical sufferings of Jesus would have had cardiac effects. The first medical writer to propose a cardiac mechanism for Jesus' death was William Stroud in 1847. Dr. Stroud proposed that Jesus died by rupture of the heart muscles as a result of severe "mental agony."[221]

Interestingly, in more recent times it has been found that severe emotional distress can affect the heart muscle. There is a rare condition called Takotsubo stress-induced cardiomyopathy, sometimes called the "Broken Heart Syndrome." This condition occurs after extreme stress. It temporarily weakens the heart muscle and actually causes the heart to balloon or dilate. When this occurs the heart is unable to beat properly and causes symptoms indistinguishable from a heart attack.

Broken Heart Syndrome is rare and the actual incidence is unknown. However, Jesus does not fit the profile of patients suffering from this syndrome. Only three percent of those affected

---

[220]St. Bridget reported the description of Jesus' death as told to her in a vision of the Virgin Mary. St. Bridget of Sweden, *The Prophecies and Revelations of Saint Bridget of Sweden,* Chapter 10.
http://www.saintsbooks.net/books/St.%20Bridget%20(Birgitta)%20of%20Sweden%20-%20Prophecies%20and%20Revelations.html (accessed February 23, 2017). See also, Zugibe, *The Crucifixion of Jesus,* 123.

[221]William A. Stroud, *Treatise on the physical cause of the death of Christ and its relation to the principles and practices of Christianity* (London: Hamilton and Adams, 1847) 334–335. Stroud also felt that spontaneous rupture arising from emotional anguish explained the appearance of water and blood from the chest stab wound, and that Jesus had already died by the time the soldier impaled his chest.

by Takotsubo stress-induced cardiomyopathy are under age fifty and cardiac rupture is thought to occur in less than two percent of these patients. Patients are typically over age fifty, ninety percent are female, and those affected generally have a good prognosis for recovery in the absence of any underlying cardiac disease.[222] The effects of extreme emotional stress on Jesus' heart muscles, and Takotsubo stress-induced cardiomyopathy specifically, are unsupportable as mechanisms for Jesus' death.

The most common cause of cardiac rupture is a heart attack, in medical terms *myocardial infarction*. Heart attacks occur when a clot (thrombosis) occurs in an artery providing blood to a portion of the heart muscle. After a heart attack, inflammatory changes and infiltration of neutrophils (a type of white blood cell) occurs in the area in the heart muscle not receiving its necessary blood supply. Unless blood flow is re-established through the clogged artery, slow disintegration of the heart muscle can occur with the potential risk of cardiac rupture.

A heart attack would be very unlikely in a healthy male in his early thirties. However, even if one were to speculate that Jesus may have had a heart attack, rupture of the heart muscle is not common and normally does not happen immediately. Rather, rupture from this mechanism typically occurs in three to five days. Still, this is not a common occurrence. Before modern treatments now available to reestablish blood flow through the clogged arteries, risk of heart rupture from a heart attack was only 1–3 percent. If a patient survives a heart attack, the area of the heart injured by the clogged artery develops a scar and the risk of rupture diminishes. In rare cases, rupture can occur within 24 hours of a heart attack but this is typically when blood accumulates between the muscle fibers of the heart (hematoma) causing the muscle fibers to separate or dissect.

---

[222]Abhiram Prasad, Amir Lerman, and Charanjit S. Rihal, "Apical ballooning syndrome (Tako-Tsubo or stress cardiomyopathy): A mimic of acute myocardial infarction." *American Heart Journal* 155, no. 3. (2008): 408–417.

If this occurs, it can lead to rapid rupture of the heart muscle.[223]

Knowledge of cardiac disease was limited in Dr. Stroud's time. The idea that Jesus' mechanism of death was spontaneous cardiac rupture is difficult to support as medically logical any longer. This explanation has largely fallen out of favor.

Fatal Stab Wound

Cardiac rupture from traumatic injury to the heart is not out of the question, however. There is logical merit in considering whether Jesus may have died from a stab wound rupturing his heart. Jesus' disciple, John, described a Roman soldier impaling Jesus' chest with a spear. John was specific, if not redundant, in stating that he was an eyewitness of the event.

Then, because it was the day of preparation, so that the bodies should not stay on the crosses on the Sabbath (for that Sabbath was an especially important one), the Jewish leaders asked Pilate to have the victims' legs broken and the bodies taken down. So the soldiers came and broke the legs of the two men who had been crucified with Jesus, first the one and then the other. But when they came to Jesus and saw that he was already dead, they did not break his legs. But one of the soldiers pierced his side with a spear, and blood and water flowed out immediately. And the person who saw it has testified (and his testimony is true, and he knows that he is telling the truth), so that you also may believe (John 19:31–36).

Some have thought that the description of blood flowing from Jesus' side indicated that he was alive at that moment, the premise being that blood does not flow from a wound in a dead body. The idea that blood cannot flow from a corpse is not necessarily true,

---

[223]Yochai Birnbaum, Michael Fishbein, Carlos Blanche, and Robert Siegel, "Ventricular Septal Rupture after Acute Myocardial Infarction," *New England Journal of Medicine* 347, no. 18 (2002) 1426-1432.

however. A large clot such as could develop in the heart at the moment of death may be unstable and re-liquefy. Additionally, the effects of traumatic shock can impair the blood's usual clotting capabilities. In cases of violent traumatic death, for example, the blood's capacity to clot can be compromised to a point where blood will ooze from the wounds of a corpse.[224] In sum, the description of blood flowing from Jesus' side does not mandate the conclusion that Jesus was alive when the spear impaled his chest.

The importance of John's eyewitness description should not be overlooked. The Jews asked Pilate to have his soldiers inflict further torture by breaking the legs of those being crucified so that their bodies would not remain on crosses during that particular Sabbath (John 19:31). Usual Roman practice was to allow bodies to remain on the cross to be consumed by scavenging animals, but this Sabbath was a "an especially important one" (John 19:31). This particular Sabbath was during a religious festival, the week-long Feast of Unleavened Bread and therefore *doubly* Holy in Hebrew culture. Pilate agreed to their request, but when the soldiers came to Jesus they did not break his legs since they found him dead already (John 19:33).

With a mandate that those being executed had to die before sundown, soldiers broke the legs of the others being crucified. They would not have hesitated to break Jesus' legs also. Roman soldiers were skilled in execution and assuring condemned prisoners were killed. We must therefore conclude that Jesus was unmistakably dead, but to assure absolute certainty a spear was thrust into his chest wall which collapsed his lung and ruptured his heart.[225] (Image 38: *Chest Wound*).

It is certain Jesus died that day. However, it is unlikely that the mechanism of Jesus' death was the chest wound based on the evidence considered previously.

---

[224]Zugibe, *The Crucifixion of Jesus*, 214.

[225] Edwards, *the Physical Death of Jesus Christ*, 1462.

Suffocation

Suffocation is the interruption of the breathing apparatus. Asphyxiation is the term given to the effects of oxygen deprivation which potentially can lead to death. Suffocation can cause asphyxiation.

The idea that Jesus died by suffocation was first proposed in 1923 by the French surgeon, Dr. Le Bec, who believed that Jesus' ribs were immobilized when his arms were held by nails in an outstretched position on the cross.[226] In 1936 the Czech surgeon, Rudolph Hynek, expanded on this idea. Dr. Hynek was aware of *Anbinden*, a type of suspension torture used during the Austro-Hungarian War where victims were suspended with their arms tied overhead with their feet unsupported. With the force of their entire body weight being supported only by arms tied directly overhead, the victims' chest walls were expanded, restricting the ribs from moving normally. Regular breathing became impossible and victims rapidly developed severe pain and muscle spasms. Due to its peculiar cruelty, Anbinden was limited to a duration of five to ten minutes at a time. Dr. Hynek believed suffocation occurred during crucifixion by this mechanism.[227]

The belief that Jesus died by suffocation was further popularized by the French surgeon Pierre Barbet in his book *A Doctor at Calvary*.[228] Dr. Barbet was aware of Anbinden torture. He knew that similar suspension torture had also been used at the Dachau

---

[226]Le Bec, "The Death of the Cross: A Physiological Study of the Passion of Our Lord Jesus Christ," *Catholic Medical Guardian*3, (1925): 126–132. (Originally published in French, *La Revue de Philosophie*. March/April 1923).

[227]Hynek, *Science and the Holy Shroud*, 80.

[228]Pierre Barbet, *A Doctor at Calvary: The Passion of our Lord Jesus Christ as Described by a Physician* (Fort Collins: Roman Catholic Books, 1953). Dr. Barbet's academic integrity should be acknowledged. While Dr. Barbet embraced and popularized the idea of suffocation as Jesus' cause of death, he did recognize differing opinions. In Appendix II, Barbet included the opinion of a friend and colleague, Dr. P.J. Smith who differed with Dr. Barbet and felt shock was the most likely cause of Jesus' death.

concentration camp as a form of torture and murder.[229] (Image 39: *Concentration camp, Dachau*). Dr. Barbet was told by an eyewitness of a Dachau prisoner pulling up with his arms in desperation trying to breathe before eventually turning blue and dying by apparent asphyxiation. Victims tortured this way died within three hours.[230] [Suspension torture was used for punishment in Nazi concentration camps and was part of their *Disciplinary and Penal Code*.[231] (Image 40: *Administrative Punishment*)] Based on the eyewitness account recorded by Dr. Barbet, Anbinden suspension punishment could be prolonged to the point of murder.

---

[229]Ibid., 174.

[230]Barbet cites an eyewitness account of Anbinden-like torture at Dachau. The description is consistent with suffocation and death by asphyxiation. In added cruelty, weights were tied to victims feet which appeared to worsen their suffocation. See Appendix I. Ibid.

[231]A form of suspension torture analogous to Anbinden called *Strappado* was part of the *Lagerordnung*, the "Disciplinary and Penal Code" for the Nazi concentration camps. Victims were suspended with arms tied behind the back, dislocating their shoulders, Wikipedia contributors, "Lagerordnung", Wikipedia, The Free Encyclopedia, July 8, 2017, https://en.wikipedia.org/w/index.php?title=Lagerordnung&oldid=789597052. (accessed August 17, 2017), and Wikipedia contributors, "Strappado", Wikipedia, The Free Encyclopedia, November 24, 2017, https://en.wikipedia.org/w/index.php?title=Strappado&oldid=811789389. (accessed December 6, 2017).

Image 39 - *Concentration Camp, Dachau*. Used with permission, Yad Vashem. www.yadvashem.org.

Image 40 - *Administrative Punishment*. Jan Komski. When something unauthorized was found on a prisoner, for example an extra piece of bread, he was subjected to this punishment. Jan Komski, the artist, hung like this an hour a day for three consecutive days, because he brought food and medicine back to the camp after a day at work. Jan Komski was a Holocaust survivor. He had been imprisoned in five concentration camps. This painting depicts punishment at Auschwitz.[232] Used with permission.

---

[232] Jan Komski, "Administrative Punishment – a painting by Jan Komski," *remember.org*. http://remember.org/komski/komski-paintings1-009. (accessed November 3, 2017)

Dr. Barbet noticed that the blood stains bifurcate on the arms in the image of the man on the *Shroud of Turin* (believed by many to be the image of the crucified Jesus). Dr. Barbet supposed that the changes in blood flow resulted from Jesus changing position on the cross, specifically from pulling himself up in an effort to breath.[233] (Image 41: *Shroud of Turin*). Dr. Barbet took this to be evidence that Jesus had to relax his rib cage in order to breathe, similar to descriptions of suspension torture at Dachau. From his knowledge of suspension torture and his inspection of the *Shroud of Turin*, Barbet agreed with doctors Le Bec and Hynek that Jesus had suffocated.

Dr. Barbet further speculated that the Roman practice of *crurifragium*, fracturing bones in the legs while on the cross (John 19:32), prevented crucifixion victims from pushing up with their legs in order to breathe.[234] Dr. Barbet's observations of the *Shroud of Turin* and his awareness of suspension torture supported his *a priori* conclusion that suffocation was the primary mechanism of death with crucifixion. Fracturing the legs (*crurifragium*) worsened the suffocation according to Dr. Barbet.

There are logical problems with suffocation being the mechanism of Jesus' death, however. *Anbinden* torture differs from crucifixion in that the arms were tied directly overhead and the feet were left dangling unsupported. Sometimes weights were also placed on the legs. When used as a form of execution, death by Anbinden-type suspension torture occurred in about three hours with unmistakable signs of suffocation and asphyxiation. In crucifixion, the arms were restrained to the side rather than directly overhead and legs were supported by being nailed in place. Crucifixion could last for days, suggesting that breathing while on the cross was not restricted in any significant way. Jesus himself spoke with the others being crucified with him (Luke 23:39–43). It is counterintuitive to think that

---

[233]Barbet, *Doctor at Calvary*, 76–77.
[234]Ibid., 77–78.

crucifixion victims could carry on a conversation if they were suffocating. Conversing during prolonged Anbinden suspension torture would be impossible.

Furthermore, there is not clear direct evidence to suggest that chest wall movement was significantly restricted during crucifixion. Dr. Frederick Zugibe performed an interesting reenactment experiment, placing subjects on a cross while monitoring their vital signs and blood chemistry. All subjects maintained normal arterial pH and oxygenation throughout the experiment.[235] Subjects fastened to the cross only by their arms with their feet dangling unsupported had severe arm pain but their breathing was unaffected. Fastening the subjects' feet to the cross provided further support which reduced their arm pain, but they continued to be without signs of difficulty breathing.[236]

It is almost certain that crucifixion victims were not able to pull themselves up with their arms. The primary muscles flexing the arms are the biceps (*Biceps brachii*). With the body leaning forward and the arms outstretched on the cross, the biceps muscles would be elongated and at a mechanical disadvantage. In a stretched or elongated position, the biceps muscles would also have diminished contractile capability.[237]

Part of Dr. Zugibe's reenactment experiments included testing subjections to see if they could pull themselves up while on the cross. None could. It is again noteworthy that difficulty in breathing was never reported in Zugibe's experiment.[238] It should not be overlooked that crucifixion victims were severely beaten and in a

---

[235]Frederick T. Zugibe, "Death by Crucifixion", *Canadian Society of Forensic Science Journal,* 17, no. 1. (1984) 1–13.

[236]Zugibe, *The Crucifixion of Jesus,* 85–89.

[237]Zugibe noticed that subjects in his reenactment studies assumed a forward leaning position shortly after being placed on the cross. Zugibe, "Death by Crucifixion," 10. See also, Arthur C. Guyton and John E. Hall, *Textbook of Medical Physiology,* 12th ed. (Philadelphia: Saunders, 2011) 77. A muscle stretched beyond its usual anatomical position has diminished *active tension* or force capability.

[238]Zugibe, *The Crucifixion of Jesus,* 116–119.

weakened condition before being placed on the cross, unlike Dr. Zugibe's young healthy subjects. If crucifixion victims could not breathe without pushing and pulling themselves up, the effects of torture and exhaustion would have led to rapid death. This was not the case, however. Crucifixion victims could remain on the cross for days, perhaps a week or more, before eventually dying.[239] The notion that crucifixion victims had to push and pull themselves up on the cross to keep from suffocating finds little empiric support.[240]

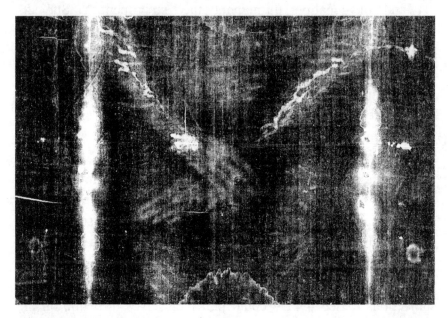

Image 41 - *Shroud of Turin (photonegative)*. Dr. Pierre Barbet believed changes in blood flow on the arms was evidence that Jesus had to pull up with his arms in order to breathe while on the cross. Image used with permission, ©1978 Barrie M. Schwortz Collection, STERA, Inc.

---

[239]There are literary references to crucifixion victims being on the cross for over a week before dying. Ibid.,57.

[240]To consider suffocation as a plausible mechanism for Jesus' death, it would be necessary that he had been suspended on a stake rather than a cross with his hands tied directly overhead with feet unsupported, in essence precisely duplicating *Anbinden* torture. However, this is inconsistent with the Gospel accounts as well as known Roman crucifixion practices in Jerusalem in Jesus' time. The *crux simplex*, or upright stake, was used to impale victims rather than as a form of crucifixion. See Chapter 5 for further discussion.

Dr. Barbet's belief that Jesus died of suffocation was based in part on his observations of the *Shroud of Turin*. An underlying premise was that the *Shroud of Turin* is the burial cloth of Jesus, assumed here for the sake of this discussion.[241] Dr. Barbet believed that the blood stain patterns indicated Jesus had to pull himself up on the cross in order to breathe. This cannot be the explanation for the blood stains on the arms of the *Shroud* image, however. Jesus' body would have been quickly washed in accordance with Jewish

---

[241] Wrapping the corpse in a linen shroud was customary in Jewish culture in Jesus' time. Hachlili, *Jewish Funerary customs*, 444. The Greek word used for Jesus' burial cloth in the synoptic Gospels is, *sindōn*. (Matt. 27:59, Mark 15:46, Luke 23:53) The primary meaning of *sindon* is "fine linen cloth." "Sindon", Strong's Exhaustive Concordance, 4616. biblehub.com. http://biblehub.com/greek/4616.htm. (accessed January 9, 2018). *Sindon* has also been translated as *shroud* (Mark 16:46, Luke 23:53, RSV). John's Gospel uses the Greek word, *soudarion* for Jesus' burial cloth translated as "face cloth" (John 20:7, NET), and states that it was rolled up lying separately from other linen strips (Greek, *othonion*) in the tomb. John uses similar language (John 11:45) when referring to Lazarus' burial cloth, stating a cloth (*soudarion*), was wrapped around Lazarus' face and his hands and feet bound with strips. Barbet proposed that John originally wrote in Aramaic and used the word *soudara*, as a more general term for a large cloth. The same wording is used both with Jesus as well as the description of Lazarus' burial cloth (John 11:44). Barbet suggests the Aramaic word *soudara* transitioned to *soudarion* when John's Gospel was written in Greek. This became *sudarium* in Latin and translated in English as *face cloth*. Barbet, *Doctor at Calvary*, 148. Archeological finds in tombs at En Gedi showed linen cloth wrapped around remains along with knotted fragments of linen, apparently consistent with John's description. Hachlili, *Jewish Funerary Customs*, 482. Barbet's supposition about possible word swapping as John's Gospel was translated from Aramaic to Greek seems credible based on known burial customs in Jesus' time. However, it is possible that any clothes soaked with Jesus' blood were buried with his body. In Jewish tradition, blood as well as amputated body parts are considered part or the individual and retained for burial along with the body. For example with terrorist attacks in Israel, the *Chevra Kadisha* (burial society) collects the remains of those killed in violent deaths including their spilled blood, to be buried with the individual's remains. Rochel Berman, "Dignity in Terrorism" excerpt from chapter 8 in *Dignity Beyond Death: The Jewish Preparation for Burial*, Brooklyn: Urim publications, 2005. kosherfuneral.com. Chevra Kadisha of Florida, http://www.kosherfuneral.com/dignitybeyonddeath.html (accessed March 3, 2018). If similar practices were followed in Jesus' time, a *sudarium* used to wipe blood from Jesus' body may have been buried with his corpse. However, a separate cloth over the face in addition to a shroud over the entire body seems unsupported by funerary customs of the time.

custom before being wrapped in a burial shroud and placed in a tomb.[242] The *Shroud of Turin* image contains blood stains only adjacent to puncture wounds but not otherwise, indicative that the body was washed prior to being wrapped in the cloth. Had Jesus' body not been washed there would have been widespread blotches of blood stains on the *Shroud*. The blood stains on the *Shroud of Turin* are more reasonably from blood oozing from puncture wounds after the body had been washed and wrapped in the burial cloth.[243] Thus, the blood stains on the *Shroud of Turin* did not occur until after the body was wrapped and placed in the tomb.

Crurifragium was the practice of fracturing the legs of crucifixion victims and may have been common practice.[244] Fracturing the legs could have several effects. Besides the obvious effect of pain and torture, further blood loss was likely. Fat globules (emboli) can sometimes enter the blood stream from fractures of long bones. If this happens, injury can occur to vital organs from blocked blood flow. If emboli enter the blood stream and reach the heart or lungs, death could occur rapidly and sometimes immediately. The intent of crurifragium was most likely further torture and punishment.[245] To suggest that breaking the legs is evidence that suffocation occurred during crucifixion is an *a prior* conclusion without adequate basis.

In sum, crucifixion and Anbinden-type suspension torture are not

---

[242]Zugibe, *The Crucifixion of Jesus*, 224–226. See also, Rachel Hachlili, *Jewish Funerary Customs, Practices and Rites in the Second Temple Period* (Boston: Brill, 2005), 384–385.

[243]Blood components have been identified in the blood stain images on the Shroud of Turin. For detailed treatment of the Shroud of Turin the reader is referred to, Raymond N. Rogers, *A Chemist's Perspective on The Shroud of Turin*, (Self-pub., Joan Rogers and Barrie M. Schwortz., Lulu, 2008). See also Chapters 11-19 in Zugibe, *The Crucifixion of Jesus*, 167-332.

[244]Fracturing the legs during crucifixion seems to have been common practice. Legs were found to have been fractured in the remains of a crucifixion victim have been found at the Giv'at ha-Mivtar near Jerusalem. V. Tzaferis, "Jewish Tombs at and near Giv'at ha-Mivtar, Jerusalem." *Israel Exploration Journal*, 20. No. ½ (1970): 18–32. (See Image 25: *Crurifragium*).

[245]Zugibe, "Death by Crucifixion," 6.

sufficiently comparable to conclude that the mechanism of death was the same with both. Furthermore, there is not clear evidence to indicate that suffocation occurred during crucifixion.

A pulmonary death is a worthy consideration, however. Jesus was beaten with a severity that could have injured his lungs. Collapse of the lungs, called *pneumothorax*, can occur from beatings to the chest wall. Also, bruising, bleeding, and fluid accumulation can occur within the lung tissue from pulmonary contusion, something called *traumatic wet lung*.[246] Such complications could impair the lungs' ability to exchange gases and absorb oxygen, potentially resulting in death. Without question, Jesus suffered severe trauma. It is possible, even likely, that his lung function may have been compromised. However, the notion that suffocation was the primary mechanism of Jesus' death is without adequate basis.

Jesus dying in six hours was faster than expected, surprising Pontius Pilate (Mark 15:44). Why did he die so much faster than the others crucified with him? The mechanism of Jesus' death must have differed from the others crucified with him in a way that was not obvious to eyewitness observers. The pathophysiological processes occurring in Jesus' body were either not present in the others, or occurred at a much faster rate with Jesus.

Shock

Shock has many meanings in the English language, from the tangible sensation of electricity to being emotionally flabbergast. In medical science *shock* refers to the effects of decreased blood

---

[246]Zugibe describes an autopsy he performed on a young male beaten with a knotted belt and an electric cord. The autopsy subject experienced both pneumothorax and traumatic wet lung as a result of his beatings. Zugibe described these findings as similar to what would occur with scourging prior to crucifixion, but most likely less severe. Zugibe commented that such a beating can cause fluid to accumulate around the lungs, something called *pleural effusion*. Zugibe, *The Crucifixion of Jesus*, 21–23.

perfusion and oxygen delivery to cells within the body.[247]This can occur by several physiologic mechanisms, including severe allergic reaction, serious infection, a mechanical obstruction limiting blood flow from the heart, and loss of blood from injury. *Traumatic Hemorrhagic Shock* is caused by decreased circulating blood volume (hypovolemia) as a result of injury and bleeding. That Jesus suffered Traumatic Hemorrhagic Shock is suggested by the descriptions of his torture and execution.

Symptoms of shock include decreased systolic blood pressure, typically less than 90 mm Hg. The heart beats faster and blood vessels in the body constrict, compensatory mechanisms by which the body seeks to maintain blood pressure and increase blood return to the heart. There can be signs of inadequate blood perfusion within the body. These may include impaired consciousness such as confusion and disorientation. Kidneys will decrease urine production. The skin becomes cold, clammy, and mottled or of blue discoloration.[248] Extreme thirst can occur during shock, as well.[249]

The human body can compensate for modest blood loss. However, shock can occur when blood loss surpasses 10 percent. At 45 percent blood volume loss, reduction in blood return to the heart and decreased resistance in the body's blood vessels will cause the blood pressure to drop to zero. A modest drop in blood pressure from shock is treatable usually with a good outcome, but there is a point beyond which blood pressure cannot fall without eventually causing death in spite of the best of medical treatment.[250] A rapid or sustained drop in blood pressure can cause irreversible shock and

---

[247]For a more expanded discussion of shock, the reader is referred to Chapter 22, "Circulatory Shock and its Treatment," in Guyton and Hall, *Medical Physiology*, 273–282.

[248]Jean-Louis Vincent and Daniel De Backer, "Circulatory Shock." *New England Journal of Medicine*, 369, no. 18 (2013): 1726–34.

[249]For a historical description of thirst during crucifixion see, Le Bec, "The Death of the Cross," 130.

[250]In experimental animals, a drop in blood pressure below 45 mm Hg was unrecoverable and ultimately resulted in death. Guyton and Hall, *Medical Physiology*, 275.

lead to death even if medical intervention temporarily normalizes blood pressure and vital signs.

The heart muscle itself requires blood flow for oxygen and nutrients like any other organ in the body. If blood supply through the arteries in the heart is inadequate, heart function can become depressed. The effects may not be immediately observable depending on the amount of blood loss since the heart has some compensatory capability. However, the heart can gradually weaken due to inadequate blood perfusion. This is called *Cardiac Depression*.

The Sympathetic Nervous System becomes activated both from the effect of blood loss as well by the anxiety and emotional duress of injury.[251] Blood vessels constrict to increase blood return to the heart and maintain blood pressure. This can have potential negative effects if constricting blood vessels further impairs circulation to soft tissue and organs. If brain function becomes significantly impaired, then the sympathetic nervous system response will diminish causing decreased vascular resistance and lower blood pressure.[252] The sympathetic nervous system also activates sweat glands, explaining why symptoms of shock include sweating and feeling clammy.

The effects of shock and decreased blood perfusion through small vessels and capillaries can cause small regions of tissue necrosis (cellular death). Inflammatory molecules and lactic acid are released due to tissue necrosis which worsens the patient's condition.[253] Diminished nutrient and oxygen supply can also affect the small blood vessels themselves and cause them to lose the ability

---

[251]The Autonomic Nervous System is the part of the nervous system that controls visceral (organ) functions. The Sympathetic Nervous System is part of the Autonomic Nervous System. Effects from sympathetic nervous system activation can be rapid and profound. Sweating and dramatic elevations in heart rate can occur within seconds for example. Ibid., 729.

[252]Ibid..

[253]Richard Dutton, "Pathophysiology of Traumatic Shock, "*International Trauma Care*, 18, no. 1 (2008): 12-15.

to contract, resulting in further drop in blood pressure. If this happens, fluid may exude through the vessel wall causing swelling, decreasing circulating blood volume. Local tissue swelling can then further impede tissue perfusion and increase the toxic chemical byproducts of ischemia (i.e. insufficient blood supply).

Inadequate blood perfusion to organ tissue causes generalized cellular deterioration. Oxygen deprivation causes cellular metabolism to shift from aerobic to anaerobic which produces inflammatory and acidic chemical byproducts. Molecular inflammatory mediators such as lactic acid, carbonic acid, and highly reactive free radicals worsen shock by their toxic effects.[254] The body's pH changes and becomes acidic.

Thus, shock creates a cascade of cellular deterioration through multiple organs and tissues in the body. The effects of shock are many. Cardiac function can become impaired, blood vessels do not function properly, inadequate oxygen supply can cause cellular death leading to widespread inflammation and toxic chemical effects. Acidity develops within the body. The effects of shock are many and each one serious, all the more when multiple effects occur simultaneously. Even more dangerous is amplification of shock through a snowball effect called *a positive-feedback-loop*. That is to say, *shock causes more shock.*

Trauma Induced coagulopathy

The body's first defense against bleeding is for blood to clot at the site of injury. A dangerous possible complication of shock is that blood can lose its normal ability to clot. It has long been observed that traumatically injured patients can have diminished blood clotting ability. This was originally assumed to be a side effect of treatment with intravenous fluids or by hypothermia (decreased core body temperature) and acidemia (decreased blood

---

[254] Ibid., 13.

pH). It wasn't until 2003 that researchers identified coagulopathy in trauma patients (i.e. impaired blood clotting specifically associated with trauma).

This has become known as *Trauma Induced Coagulopathy*.[255]It is present in one in three trauma patients admitted to emergency departments and carries a markedly increased risk of death.[256]Trauma patients admitted to emergency departments are four times more likely to die if coagulopathy is present. Causative factors that trigger coagulopathy during trauma are tissue injury with bleeding, hypothermia, and acidemia.[257]

Tissue injury

There are four major physiologic processes that stop bleeding; blood vessel constriction at the point of injury, blood cells called platelets form a plug, chemical reactions occur that cause clot formation, and finally chemical reactions occur to control excessive clotting and dissolve unnecessary clots. These processes occur simultaneously but independently.

Patients with more extensive injuries have greater risk of developing coagulopathy because the extent and degree of tissue injury is a major trigger. Injured endothelial cells (i.e. cells that line blood vessels) initiate the clotting mechanisms. With diffuse injury and widespread activation the blood clotting mechanisms, necessary blood cells and chemical factors can be depleted and cause an imbalance between the blood's ability to clot and dissolve

---

[255]Mitchell J Cohen and S. Ariene Christie, "Coagulopathy of Trauma," *Critical Care Clinics* 33, no. 1 (2017): 101–118.

[256]E. Gonzales, E.E. Moore, H.B. Moore, M.P. Chapman, C.C. Silliman, and A. Banerjee, "Trauma-induced Coagulopathy: An institution's 35 Year Perspective on Practice and Research," *Scandinavian Journal of Surgery*,103, no.2 (2014): 89–103.

[257]Brandon H. Tieu, John B. Holcomb, and Martin A. Schreiber, "Coagulopathy: It's Pathophysiology and Treatment in the Injured Patient," *World Journal of Surgery*, 31, (2007): 1055-1064. See also Guyton and Hall, "Hemostasis and Coagulation," in *Medical Physiology*, 451-461.

unnecessary clots.[258] This is a detrimental amplification of the body's natural process of dissolving unneeded blood clots, just when the blood's ability to clot is needed most. That is to say, the body shifts to dissolving clots abnormally, when it should be producing more clots where needed instead.

Hypothermia

Normal body temperature is 37 degrees Celsius (98.6 degrees Fahrenheit). Hypothermia (decreased core body temperature to 36 Celsius or below) impairs blood coagulation. Two-thirds of trauma patients have hypothermia, and 9% of trauma patients have severe hypothermia (33 Celsius or below).[259] Enzyme activity is sensitive to changes in temperature. In the human body, a decrease in body temperature slows the activity of enzymes associated with blood clotting. It also impairs platelet (tiny blood cells involved in clotting) activation. This becomes clinically significant at a body temperature of 34 degrees Celsius. The risk of death from trauma markedly increases when the body temperature falls to 33 degrees Celsius or below.[260]

Acidemia / Acidosis

Another inciting factor that contributes to coagulopathy is when the blood becomes acidic, called *Acidemia*, (decreased blood pH which makes the blood more acidic; the process leading to this is called acidosis). Increased blood acidity is the result of cellular ischemia from decreased blood flow and oxygen deprivation. (If the lungs are injured or collapsed and unable to normally exhale carbon

---

[258]Tieu, "Coagulopathy: It's Pathophysiology and Treatment," 1056.

[259]Cohen and Christie, "Coagulopathy of Trauma," 101–118.

[260]John R Hess, et al., "The Coagulopathy of Trauma: A Review of Mechanisms," *Journal of Trauma Injury, infection, and critical care*, 65, no. 4 (2008): 748–754.

dioxide, acidemia can further worsen by a separate mechanism called *respiratory acidosis*). Like decreased temperature, acidity in the blood slows the enzyme activity associated with clotting. Normal human pH is 7.4. At a pH of 7.2 the clotting enzyme cascade is reduced by 50 percent and is reduced by 90 percent below a pH of 7.0.[261]

Trauma Induced Coagulopathy is an ominous potential complication of Traumatic Hemorrhagic Shock and markedly increases the risk of death. The greater the tissue injury and bleeding, the greater the risk. Acidemia and hypothermia are also triggering factors and common during shock. When tissue injury with bleeding, acidemia, and hypothermia occur simultaneously they create a positive-feed-back loop of progressively worsening coagulopathy. This has been called a *lethal triad*.[262] (Image 42: *Lethal Triad*). Trauma Induced Coagulopathy is difficult for physicians to treat in the best modern trauma centers. In Jesus' time, death would be certain and rapid.

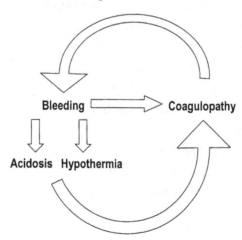

Image 42 - *Lethal Triad*. The combination of injury with bleeding, acidosis and hypothermia can lead to a spiraling progression coagulopathy by a positive feedback loop. Image used with permission.

---

[261]Ibid., 751.

[262]Martin A. Schreiber, "Damage Control Surgery," Critical Care Clinics, 20, (2004): 102.

Evidence of Shock in Jesus

Jesus suffered extensive injury and blood loss prior to crucifixion making him susceptible to shock. Initially after his arrest, he was on trial before members of the Jewish ruling tribunal, the Sanhedrin. He was beaten by the Temple Guard (Luke 22:63, Matt. 26:67, Mark 14:65, John 18:22). The Sanhedrin found Jesus guilty of blasphemy which was punishable by death (Mark 14:63–65). By this time, however, the Sanhedrin had lost autonomous authority for capital punishment.[263] Since Jewish execution of criminals was generally not permitted by Roman authorities, it is likely that Jesus received the maximum beating permitted by Hebrew law prior to being delivered to Roman authorities. Luke's Gospel implies that Jesus received a particularly harsh thrashing from the Temple Guard prior to being sent to Roman authorities (Luke 22:63. See also Chapter 6).

After Pontius Pilate ordered Jesus' execution, Roman soldiers again scourged Jesus prior to crucifixion. Unlike Jewish scourging, Romans had no lash limit. Roman scourging was done with a *flagellum*, a whip comprised of leather strips with dumbbell shaped pieces of lead sewn to the ends (Image 18: *Roman Scourging*). The entire body would be scourged. Romans had known anti-Semitic sentiments which were allowed free and full expression during crucifixion.[264] In Jesus' case, his Roman scourging was most likely particularly brutal.

Jesus was executed as a political insurgent, his stated crime being "the King of the Jews." Roman soldiers would have viewed this as defiance against Caesar, increasing their ire. After scourging him, "the whole cohort" of soldiers gathered to mock and beat him. Notably, he was "struck on the head with a staff" which they had placed in his hand to mimic a royal scepter. A crown of thorns added to the mockery and caused puncture wounds to the scalp (Mark 15: 16–20).

---

[263]Stewart, "Judicial Procedure in New Testament Times," 95.
[264]See fn 214.

The severity of Jesus' beatings has medical significance as a precipitating factor for shock. Besides the loss of blood, widespread soft-tissue injury is a trigger for developing Trauma Induced Coagulopathy. The severity of his beating caused diffuse cellular tissue injury to the musculoskeletal system, and probably internal organ injury as well.

Internal organ injury is suggested by the description of the spear wound to Jesus' chest wall. The appearance of clear fluid from the chest wound (John 19:35) indicates that fluid had accumulated around the lungs (pleural effusion). The pleural effusion would have been caused by beatings to the thorax. Fluid around the lungs typically has a clear appearance and would look like water when the spear initially entered the chest. Once the spear ruptured the heart, blood would mix with the fluid in the chest cavity making the fluid flowing from the chest wound appear to be blood.[265]

Since Jesus' beatings caused fluid to accumulate around his lungs, it is plausible to consider that the lungs themselves may have been injured. If so, blood and fluid could have accumulated within the lung tissue, namely pulmonary contusion and Traumatic Wet Lung. *Pneumothorax* (collapse of the lungs) is also possible in this context. If the lungs were injured and unable to normally exchange oxygen and carbon dioxide, *respiratory acidosis* from lung dysfunction would have made the acidemia worse. Breathing would become labored. Injury to other internal organs was also possible.[266]

Symptoms of shock are suggested in the Gospel accounts. After

---

[265]The heart sits in a sac called the pericardium. Clear fluid can also develop in the pericardial space. However, once a blunt instrument like a spear entered the pericardium it would immediately rupture the heart and mix with the pericardial fluid. It is, therefore, not possible that the clear fluid John described emanating from Jesus' chest wound was pericardial fluid. Zugibe, *The Crucifixion of Jesus*, 139–143.

[266]Traumatic Wet Lung was initially described during World War II when physicians noticed the presence of mucus, blood, and serum in the tracheobronchial tree and lung tissue in those experiencing thoracic trauma. This can potentially worsen the effects of shock by impairing lung function and gas exchange. Earl Sanborn, "Clinico-pathologic aspects of traumatic wet lung, "*American Journal of Surgery*, 87, no. 3, (1954): 457–461.

the Roman flogging, Jesus was compelled to carry the *patibulum* to the crucifixion site, either 300 or 1000 meters.[267] (Image 43: *Jerusalem in the Time of Christ*). Jesus was unable to do so, however. Jesus appears to have been in a weakened condition beyond what was typical for crucifixion victims.

One of Jesus' last statements on the cross was, "I am thirsty!" (John 19:28). It can be assumed that Jesus was denied anything to drink after his arrest. However, the thirst experienced in shock exceeds the typical experience of thirst in a way that is difficult to fully appreciate.

Thirst from hemorrhagic shock is the result of decreased blood volume (hypovolemia). This stimulates *thirst centers* in the brain by two separate mechanisms. Pressure sensors in arteries (baroreceptors) react to decreased blood volume and trigger *thirst centers* in the brain. Decreased blood flow to the kidneys will activate the renin-angiotensin system (a hormone system that regulates body fluid and blood pressure) and also stimulate *thirst centers* in the brain.[268] Literary references of thirst during crucifixion describe a maddening agony.[269] When Jesus said "I am thirsty!", it was almost certainly as a scream.

The environmental conditions were present for Jesus to develop hypothermia. Sympathetic Nervous System activation caused him to be anxious, sweaty, have a rapid heart rate and cause blood vessel constriction. He would have been cold and clammy. Jesus' clothes were taken from him at the crucifixion site leaving him exposed to ambient temperatures (Luke 23:34).

Temperatures were cold in the early morning hours after Jesus' arrest. Peter followed the Temple Guard with Jesus to the Palace of

---

[267]The location of Jesus' burial, and by association the site of his crucifixion, is not known with certainty. Many feel the location of Jesus' tomb is at the *Church of the Holy Sepulchre*, others believe is was *The Garden Tomb*. Holden and Geisler, *Handbook of Archeology and the Bible*, 315-318.

[268]Guyton and Hall, *Medical Physiology*, 358–359.

[269]Le Bec, "The Death of the Cross," 130-131.

the High Priest. He stayed some distance away but tried to monitor what was happening. Yet, it was cold enough that Peter lost his hesitation and joined the Temple Guard to warm himself by a fire, *"slaves and the guards were standing around a charcoal fire they had made, warming themselves because it was cold. Peter also was standing with them, warming himself"* (John 18:18).

Average temperatures in Jerusalem during the first week of April ranges from 8–20 degrees Celsius (46 to 67 degrees Fahrenheit), but can drop as low as minus one degree Celsius (30 degree Fahrenheit).[270] It was cold the day Jesus was crucified. Hanging naked on the cross in cool ambient temperatures, sweaty, and with arms and legs cold due to blood vessel constriction from the effects of blood loss, make it likely that Jesus was hypothermic.

The *Lethal Triad* of causative factors for Trauma Induced Coagulopathy were present, namely, tissue injury with blood loss, acidemia, and hypothermia. Coagulopathy may have been a contributing factor as to why Jesus died so rapidly. It could also explain why blood flowed from the spear wound in Jesus' chest even though he was already dead. If coagulopathy were present, Jesus' blood had lost its normal ability to clot.

Trauma Induced Coagulopathy is a life-threatening complication of shock and is challenging to manage even in modern times. Trauma physicians seek to control bleeding, plus provide treatment with intravenous fluids, coagulation products, blood and plasma transfusions, warm the body, and rigorously monitor and correct blood chemistry. Still, risk of death remains elevated even with aggressive treatment. Without medical treatment, coagulopathy would worsen by a positive feedback loop (snowball-effect), progressively diminishing the blood's ability to clot.

---

[270]Staff writer, "Historic Average, Jerusalem, Israel," *Intellicast, The Authority in Expert Weather.*http://www.intellicast.com/Local/History.aspx?unit=F&month=4. (accessed December 5, 2017). Staff writer, "Jerusalem Climate History," *myweather2.com.* Weather2, http://www.myweather2.com/City-Town/Israel/Jerusalem/climate-profile.aspx. (accessed April 18, 2018).

In Summary

Crucifixion was designed to delay death as long as possible by sparing direct injury to vital organs. The mechanism of death from crucifixion was therefore not obvious. Without objective medical data such has laboratory and hospital records, the mechanism of death cannot be known with absolute certainty and may have differed among crucifixion victims. Suffocation as the mechanism of death with crucifixion is untenable, however. Spontaneous cardiac rupture as a cause of Jesus' death is implausible, as well.

We do not have data of Jesus' physiologic status during his final hours. We must therefore rely on observations in the biblical accounts to form the basis of a forensic reconstruction of the physiological events. Jesus was severely beaten beyond what was typical of crucifixion victims. He exhibited symptoms of shock. Pathophysiological processes were rapidly occurring in Jesus' body. He died much faster than the others crucified with him. Even Pontius Pilate was surprised by Jesus' death in six hours, since crucifixion often lasted for days. The driving mechanisms of Jesus' death were either not present in those crucified with him or were occurring at a much faster in Jesus.

Shock is the most plausible explanation for Jesus' death. Trauma Induced Coagulopathy was a possible contributing factor and may have hastened his death. Forensic pathologist and Medical Examiner, Frederick Zugibe pronounced Jesus' death this way: *Cause of death: Cardiac and respiratory arrest, due to hypovolemic and traumatic shock, due to crucifixion.*[271] Compared to other proposed mechanisms of Jesus' death, shock is the most plausible explanation and is consistent with both current medical understanding and the biblical descriptions.

The Bible contains detailed descriptions of Jesus' execution written by four different authors at different times and in different

---

[271]Zugibe, *The Crucifixion of Jesus*, 135.

locations.[272] If the descriptions were fabricated, it would be detectible with medical scrutiny. However, the biblical accounts of Jesus' execution are essentially the same and can be corroborated with medical science. This is internal evidence of the historical authenticity of the Gospels. The descriptions of Jesus' execution written by ancient observers without medical education can be explained as consequences of Traumatic Hemorrhagic Shock. From a medical perspective, the Gospel accounts of Jesus' death appear genuine.

Knowing that he would be crucified the next day, Jesus reiterated to his disciples during the Last Supper that the purpose of his death was to bring forgiveness to mankind. He gave his disciples bread and wine as emblems of his body and blood. Throughout the world, Christians remember Jesus' Last Supper by celebrating the Eucharist or Holy Communion.

In a somewhat macabre statement at the Last Supper, it's as if Jesus seemed to say that the mechanism of his death would be exsanguination:

---

[272]The date of authorship for each Gospel is not known with certainty and therefore subject to disagreement. Many date the synoptic Gospels (Matthew, Mark, Luke) to prior to 70 AD. John's Gospel is thought to be the latest dated to the 80s–90s. Matt Slick, "When were the Gospels written and by whom?" Christian Apologetics & Research Ministry, CARM.org. https://carm.org/when-were-gospels-written-and-by-whom. (accessed November 3, 2017). Mark is traditionally held as the first written Gospel thought to be written prior to 70 AD. If the Q-source existed, it is thought to have been assembled in the 40–50s AD (see also Chapter 2, fn 35). Matthew's Gospel may have been written in the mid-80s and is traditionally thought to have originated in Antioch, Syria. Luke's Gospel is considered contemporary with Matthew's Gospel and thought to have originated around the Aegean Sea or in Asia Minor. Scholars generally concur that the Gospels were separately authored. Boston College staff, "The Birth of Jesus: Two Gospel Narratives", Boston College, BC.edu.

http://www.bc.edu/schools/stm/crossroads/resources/birthofjesus/intro/the_dating_o f_thegospels.html. (accessed November 3, 2017). It is traditionally held that John wrote his Gospel while living in Ephesus (see Chapter 2, fn 29). For further discussion on Gospel authorship see chapter 2.

Then he [Jesus] took a cup, and when he had given thanks, he gave it to them [his disciples], saying, "Drink from it, all of you. This is my blood of the covenant, which is poured out for many for the forgiveness of sins" [273 and 274] (Matt. 26:27–28, NIV).

---

[273]Although not part of the first Passover meal (Ex. 12:8-11), by the time of the Mishna (c. early third century) it had become Hebrew tradition to raise four cups of wine during the Passover Seder (feast). The feast begins with the first cup, the *Kiddush*. The second cup is the *cup of plagues*, in remembrance of the time of Moses and the plagues God used to free Israel for Egyptian slavery. The third is the *cup of redemption* or *cup of blessing*. The fourth is the *Hallel*, or *cup of praise*. Jesus appears to have followed the same or similar tradition. Luke's Gospel records two times during the Seder when Jesus lifted a cup of wine (Luke 22:17, 20). Paul confirms that it was the third cup, the *cup of blessing*, that Jesus lifted when he announced that the shedding of his blood would grant forgiveness and inaugurate a new covenant between God and mankind (1 Cor. 10:17, 11:25, Luke 22:20). The prophet Jeremiah had foretold that God would one day make a new covenant with man that would transform the hearts of people and forgive their sins (Jer. 31: 31-34). God's new covenant with humanity was enacted by the crucifixion of Jesus (Matt. 26:28). Christians commemorate the *cup of blessing* lifted by Jesus at his Last Supper (Passover Seder)when celebrating the Eucharist and Holy Communion (1 Cor. 11:25-26). David Brickner, "The Mystery of the Passover Cup," *jewsforjesus.org*. Jews for Jesus, March 1, 2002. https://jewsforjesus.org/publications/newsletter/newsletter-mar-2002/the-mystery-of-the-passover-cup/. (Accessed February 13, 2018).

[274] Shedding blood when forming a covenant was customary in the ancient world and in Hebrew culture. To *cut the covenant*, each party would cut their arms and mix their blood to signify they were *brothers of the covenant*. Alternatively, covenants may be solemnized by sacrificing animals after cutting them into two parts. Each party would eat the meat together to bind the covenant. Abraham cut sacrificial animals in two when making his covenant with God, for example (Gen 15:9-10). Salt with bread was taken at the conclusion of solemnizing the covenant. Jewish Encyclopedia editorial committee, "Covenant" in Jewish Encyclopedia, vol 4, 318-322 (New York: Funk and Wagnalls, 1906), *JewishEncyclopedia.com*http://www.jewishencyclopedia.com/articles/4714-covenant. (accessed March 20, 2018).

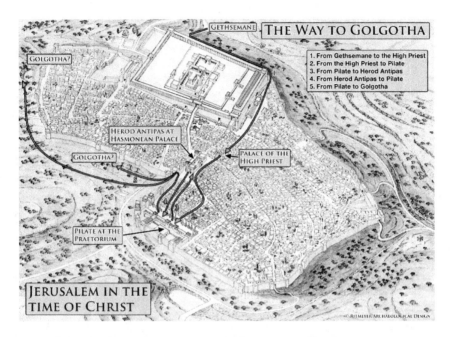

Image 43 - *Jerusalem in the Time of Christ*. Jesus walked approximately 3.5 km (2.2 miles) from his arrest until his crucifixion. Jesus was first taken 1000 m from Gethsemane to the Palace of the High Priest, a multigenerational mansion and likely location of Jesus' meetings with Annas, Caiaphas and the Sanhedrin trial (1). He was then taken 500 m to Pilate (2), from Pilate he walked500 m to Herod Antipas (3), then 500 m back to Pilate (4). Jesus was scourged by Roman soldiers then finally walked either 300 or 1000 meters to the crucifixion site, Golgotha (5).[275] Reconstruction by Dr. Leen Ritmeyer. Image used with permission.

---

[275]Described distances are based on the reconstruction of Jerusalem in the Time of Christ. There are two potential locations for Golgotha, the crucifixion site, either near the Church of the Holy Sepulchre or near the Garden Tomb. Distance from the Praetorium to the Church of the Holy Sepulchre was 300 m and distance to the Garden Tomb was 1000 m. The location of the Last Supper (not on the map) is thought to be near the Pool of Siloam, approximately 1000 m from Gethsemane. Personal communication by email to the author from Dr. Leen Ritmeyer, March 22, 2018.

CHAPTER 8
THE RESURRECTION

Studying the torture and death of Jesus Christ is much like the forensic analysis of a murder case. The historical and medical facts are relatively straightforward. The story of Jesus' execution has one enormous sticking point, however. Orthodox Christianity claims as a core fundamental belief that Jesus was resurrected from the dead to bodily life again by a supernatural act of God. Perhaps nothing has been intellectually attacked with as much fervor as the Christian proposition that Jesus rose from the dead.

Christians celebrate the resurrection of Jesus at Easter. Here are the Gospel accounts of Jesus' resurrection:

Matthew:

Now after the Sabbath, at dawn on the first day of the week, Mary Magdalene and the other Mary went to look at the tomb. Suddenly there was a severe earthquake, for an angel of the Lord descending from heaven came and rolled away the stone and sat on it. His appearance was like lightning, and his clothes were white as snow. The guards were shaken and became like dead men because they were so afraid of him. But the angel said to the women, "Do not be afraid; I know that you are looking for Jesus, who was crucified. He is not here, for he has been raised, just as he said. Come and see the place where he was lying. Then go quickly and tell his disciples, 'He has been raised from the dead. He is going ahead of you into Galilee. You will see him there.' Listen, I have told you!" So they left the tomb quickly, with fear and great joy, and ran to tell his disciples. But Jesus met them, saying, "Greetings!" They came to him, held on to his feet and worshiped him. Then Jesus said to them, "Do not be afraid. Go and tell my brothers to go to Galilee. They will see me there" (Matt. 28:1–10).

Mark:

When the Sabbath was over, Mary Magdalene, Mary the mother of James, and Salome bought aromatic spices so that they might go and anoint him. And very early on the first day of the week, at sunrise, they went to the tomb. They had been asking each other, "Who will roll away the stone for us from the entrance to the tomb?" But when they looked up, they saw that the stone, which was very large, had been rolled back. Then as they went into the tomb, they saw a young man dressed in a white robe sitting on the right side; and they were alarmed. But he said to them, "Do not be alarmed. You are looking for Jesus the Nazarene, who was crucified. He has been raised! He is not here. Look, there is the place where they laid him. But go, tell his disciples, even Peter, that he is going ahead of you into Galilee. You will see him there, just as he told you." Then they went out and ran from the tomb, for terror and bewilderment had seized them. And they said nothing to anyone, because they were afraid (Mark 16:1–8).

Luke:

Now on the first day of the week, at early dawn, the women went to the tomb, taking the aromatic spices they had prepared. They found that the stone had been rolled away from the tomb, but when they went in, they did not find the body of the Lord Jesus. While they were perplexed about this, suddenly two men stood beside them in dazzling attire. The women were terribly frightened and bowed their faces to the ground, but the men said to them, "Why do you look for the living among the dead? He is not here, but has been raised! Remember how he told you, while he was still in Galilee, that the Son of Man must be delivered into the hands of sinful men, and be crucified, and on the third day rise again." Then the women remembered his words, and when they returned from the tomb they told all these things to the eleven and to all the rest. Now it was

Mary Magdalene, Joanna, Mary the mother of James, and the other women with them who told these things to the apostles. But these words seemed like pure nonsense to them, and they did not believe them. But Peter got up and ran to the tomb. He bent down and saw only the strips of linen cloth; then he went home, wondering what had happened (Luke 24:1–12).

John:

Now very early on the first day of the week, while it was still dark, Mary Magdalene came to the tomb and saw that the stone had been moved away from the entrance. So she went running to Simon Peter and the other disciple whom Jesus loved and told them, "They have taken the Lord from the tomb, and we don't know where they have put him!" Then Peter and the other disciple set out to go to the tomb. The two were running together, but the other disciple ran faster than Peter and reached the tomb first. He bent down and saw the strips of linen cloth lying there, but he did not go in. Then Simon Peter, who had been following him, arrived and went right into the tomb. He saw the strips of linen cloth lying there, and the face cloth, which had been around Jesus' head, not lying with the strips of linen cloth but rolled up in a place by itself. Then the other disciple, who had reached the tomb first, came in, and he saw and believed. (For they did not yet understand the scripture that Jesus must rise from the dead.) So the disciples went back to their homes (John 20:1–10).

Image 44 - *Returning from the Burial of Christ.* Nikolai Ge.

Synopsis of the Gospel Accounts of Jesus' Resurrection

On the day of his death prior to the beginning of the Sabbath (i.e. before sundown on Friday evening), Jesus' body had been placed in the tomb after a cursory and incomplete preparation. On the day after the Sabbath (i.e. Sunday morning), a group of women, most notable among them Mary Magdalene, went to Jesus' tomb at day break to finish the usual embalming customs. The women brought aromatic spices that they had compounded (Luke 23:56, 24:1). The biblical accounts are consistent with known Jewish funerary customs in Jesus' time. Preparation for burial began immediately after death in order to bury the body the same day (Deut. 21:23). Funerals could not be performed on the Sabbath, however. Embalming practices included washing the body, anointing the body with water and oil, and sprinkling perfume on the corpse before wrapping it in a shroud. Spices may also be sprinkled over the body prior to wrapping. Once finished and the body wrapped, spices were sprinkled in the tomb and over the deceased.[276]

An angel rolled away the stone from the tomb entrance and Jesus departed. When the women arrived, they were therefore bewildered to find that the stone had been rolled away and the tomb empty. The Jewish Temple Guard standing watch over the tomb fainted when they saw the angel and left the scene after they had regained consciousness. The women encountered Angels, then left to go tell the disciples but met Jesus on the way. (The Synoptic Gospels include Mary Magdalene in the group of women. John's Gospel states Mary Magdalene left the empty tomb to go find Peter and John, thinking Jesus' body had been stolen). Mary Magdalene returned to the tomb with Peter and John. Peter and John were perplexed by the empty tomb and departed to their respective homes. Mary Magdalene stayed at the tomb weeping and encountered Jesus, initially mistaking him to be a gardener.

Why the Variation in Details?

There are variations in detail and sequencing of events among the Gospels regarding the discovery of Jesus' resurrection. This is not unusual for eyewitness testimony according to cold-case murder detective J. Warner Wallace. Eyewitnesses frequently recall or emphasize certain aspects of the same event differently. This does not indicate any of the witnesses are lying, rather it is consistent with variations of individual perception and memory of the most important features of an event.[277]

The Gospel accounts were written by different people at different

---

[276] Rachel Hachlili, *Jewish Funerary Customs, Practices and Rites in the Second Temple Period* (Leiden: Brill, 2005), 384-385, 444, 480.

[277] J. Warner Wallace, *Cold-Case Christianity: A Homicide Detective Investigates the Claims of the Gospels,* (Colorado Springs: David C. Cook, 2013), 69-86

times and in different locations.[278]Some variations in the story would be expected. If all the biblical accounts were identical in every detail, it would raise suspicion of deliberate corroboration. This is not the case, however. Rather, the unifying big picture of each Gospel account is that Jesus was resurrected to bodily life and that his resurrection was discovered by multiple persons the same day. Jesus' resurrection was later verified by additional subsequent meetings with his followers both separately and in groups.

Appearances of Jesus after the Resurrection

Many meetings with Jesus after Easter are recorded in the New Testament. Jesus met with two of his followers later on the day of his resurrection while they were walking to the nearby town of Emmaus (Luke 24:13–31). Jesus met with his disciples without Thomas (called Didymus or "the twin," commonly known as "Doubting Thomas") present (John 20:19–23). He again met his disciples when Thomas was also present. Jesus demonstrated to Thomas that his physical body had been resurrected to life again by asking Thomas to feel the nail and spear wounds for himself (John 20:26–29). Jesus met with Peter (Luke 24:34). He cooked breakfast for his disciples Simon [Peter], James, John, Nathanial, and Thomas (Didymus), and ate with them (John 21:1–16). Paul, on his way to Damascus intending to persecute Christians there, encountered Jesus. This resulted in Paul believing Jesus to be the Messiah (Acts 9:3–6). Paul noted later that after his resurrection Jesus met with Peter, James, and all the apostles, plus spoke to a crowd of over 500 people at once (1 Cor. 15:3–7). Jesus also met with an unnumbered group of disciples prior to his ascension into Heaven (Acts 1:6–9). It should also be noted that the Gospels provide only a partial list of Jesus' appearances and activities after the resurrection (John 20:30–31; Acts 1:3).

---

[278]See fn 272.

Analysis

Forensic homicide detective, J. Warner Wallace notes that every well-documented and successfully prosecuted criminal case has its weak points, limitations of evidence, and unanswered questions. Jurors are able to weigh the evidence and determine the superior explanation for the facts. With Christianity, the stumbling block is the bodily resurrection of Jesus.[279]

Many are unable to consider the possibility of a supernatural explanation for the disciples' belief that Jesus had risen from the dead. This is an understandable position. Yet if the resurrection story is a fabrication, it is difficult to explain the disciples' unwavering commitment to preach about Jesus' resurrection in spite of great personal risk. Is there a plausible alternate explanation for the disciples' beliefs and actions?

The strength of any hypothesis lies in its ability to explain all the facts and predict observed data. The claims of Jesus' resurrection from the dead to bodily life again should be able to withstand logical scrutiny even though special assumptions are required.

Human proclivity is to favor naturalistic explanations and turn a blind eye to the possibility of a supernatural explanation. To objectively consider all proposed explanations for Jesus' resurrection, however, prejudices must be set aside. The existence of God and the occurrence of an event outside the bounds of natural laws must be considered at least possible. The logical merits of the biblical accounts of Jesus' resurrection can then be compared to alternative naturalistic explanations. First, let's consider the alternative explanations.

---

[279]J. Warner Wallace, "The Problem with the Christian Explanation," ColdCaseChristianity.com, August 24, 2017 http://coldcasechristianity.com/2016/the-problem-with-the-christian-explanation/?utm_source=feedburner&utm_medium=email&utm_campaign=Feed%3A+ColdCaseChristianity+%28Cold+Case+Christianity%29 (accessed March 3, 2017).

Naturalistic Explanations for Jesus' Resurrection

Alternate explanations to the biblical accounts of the disciples' post-crucifixion encounters with Jesus fit into three general categories. Namely, (1) Jesus didn't actually die, (2) the disciples perpetrated a hoax, or (3) the disciples were deceived somehow into thinking Jesus had risen from the dead either by finding an empty tomb or by seeing hallucinations.

Some believe Jesus did not die when he was crucified. They suppose that he either revived or was nursed back to health and eventually went on to live out his life; speculative stories range from Jesus moving to France with Mary Magdalene to living in an ashram in India.[280] Speculations that Jesus did not actually die on the cross have been collectively referred to the "swoon theory."

Others accept that Jesus died by crucifixion but propose that his disciples perpetrated a hoax by removing his body from the tomb. The disciples then spread the story of Jesus' resurrection.

Some propose that Jesus' body was stolen or that his disciples went to the wrong tomb. Happening upon an empty tomb, the disciples mistakenly believed that Jesus had risen from the dead.

Finally, psychiatric phenomena (hallucinations) have also been proposed as a possible explanation for the disciples' belief that Jesus was resurrected from the dead. The diagram below illustrates proposed explanations for the disciples' testimony that Jesus rose from the dead (Image 45: *Tree Diagram*).

---

[280] Zugibe, *The Crucifixion of Jesus*, 146–163.

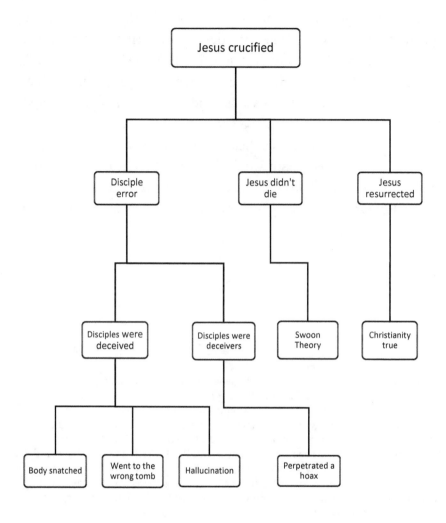

Image 45: *Tree Diagram* - potential explanations for Jesus' resurrection.

The Swoon Theory

Logical problems with non-biblical explanations are immediately apparent. Roman crucifixion practices are described in Chapter 5. Jesus' torture and death are described in detail in Chapters 6 and 7. To suggest that Jesus did not die when crucified is untenable. Moreover, to assure that Jesus was dead a Roman soldier delivered the *coup de grace* of plunging a spear into Jesus' chest, collapsing his lung and rupturing his heart (John 19:34).[281] Only after verification of Jesus' death would his body be released for burial (Mark 15:44–45). The reports of those at the scene, as well as known Roman crucifixion practices, make the proposition that Jesus

---

[281]Quintilian, a first century educator in Roman rhetoric, makes a passing reference to crucifixion in his writings, *The Major Declamations*, 6:9. The declamations (speeches) are framed as arguments in court cases, whether actual or fictitious is unknown. Quintilian noted that, "Crosses are cut down, the executioner does not prevent those who have been struck/pierced from being buried", John G. Cook, *Crucifixion in the Mediterranean World*, (Tubingen: Mohr Siebeck, 2014), 111. It should be noted that this passage has been alternately translated, "But bodies are cut down from crosses, executioners do not prevent executed criminals from being buried", Quintilian, Lewis Sussman translator, *The Major Declamations ascribed to Quintilian*, (Bern: Lang, 1987) 75. The latter translation omits piercing the crucifixion victim prior to release of remains for burial. While Quintilian is not known to have been in the Roman military, it can be assumed that he was aware of Roman crucifixion practices. A stab wound to the chest puncturing the heart could be easily implemented by soldiers on the crucifixion team and is the most likely the *coup de gras* used by Roman soldiers. The executioners were soldiers and the implements at hand to deliver a death blow would be either a sword or spear. While this passage from Quintilian can be translated to indicate that a death blow by stabbing was required prior to releasing the body, there is some disagreement among translators. However, this passage does offer extra-biblical historical evidence of the Roman practice of releasing the crucifixion victim's body for burial after death had been verified, concordant with the Gospel account of Pilate releasing Jesus' remains for burial (Mark 15:44-45).

survived crucifixion impossible.[282]   The *Swoon Theory* is simply balderdash!

Was Jesus' Resurrection a Hoax?

What possible motive would the disciples have for perpetrating a hoax of Jesus' resurrection? There was no incentive of fame and fortune. The personal risks of such a hoax were great, evidenced by the torture and executions of many of Jesus' disciples. All of Jesus' original inner circle of disciples were killed except for one, John. Would his disciples have persisted in perpetrating a hoax knowing that it would almost certainly get them killed?

The notion that the disciples were hucksters is not logically supportable. Blaise Pascal, the seventeenth century French mathematician, physicist, and Catholic theologian stated the problem this way:

The supposition that the apostles were impostors is very absurd. Let us think it out. Let us imagine those twelve men, assembled after the death of Jesus Christ, plotting to say that He was risen. By this they attack all the powers. The heart of man is strangely inclined to fickleness, to change, to promises, to gain. However little any of them might have been led astray by all these attractions, nay more,

---

[282]By the time a victim was actually suspended on a cross, death was imminent. Josephus recalled "...I saw many captives crucified, and remembered three of them as my former acquaintance. I was very sorry at this in my mind, and went with tears in my eyes to Titus, and told him of them; so he immediately commanded them to be taken down, and to have the greatest care taken of them, in order to their recovery; yet two of them died under the physician's hands, while the third recovered." In spite of the best medical care Rome could offer, two of Josephus' three friends died from the effects of torture even though they had a stay of execution from Caesar. Flavius Josephus, *The Life of Flavius Josephus*, William Whiston translator, 75. http://www.perseus.tufts.edu/hopper/text?doc=Perseus:abo:tlg,0526,002:75 (accessed March 23, 2017). To the author's knowledge, this reference from Josephus is the only recorded case of anyone surviving after being placed on a cross.

by the fear of prisons, tortures, and death, they were lost. [283]

Any conceivable reason to perpetrate a hoax would have vanished with the threat of personal suffering and death.

Charles Colson was special counsel to President of the United States, Richard Nixon. As an accomplice in the Watergate Scandal that led to Nixon's resignation, Colson frequently commented on the willingness of those caught up in the scandal to testify against the President in the interest of self-preservation.

Colson said:

Yet even at the prospect of jeopardizing the President, even in the face of all the privileges of the most powerful office in the world, the threat of embarrassment, perhaps jail, was so overpowering and the instinct for self-preservation so overwhelming, that one by one, those involved deserted their leader to save their own skin.

What has that got to do with the resurrection? Simply this: Watergate demonstrates human nature. No one can ever make me believe that 11 ordinary human beings would for 40 years endure persecution, beatings, prison, and death, without ever once renouncing that Jesus Christ was risen from the dead.

Only an encounter with the living God could have kept those men steadfast. Otherwise, the apostle Peter would have been just like John Dean, running to the prosecutors to save his own skin. [284]

Who knowingly sacrifices their life for a lie? It can be reasonably assumed that any hoax of Jesus' resurrection would have been

[283]Blaise Pascal, *Pensées*, 800, Gutenberg.org, Gutenberg project, April 27, 2006, http://www.gutenberg.org/files/18269/18269-h/18269-h.htm. (accessed January 12, 2018).

[284]Charles Colson, "Watergate and the Resurrection of Christ", from a speech delivered at the National Religious Broadcasters Convention, Feb 1984. David and Tim Bayly, "Chuck Colson on the Resurrection" BaylyBlog April 24, 2012. http://baylyblog.com/blog/2012/04/chuck-colson-resurrection. (accessed April 3, 2017).

abandoned as soon as the disciples started getting killed. That the disciples would unite and commit to a life-long hoax of Jesus' resurrection at the cost of personal injury and death is an impossibility.

Body Snatchers?

Could finding an empty tomb have caused the disciples to believe Jesus had been resurrected?

The 1876 attempt to steal Abraham Lincoln's body from the grave was bungled and unsuccessful.[285] But what if the body snatchers had succeeded? Would anyone have believed that Mr. Lincoln had risen from the dead?

A physician, Dr. Charles Leale, was at Lincoln's side within seconds of the assassination. He found Lincoln without a detectable pulse. While examining Lincoln, Dr. Leale removed a blood clot from the back of Lincoln's head, found the gunshot wound and probed it with his left small finger. Mr. Lincoln showed some signs of life after Dr. Leale's resuscitation efforts, but he remained paralyzed and comatose. Recognizing that there was no chance that Mr. Lincoln could survive, Dr. Leale held Lincoln's hand through the night until he died nine hours later. Dr. Leale knew that people sometimes rally at the moment of death, a phenomenon called *Terminal Lucidity*. If Mr. Lincoln were to become conscious at the moment of death, Dr. Leale wanted him to know that "he was in touch with humanity and had a friend."[286] Would finding Lincoln's

---

[285]Thomas J. Craughwell, "A Plot to Seal Lincoln's Body: A posthumous kidnapping attempt shaped the Secret Service." *usnews.com*. June 24, 2017, https://www.usnews.com/news/articles/2007/06/24/a-plot-to-steal-lincolns-body. (accessed May 10, 2017).

[286]Charles A. Leale, "Lincoln's Last Hours", Speech delivered to the Commandery of the State of New York, Military Order of the Loyal Legion, Feb 1909. p. 11. https://archive.org/stream/lasthours00lealrich/lasthours00lealrich_djvu.txt. (accessed May 12, 2017).

tomb empty have convinced Dr. Leale that Mr. Lincoln had risen from the dead?

Had Jesus' body been taken by body snatchers, would this give rise to the story of his resurrection? Actually, when Mary Magdalene found Jesus' grave empty she thought his body had been stolen. She immediately went to Peter and John and told them, "They have taken the Lord from the tomb, and we do not know where they put Him!" (John 20:2). A missing body does not suggest the idea of resurrection from the dead. It would take more than a missing body for eyewitnesses of Jesus' crucifixion to believe he had risen from the dead. They watched his grisly execution and knew he had died (Luke 23:49).

Jesus foretold his crucifixion and resurrection but the disciples never seemed to understand. In fact, Jesus and Peter even got into an argument ultimately ending in a harsh rebuke of Peter by Jesus.

From that time on Jesus began to show his disciples that he must go to Jerusalem and suffer many things at the hands of the elders, chief priests, and experts in the law, and be killed, and on the third day be raised. So Peter took him aside and began to rebuke him: "God forbid, Lord! This must not happen to you!" But he turned and said to Peter, "Get behind me, Satan! You are a stumbling block to me, because you are not setting your mind on God's interests, but on man's" (Matt. 16:21–23).

While some Jews believed in the resurrection of the dead at the end of time, others did not believe in any resurrection at all. A near term resurrection from death, however, was not part of their religious culture and was not something anyone would be expecting

---

Dr. Leale's initial medical report of attending Lincoln after the assassination was found in June 2012 in the National Archives. See, John O'Connor, "Report of first doctor to reach shot Lincoln Found" June 5, 2012. Yahoo News.
https://www.yahoo.com/news/report-first-doctor-reach-shot-lincoln-found-175353998.html?ref=gs. (accessed May 12, 2017).

in Jesus' day.[287] The idea was too far-fetched even to Jesus' closest followers. To think Jesus' disciples had excited expectations of his resurrection is not supportable. It is inconsistent with cultural beliefs of the time as well as the biblical accounts (Luke 24:10–11, 17, 21). After Jesus was crucified, the disciples were forlorn and in hiding (John 20:19).

Did They Go to the Wrong Tomb?

How can going to the wrong tomb lead to the conclusion that Jesus had been resurrected from the dead? Again, an empty tomb simply does not suggest the idea that the dead have been resurrected. In the case of Jesus' burial, the tomb was the family property of a wealthy and socially prominent Sanhedrin member, Joseph of Arimathea. The tomb was intended for the burial of several generations of family members. Joseph's family tomb would be easily identifiable. It was new, large, cut in stone, and empty.[288] Jesus' body was taken to Joseph's family tomb specifically because it was near the crucifixion site and it was late in the day just prior to the beginning of Sabbath (John 19:41). Mary Magdalene and others saw Jesus' body put in the tomb (Mark 15:47, Matt. 27:61, Luke 23:55). They knew where the tomb was. They had to. It was the women's task to return to Jesus' tomb after the Sabbath and complete customary embalming.[289]

Even in the implausible scenario that Mary Magdalene and the

---

[287]N.T. Wright, *The Resurrection of the Son of God; Christian Origins and the Question of God,* volume 3 (Minneapolis: Fortress Press, 2003), 205.

[288] Family tombs were a cultural norm for those who could afford them and might contain remains from several generations. This is exemplified by biblical statements such as, "laid to rest with his ancestors" (1 Kings 1:21, NIV). Hachlili, *Jewish Funerary Customs,* 523. Stone cut tombs typically had a round central room with small separate cavities (loculi) cut into the walls to accommodate the remains of multiple individuals. V. Tzaferis, "Jewish Tombs at and near Giv'at ha-Mivtar," *Israel Exploration Journal,* 20, no. 1/2 (1970): 30.

[289]Washing the body and anointing it with oils and perfumes was typically the task of women. Hachlili, *Jewish Funerary Customs,* 480.

other women could not find the correct tomb, the logical next step would be to inquire of the cemetery staff. If no staff were available, surely one of the other disciples would have remembered where the correct tomb was. If all else failed, they could inquire of Joseph of Arimathea to direct them to the location of his family's new stone cut tomb.[290]

In actual fact, the location of the tomb was known and could be easily located. The resurrection of Jesus cannot be explained away by the proposition that the women mistakenly went to the wrong tomb on their way to complete the usual funeral customs.

It is noteworthy that the Chief Priests went to great effort to see that Jesus' body stayed in the tomb. They asked Pontius Pilate to place soldiers at Jesus' tomb to ensure that the body was not stolen. Pilate told them, "You have a guard. Go your way. Make it as secure as you can" (Matt. 27:65, MEV). But, the Temple Guard soldiers fainted when they saw an Angel remove the stone from the entrance to the tomb. When the guards regained consciousness they went to the chief priests and informed them of what they had seen. The soldiers were then bribed by the Chief Priests to spread the story that Jesus' body had been stolen.

While they were going, some of the guard went into the city and told the chief priests everything that had happened. After they had assembled with the elders and formed a plan, they gave a large sum of money to the soldiers, telling them, "You are to say, 'His disciples came at night and stole his body while we were asleep.' If this matter is heard before the governor, we will satisfy him and keep you out of trouble." So they took the money and did as they were instructed. And this story is told among the Jews to this day (Matt. 28:11–15).

---

[290]Stone cut tombs were intended to hold the remains of multiple family members. See fn 288, above.

The story that Jesus' body had been stolen seems to have been widely circulated. Justin Martyr, a second century Christian apologist, said that this was still commonly reported in his time.[291]

The obvious must not be overlooked. To disband Jesus' followers and put an immediate end to the story of his resurrection, all that was needed was to exhume Jesus' body. Jesus' body was placed in a new stone cut tomb belonging to Joseph of Arimathea, a prominent social figure. Joseph was a well-respected, wealthy member of the Sanhedrin but had not been complicit with their plans to kill Jesus (Mark 15:43, Luke 23:51). It was not a secret that Joseph had obtained Jesus' remains for burial. He had to obtain permission from Pontius Pilate to take Jesus' body away for burial (Mark 15:43–45). The location of the tomb was known. The chief priests placed military surveillance at the tomb, after all. It would have been a simple matter for the chief priests and Sanhedrin to compel Joseph to exhume Jesus' body. Why did the chief priests perpetrate a lie about body snatchers rather than simply exhume Jesus' body for public display?

It was customary for the remains of crucifixion victims to be left on the cross and eaten by scavenging animals. This usual protocol was not followed the day of Jesus' execution because the next day was an "especially important" Sabbath, namely the Sabbath during Passover week (John 19:31). However, to prove a point the authorities could have suspended Jesus' body on the cross again the day after the Sabbath. Had Jesus' corpse been exhumed, put back up on the cross, and left on public display until consumed by scavenging animals, Christianity would not exist.

---

[291]Gary Habermas and Michael Licona, *The Case for the Resurrection of Jesus* (Grand Rapids: Kregel, 2004) 93, fn 36.

The Hallucination Hypothesis

Recognizing the logical problems with "swoon theories," wrong tomb or body snatching explanations, "hallucination hypotheses" have been embraced by some to explain the disciples' meetings with the resurrected Jesus.[292]   Could the disciples have experienced psychological phenomena leading them to believe Jesus had been resurrected from the dead to bodily life?   Such arguments are inherently problematic.

What Are Hallucinations?

A hallucination is an experience in one or more of the five senses in the absence of external stimuli, yet it is perceived by the conscious mind as real.[293] It is a symptom of an underlying problem.   Why hallucinations are occurring must be identified.   This is the underlying flawed premise of most writers who embrace a hallucination hypothesis for Jesus' resurrection.[294] The most important question is not addressed. Specifically, what underlying pathology (diagnosis) caused the hallucination? A medical explanation for hallucinatory symptoms is mandatory. *Hallucination* as a stand-alone explanation for Jesus' resurrection is unacceptable. Could Jesus' disciples have suffered from the types

---

[292]The first literary reference to a hallucination hypothesis occurred in a debate between a second century philosopher, Celsus, and the Church Father, Origen. In more recent times, several authors have proposed psychiatric phenomena to account for the disciples' belief in Jesus' resurrection. Bergeron and Habermas, "The Resurrection of Jesus," 158–168.

[293] Benjamin J. Sadock, Virginia A. Sadock, and Pedro Ruiz, Kaplan and Sadock's Synopsis of Psychiatry, Behavioral Science/Clinical Psychiatry, 11th ed. (Philadelphia: Wolters Kluwer, 2015), 452-453.

[294]Hallucination hypotheses for the story of Easter are found in books or transcribed debates primarily by critical theological scholars. These writers have not been exposed to peer review within the broader medical community. As would be expected, search of medical literature fails to find academic medical discussion on this topic. Bergeron and Habermas, "The Resurrection of Jesus," 161.

of medical conditions that cause hallucinations?

Hallucinatory symptoms can be thought of as arising from one of three general medical categories; psychophysiological, psychobiochemical, and psychodynamic. Psychophysiological causes of hallucination are due to changes in brain structure or function, for example hallucinations due to a brain tumor or occurring after a seizure. Psychobiochemical causes of hallucinations arise from chemical derangement, for example hallucinations during *delirium tremens* from alcohol withdrawal. Psychodymanic causes of hallucinations refer to intrusion of abnormal thoughts and perceptions into the conscious mind. This occurs in psychiatric illnesses such as schizophrenia.

In Jesus' time there was little to no treatment for the kinds of medical conditions that cause hallucinations. Those with severe brain or psychiatric disorders were considered lunatics or demonized and were shunned and ostracized. Who would listen to the severely mentally ill and consider their testimony reliable? Could so many different people at different times and different locations have had physical, biochemical or psychiatric disturbances causing them to have similar, even identical hallucinations?

Hallucinatory symptoms are often associated with those suffering from more severe psychiatric disorders.[295] The rapid spread of Christianity in the first century required organized planning and deliberate action by capable individuals. Christianity spread so fast that Christians were a recognized religious minority by the early 60's AD. Nero blamed them for the great fire in Rome. In 64 AD Nero launched the first mass persecution campaign by Romans against Christians.[296] Could a band of lunatics with severe untreated psychiatric illnesses have deployed such a rapid and successful widespread expansion of Christianity?

---

[295]Bryan Teeple, Jason Caplan, and Theodore Stern, 'Visual Hallucinations: Differential Diagnosis and Treatment,' *Journal of Clinical Psychiatry* 11 (2009): 26–32.
[296]See fn 28.

Did the Apostle Paul have Conversion Disorder?

The Apostle Paul had persecuted and killed Christians when he was a Pharisee (Acts 9:1–2). While traveling to Damascus intent on persecuting the Christians there, he met Jesus on the road and became blind for three days (Acts 9:7–9). Could this be an example of Conversion Disorder? Conversion Disorder is the impairment or suspension of neurologic function due to psychological trauma.[297] (Conversion Disorder is completely unrelated to religious conversion). The psychologist Carl Jung believed that Conversion Disorder was the cause of Paul's blindness. Jung hypothesized that Paul had really been a Christian for some time subconsciously even though he vigorously persecuted Christians. Paul's internal conflict eventually broke into his "ego-consciousness" resulting in a vision of Jesus followed by blindness from psychiatric causes, namely Conversion Disorder.[298] This, however, is an antiquated perspective since visions are not considered to accompany Conversion Disorders. Namely, the concept of a *Conversion-Vision* is discordant with current psychiatric nomenclature and understanding.[299]

Paul's blindness resolved in three days. He later went on to become the primary advocate of Christianity to the Western World of his time. This was a radical change for someone who previously persecuted and killed Christians. Had Paul actually experienced blindness from Conversion Disorder, one would expect that he would eventually come to himself after regaining sight. It would be more reasonable to expect that Paul would resume his vigorous

---

[297]Conversion Disorder has nothing to do with religious conversion. Sigmund Freud believed that subconscious conflicts were at times "converted" into neurological symptoms, hence the term *conversion disorder* for psychiatrically mediated neurological symptoms in the absence of identifiable physiologic cause. Josef Breuer and Sigmund Freud, *Studies in Hysteria*, trans. James Strachey (New York: Basic Books, 1957), 206.

[298]Carl G. Jung, *Contributions to Analytical Psychology* (New York: Harcourt, Brace, 1928), volume 9, 258–60.

[299]Bergeron and Habermas, "The Resurrection of Jesus," 167.

persecution of Christians. Instead, Paul demonstrated a radical and life-long change in belief and purpose. As a Pharisee, he would not have even associated with Gentiles. Yet, Paul became the most prolific evangelist to the non-Jewish world in his time, both through extensive doctrinal writing and itinerant preaching (Acts 9:20–22). He demonstrated an unwavering commitment to Christian faith in spite of repeated persecution, legal entanglements, and assassination attempts.

Paul is thought to have been tried before Caesar and ultimately killed (traditionally believed by beheading) for his religious activities.[300] He relentlessly championed Jesus' resurrection to the end of his life. Conversion Disorder is not a plausible explanation for Paul's radical change.

Mass Hysteria

Could the disciples and others have experienced some kind of *mass hysteria*? Mass Hysteria is perhaps more accurately termed *Mass Sociogenic Illness* in modern medical parlance. It is known that collective psychological experiences can occur and cause similar physical symptoms to multiple persons within a group. In rare cases groups can even have simultaneous visual experiences that are psychologically mediated. Mass Sociogenic Illness can occur within groups where there is a heightened sense of unique cultural or social expectation.[301] This is unlike the group psychosocial dynamics of Jesus' disciples after the crucifixion, however. They were frightened and in hiding (John 20:19).

It is important to note that even when simultaneous visual experiences occur within groups, no two individuals within the

---

[300]Philip Schaff, "Latin Christianity: It's founder, Tertullian," *Christian Classics Ethereal library*, June 1, 2005. http://www.ccel.org/ccel/schaff/anf03.v.iii.xxxvi.html. (accessed, November 29, 2017)

[301] Erica Weir, "Mass sociogenic illness," *Canadian Medical Association Journal*, 172, no. 1 (2005): 36. doi: 10.1503/cmaj.045027. (accessed January 5, 2018).

group experience the exact the same vision.[302]This is as would be expected. It is counterintuitive to think that any two individuals would have identical visions. Hallucinatory symptoms, or any other psychologically mediated experience, are generated within the internal milieu of the individual's mind. They are private personal experiences. Hallucinations, whatever the cause, offer no credible explanation for the biblical accounts of group meetings with the resurrected Jesus.

Bereavement

Could the disciples have seen visions of Jesus due to a deep state of grief and bereavement? It is not unusual for a spouse to describe hallucinatory experiences of their deceased partner.[303] The most common description of this kind of grief experience is a *sense of closeness*. However, auditory and visual experiences can occur. Visual encounters of a deceased spouse are rare, but when they occur are rapidly transient and not interactive. These kinds of grief experiences are psychologically mediated, as are hallucinations, but they are not considered pathological (i.e. related to illness). Rather, they are within the bounds of the normal sequelae of grief and bereavement.

These kinds of bereavement hallucinations do not compare with the disciples' meetings with the resurrected Jesus, however.

---

[302]Bergeron and Habermas, "The Resurrection of Jesus," 162, *fn* 19.

[303]Dewi Rees, a Welsh physician, made important contributions to the medical understanding of bereavement experiences in widowhood, W. Dewi Rees, 'The Hallucinations of Widowhood,' *British Medical Journal* 4 (1971): 37–41. In a later book without medical peer review, Rees proposed that hallucinatory bereavement experiences of a deceased spouse had spiritual significance and offered confirmation of life after death. Dewi Rees, *Pointers to Eternity* (Talybont: Y Lolfa, 2010). Rees' later writing is an overreach of the clinical data from the standpoint of medical logic. Rees feels that the disciples' experiences of Jesus should not be ruled out as possible bereavement phenomena, but admits that bereavement experiences cannot account for the disciples' simultaneous group encounters with the resurrected Jesus, Dewi Rees, *Pointers to Eternity,*193–195, 205.

Bereavement experiences of this kind usually occur with the spouse of the deceased, not friends and associates. Also, bereavement hallucinations cannot explain Jesus' simultaneous meetings with groups of people. Again, psychologically mediated visual experiences including those related to bereavement are private and personal experiences. Biblical accounts describe the resurrected Jesus meeting with individuals and groups, eating with them, and having extended conversations and personal contact with them. The numerous and variable nature of the disciples' meetings with Jesus make them unlike bereavement hallucinations.

It is noteworthy that hallucinations from bereavement, even when they are auditory or visual, never lead the living spouse to conclude that the deceased has been resurrected from the dead. Rather, they are personal experiences about which the living spouse is reluctant to speak.

Bereavement experiences are most common among widowed spouses, and more prevalent among those who had happy relationships with the deceased. Bereavement experiences among friends are possible but would be unusual. In short, bereavement hallucinations are rare and unlike the biblical accounts of the resurrected Jesus. A bereavement vision hypothesis for the resurrection of Jesus is not supportable.

Minimal Proofs Argument for Jesus' Resurrection

There are ample reasons to consider the Gospels as reliable eyewitness accounts. However, we need not solely rely on the authenticity of the Gospels to assess the Christian claims of Jesus' resurrection. For the sake of argument, let us consider the Bible as an unexceptional piece of evidence alongside other ancient literary references of Jesus.

There are a handful of facts about Jesus accepted by essentially all historical scholars, Christian or not, that do not rely on the biblical texts. These form the basis of the *Minimal Proofs Argument* for the resurrection of Jesus.[304] Accepted historical facts about Jesus allow us to form some conclusions. No faith required.

There are at least five facts accepted as historically valid that form the basis of the minimal proofs argument that Jesus was resurrected from the dead: (1) Jesus was a historical figure who was executed by crucifixion; (2) Jesus' disciples experienced *something* that made them believe Jesus had been bodily resurrected to life after his execution; (3) the Apostle Paul had a radical transformation after allegedly meeting the resurrected Jesus. It changed him from a ruthless and inhumane murderer of Christians to a prolific proponent of faith in Jesus as the Messiah; (4) Jesus' brother James changed from a skeptic to a leader in the early Church after encountering the resurrected Jesus; and finally (5) a majority of historians agree that an empty tomb was discovered the day of Jesus' reported resurrection.

Historicity

To suggest that Jesus never really existed is academically unfounded. Historical scholars, Christian or not, generally agree that Jesus was a historical figure who was executed by crucifixion and that his followers experienced *something* that made them believe he had risen from death to bodily life.[305]The most detailed descriptions of Jesus' life and teachings are found in the Gospels. However, there is convincing historical evidence outside the Bible pointing to the validity of Jesus as a historical figure.

Tacitus was a first century Roman historian and no friend of Christianity. His writings attest to the rapid spread of Christianity

---

[304]Habermas and Licona, "A Quintet of Facts: the First Two" and "A Quintet of Facts, the Last Three" in *The Case for the Resurrection of Jesus*, 48-77.

[305]Michael R. Licona, *The Resurrection of Jesus: A New Historiographical Approach* (Downers Grove, IL: IVP, 2010), 318. Gary R. Habermas, "Experiences of the Risen Jesus: The Foundational Historical Issue in the Early Proclamation of the Resurrection, "*Dialog: A Journal of Theology,*45 (2006): 288–97.

in the Roman Empire. "Christians" as they had become known, were followers of a person called Christ who had been crucified by Pontius Pilate. Christians became a recognized and hated minority in the Roman Empire.

...Nero fastened the guilt and inflicted the most exquisite tortures on a class hated for their abominations, called Christians by the populace. Christus [Christ], from whom the name had its origin, suffered the extreme penalty[306] during the reign of Tiberius at the hands of one of our procurators, Pontius Pilatus, and a most mischievous superstition, thus checked for the moment, again broke out not only in Judaea, the first source of the evil, but even in Rome...[307]

Tacitus refers to Christians believing "a most mischievous superstition," almost certainly a reference to the Christian belief that Jesus resurrected from the dead after crucifixion.

Tacitus' writings on Christianity are of particular importance because he corroborates the Gospel accounts of Jesus' crucifixion by Pontius Pilate. He further attests that early Christians believed Jesus had risen from the dead, that Christianity had spread widely through the empire, and that Christians were hated and persecuted. As a non-Christian Roman author, Tacitus provides important historical documentation.[308] Tacitus' anti-Christian tone makes it virtually impossible for this passage to be a Christian forgery. Literary evidence outside the Bible for the historicity of Jesus is discussed in further detail in Chapter 2.

---

[306] "The extreme penalty" (*summa supplica*) is a reference to crucifixion. Hengel, *Crucifixion*, 33.

[307] See fn 28.

[308] This passage from Tacitus' *Annals* is generally accepted by scholars as accurate and valid. Craig A. Evans, *Jesus and His Contemporaries: Comparative Studies*, (Leiden: Brill, 2001) 42.

Disciples Meeting the Resurrected Jesus

The disciples experienced *something* that made them believe Jesus had risen from the dead. Naturalistic hypotheses seeking to explain away the biblical accounts of Jesus' resurrection lack logical merit. Swoon Theories, body snatching or going to the wrong tomb are simply unsatisfactory.

Hallucination hypotheses for Jesus' resurrection are fraught with greater difficulty than is often realized. Hallucination explanations for the disciples' meetings with Jesus are not medically logical. Proponents of hallucination hypotheses are naïve to the medical understanding of causation for hallucinatory symptoms. It is untenable to think that all the disciples were suffering from severe medical or psychiatric illnesses causing them to hallucinate. Jesus' disciples also do not fit the profiles or group psychodynamics of those experiencing Mass Sociogenic Illness (mass hysteria) or bereavement visions. Perhaps most importantly, hallucination hypotheses offer no acceptable explanation for the biblical accounts of group meetings with the resurrected Jesus.

Naturalistic explanations are unable to explain away the biblical accounts of Jesus' resurrection, nor offer superior alternative explanations for the historical rise of Christianity in the first century. The biblical accounts best explain why the disciples placed their lives in peril to preach that Jesus was the Messiah and that he had risen from the dead.

The Apostle Paul

The Apostle Paul had been an ardent persecutor of Christians. He was an intellectual and rising star in the Hebrew religious culture of his time. He was famous for his religious fervor in persecuting and murdering Christians, ostensibly in the *name of God*. How is it that someone like Paul would turn 180 degrees to become the most influential proponent of Jesus' resurrection to the Western World?

Paul's religious fervor to spread Christianity was relentless in spite of enormous resistance and persecution (2 Cor. 11:23–27). He was ultimately martyred.

So far as Paul was concerned, he had met the resurrected Jesus (1 Cor. 15:8). A consensus of scholars also concur that Paul believed Jesus was actually physically alive when they met.[309] Attempts to explain Paul's drastic and lifelong change as arising from a psychological event, such as Conversion Disorder, are untenable. Paul's commitment to the arduous task of spreading Christianity is difficult to explain apart from Paul's own report that he had met the resurrected Jesus and believed that he was the Messiah.

James

James, the brother of Jesus, didn't buy into Jesus' claims. "For not even his own brothers believed in him" (John 7:5). Who would believe their sibling was the Messiah, the epic leader foretold in Hebrew prophecy, who also claimed to be God incarnate? The unhappy but obvious suspicion would be that brother was psychologically deranged. With the likely exception of Jesus' mother, his family thought he was a lunatic. "When his family heard this they went out to restrain him, for they said, 'He is out of his mind'" (Mark 3:21). Worse than having a sibling with psychiatric illness would be the tragedy of seeing your mentally ill brother crucified by Roman soldiers.

Jesus appeared to James after the resurrection (1 Cor. 15:7). James' belief that he had encountered the resurrected Jesus produced a radical change of heart. James became the leader of the Christian Church in Jerusalem (Acts15:13). Paul referred to James, the Lord's brother, as an Apostle in the church (Gal. 1:19). James' commitment to leading the church in Jerusalem and preaching

---

[309]Bergeron and Habermas, "The Resurrection of Jesus," 163.

Jesus' resurrection was unswerving. He was eventually executed for his religious activity according to Josephus:

Festus was now dead, and Albinus (Procurator of Judea after Porcius Festus) was but upon the road; so he assembled the Sanhedrin of judges, and brought before them the brother of Jesus, who was called Christ, whose name was James, and some others, [or, some of his companions]; and when he had formed an accusation against them as breakers of the law, he delivered them to be stoned.[310]

Josephus, a Jewish historian and naturalized Roman citizen wrote for a Roman audience. He had no sympathy for Christians. The historical validity of Josephus' record of James' execution is not questioned.[311] It is clear that James believed he met the resurrected Jesus. His behavior is difficult to explain otherwise.

The Empty Tomb

A consensus of scholars, Christian or not, concur that finding an empty tomb was within the sequence of events that day.[312] Is there a reasonable explanation apart from the Bible? Suggestions that the disciples couldn't find the tomb or went to the wrong tomb simply don't make sense.

Joseph of Arimathea was a Sanhedrin member and prominent social figure. It was no secret that he had obtained permission to inter Jesus' body. The location of the tomb was known.

Was Jesus' body stolen? Jesus was a highly visible public figure. He had a controversial trial with high-level hearings before the

---

[310]See chapter 2, fn 36, 37.

[311]Michael Licona, *The Resurrection of Jesus: A new historiographical approach.* (Downers Grove: Intervarsity Press, 2010), 457.

[312]Habermas and Licona, *The Case for the Resurrection of Jesus,* 70.

Sanhedrin, Pontius Pilate, and Herod Antipas. He was publicly beaten and executed. Temple Guard soldiers were placed at his tomb to assure the body was not stolen. Tales of body snatchers seem impossible.

That Jewish leaders did not exhume Jesus' corpse is significant. Why didn't they? It would have been the quickest and most direct way to destroy the religious movement Jesus started. The Sanhedrin could have compelled Joseph of Arimathea to open the tomb and exhume Jesus' body.

Jewish leaders desperately wanted to refute the reports that Jesus had been resurrected from the dead but were unable to definitively do so. Evidence would suggest they were incapable of producing his corpse for public display.

The First Christian Creed

A creed is an authoritative, formulated statement or confession of shared beliefs within a religious community. The first Christian creed is recorded for us by the Apostle Paul. Interestingly, it contains components of the minimal proofs arguments.

...Christ died for our sins according to the scriptures, and that he was buried, and that he was raised on the third day according to the scriptures, and that he appeared to Cephas [Peter], then to the twelve. Then he appeared to more than five hundred of the brothers and sisters at one time, most of whom are still alive, though some have fallen asleep. Then he appeared to James, then to all the apostles (1 Cor. 15:3–7).

This creed was adopted very early in Christian worship, probably within five years of Jesus' crucifixion.[313] Paul states that the creed did not originate with him but was something he learned (1 Cor.

---

[313]*Ibid.*, 56, 53 fn 25.

15:3). Paul most likely learned the creed three years after his conversion when visiting Peter and James in Jerusalem.[314] The creed states that there were many eyewitnesses of Jesus' death and resurrection and specifically names James, Peter, the original twelve disciples, and also that Jesus spoke to a group of 500 at once after his resurrection. Paul goes on to say, "he appeared to me also" (1 Cor. 15:8).

This first Christian creed was not only a statement of faith but also attested to verifiable evidence. It can no longer be recited today since anyone who saw Jesus has long ago passed away, but in the first century many who knew Jesus were still living. The creed contains core beliefs shared by the earliest Christians, that Jesus was the Messiah and that he died for the forgiveness of the sins of humanity. Perhaps most important, the creed pointed to proof in the form of then living eyewitnesses that Jesus had risen from the dead.

The Differential Diagnosis

In medical practice, steps to finding the correct diagnosis involve formulating a *differential diagnosis*, in essence brainstorming a list of possible diagnoses that could explain a patient's symptoms. The *Differential Diagnosis Method* is a systematic logical process where the list of potential diagnoses shrinks as the physician is able to eliminate less likely diagnoses by scientific method. The doctor collects facts, such as symptoms reported by the patient, physical examination findings, and review of medical records. This initial step often enables the physician to narrow the list of possible diagnoses. The doctor may request additional information via

---

[314]Paul's first introduction to any of the other Apostles was three years after his conversion. He visited Jerusalem to meet Peter where also met James, the Lord's brother. Paul did not meet any of the other Apostles at that time (Gal. 1:18). Paul spent fourteen days with Peter and most likely learned the traditions of the church in Jerusalem from him. Richard Bauckham, *Jesus and the Eyewitnesses: The Gospels as Eyewitness Testimony*. (Grand Rapids, MI: Eerdmans, 2006), 266.

supplemental special tests, for example X-rays, MRIs, lab tests, etc. The list of potential diagnoses is stratified by logical merit and refined, step by step. The physician gradually eliminates potential diagnoses from the list in favor of those that better explain the data. This process generally leads the skilled physician to the correct diagnosis and appropriate treatment.

Occam's razor is a powerful tool of logic taught in medical schools as part of the differential diagnosis approach to medical diagnosis. Occam's razor simply stated is that the explanation with the fewest number of special assumptions is most likely correct.

Through a similar logical process, consideration can be given to which hypothesis best fits the historical facts about Jesus and his followers. In examining the naturalistic hypotheses attempting to replace the biblical accounts of Jesus' resurrection, it is difficult to retain any as plausible options in a *differential diagnosis* for the explanation of Jesus' resurrection.

In Summary

The orthodox Christian belief that Jesus was resurrected from the dead requires acceptance of a supernatural event. Many find this too farfetched to consider. Yet, alternate explanations seem inherently flawed.

Efforts to naturally explain away the death and resurrection of Jesus are found to be unsatisfactory. The disciples' unrelenting belief that Jesus had risen from the dead is difficult to explain without a supernatural option. Swoon theories, going to the wrong tomb, body snatchers or pervasive unbridled psychiatric illness among the disciples are not credible explanations for the disciples' beliefs and actions.

Jesus had an overwhelming effect on his disciples. They preached that Jesus had been crucified, raised from the dead to bodily life, and that he was the Messiah. There was no potential for personal gain, financially or politically. The disciples exhibited reckless disregard for their personal safety. Their efforts produced the rapid expansion of Christianity in the first century.

Is it possible to mistake that a man has risen from the dead? What could possibly have motivated the disciples to act in the way they did? Blaise Pascal framed the conundrum this way:

The apostles were either deceived or deceivers. Either supposition has difficulties; for it is not possible to mistake a man raised from the dead ... While Jesus Christ was with them, He could sustain them. But, after that, if He did not appear to them, who inspired them to act?[315]

Could the biblical accounts of Jesus actually be true? Admittedly, supernatural special assumptions are required. Yet, the rise of Christianity is best explained by the biblical accounts. In the Scientific Method, the fallacy of *non sequitur* can never be permitted. Naturalistic hypotheses seeking to explain away Jesus' resurrection simply lack the logical merit to be considered credible.

---

[315]Blaise Pascal, *Pensées*, 801. Gutenberg.org. Project Gutenberg. April 27, 2006, http://www.gutenberg.org/files/18269/18269-h/18269-h.htm. (accessed January 12, 2018).

How would humans know about the existence of God? Mankind is lost in this regard. The responsibility sits squarely with God to reach out to humanity. C.S. Lewis, writer and professor of English literature at Oxford and Cambridge drew this analogy, "If Shakespeare and Hamlet could ever meet, it must be Shakespeare's doing."[316] That is to say, Shakespeare as the author could write himself into the play and initiate a dialogue with Hamlet but not the other way around. Could it be that God has written himself into human history?

Lewis was a committed atheist and deeply resisted the idea of the existence of God. Yet, as a literary scholar he knew that the Gospels did not appear to be mythological literature. One day an atheist friend made the inadvertent comment to Lewis that, "All that stuff,…about the Dying God,….It almost looks as if it had really happened once." Somehow, that comment from the most unexpected source put an end to years of objection and cognitive resistance. For Lewis, it evoked the epiphany that God existed. Lewis said he must have been the most "reluctant convert in all England."[317]He later went on to become a prolific proponent of Christianity, much of his writing directed to answering common objections to Christian faith.

Blaise Pascal was a seventeenth century French mathematician, physicist and Christian philosopher. A collection of his thoughts published posthumously, *Pensées* (Thoughts), contains a logical argument by Pascal that has become known as Pascal's Wager. Pascal draws an analogy to the decision of faith with betting on a coin toss.

---

[316]Clive Staples Lewis, *Surprised by Joy: the shape of my early life* (London: HBJ pub, 1955), 227.
[317]Ibid., 224, 229.

Let us then examine this point, and say, "God is, or He is not."
But to which side shall we incline? Reason can decide nothing here.
There is an infinite chaos which separated us. A game is being
played at the extremity of this infinite distance where heads or tails
will turn up. What will you wager? According to reason, you can do
neither the one thing nor the other; according to reason, you can
defend neither of the propositions.

Do not then reprove for error those who have made a choice; for
you know nothing about it. "No, but I blame them for having made,
not this choice, but a choice; for again both he who chooses heads
and he who chooses tails are equally at fault, they are both in the
wrong. The true course is not to wager at all."

—Yes; but you must wager. It is not optional. You are embarked.
Which will you choose then? Let us see. Since you must choose, let
us see which interests you least. You have two things to lose, the true
and the good; and two things to stake, your reason and your will,
your knowledge and your happiness; and your nature has two things
to shun, error and misery. Your reason is no more shocked in
choosing one rather than the other, since you must of necessity
choose. This is one point settled. But your happiness? Let us weigh
the gain and the loss in wagering that God is.[318]

In a way it seems mundane to compare a decision of faith to
wagering on a coin toss. If Pascal were explicitly comparing the
decision of faith to gambling it would be a trivialization. This was
not Pascal's intent. Sincere faith cannot be feigned nor can God be
impressed with superficial appearances. Rather, the practicality of
Pascal's argument is compelling. He defines an inescapable
decision having inherent components of uncertainty. Pascal bids us
to choose faith in God.

---

[318]Blaise Pascal, "Of the Necessity of the Wager", in *Pensées* (Thoughts), trans. William
Finlayson Trotter, (London: Collier and Son, 1910), Section 3, 233: 84,85. (Originally
published in French, 1670).
https://en.wikisource.org/wiki/Blaise_Pascal/Thoughts/Section_3. (accessed 1/5/2018).

One may say, "I choose not to wager." An agnostic position is illogical, however. Peter Kreeft makes the analogy of a ship embarked on a journey. The captain of a ship at sea may see a harbor with a sign stating, *Home and Happiness.* The agnostic captain may choose not to put into port but also to not to depart from it. Rather, he decides to anchor at a distance offshore hoping the weather may clear so that he may see the sign more distinctly. Such an attitude is flawed, however. There will come a point of no return when it is too late to come into port.[319] The eventual cessation of life mandates a decision. Indecision is an illogical choice.

I would be remiss if I did not provide some comment on how to acquire forgiveness from God and eternal security in heaven. It is tempting to provide some kind of one-size-fits-all prayer or formula that certifies the participant as a bona fide Christian. This would trivialize the process, however. Entre to Christian faith is profoundly simple yet at the same time messy and uncomfortable. It requires introspection, the recognition of one's personal moral bankruptcy, and acknowledgment of the need for God's forgiveness.

The first Christian convert serves as an example and guide on how to receive forgiveness from God and eternal life. Jesus was not crucified alone. A man crucified next to Jesus blasphemed him and said, *"Aren't you the Christ? Save yourself and us!"* However, another convicted felon crucified that day rebuffed the man who derided Jesus saying, *"Don't you fear God, since you are under the same sentence of condemnation? And we rightly so, for we are getting what we deserve for what we did, but this man has done nothing wrong."* After this, he spoke directly to Jesus with perhaps the simplest of any prayer, *"Jesus, remember me when you come in your kingdom."* Jesus responded that he would be in paradise with him later that day.[320] That convicted felon became the first Christian. He knew he deserved the death sentence, but he

---

[319]Kreeft, *Fundamentals of the Faith,* 50
[320]Luke 23:39-43

recognized Jesus as the Messiah and the person who could grant him forgiveness and entry to heaven upon death. Your own prayer need not be more complex. However, the same recognition of moral insufficiency and the humility to ask forgiveness from Jesus Christ is required. Such a prayer is never rejected.

Christianity would not exist without the death and resurrection of Jesus. It is unique among religions in that its origin can be traced to historical events. Christian faith is not blind, irrational or contradictory to the historical record.

There is a logical basis for belief in Jesus. May the peace of forgiveness and the assurance of eternal life be with you through Jesus Christ.

BIBLIOGRAPHY

Allen, Steven W. *The Illegal Trial of Christ.* Mesa: Legal
Awareness Series, 2005

Anitei, Stephan. "Colosseum, the Largest Amphitheater,"
softpedia.com. Softpedia News. April 2, 2008.
http://news.softpedia.com/news/Colosseum-the-Largest-
Amphitheater-82326.shtml. (accessed March 30, 2018).

Anonymous, "Grisly Roman Army Discipline", Great Names in
History, August 28, 2008.
https://100falcons.wordpress.com/2008/08/28/grisly-roman-
army-discipline/. (accessed November 11, 2016).

Archer, Gleason L. *A Survey of Old Testament Introduction.*
Chicago: Moody Press, 1974

Ashby, Chad. "Magi, Wise Men or Kings? It's Complicated."
Christianitytoday.com. Christianity Today, August 8, 2008.
http://www.christianitytoday.com/history/holidays/christmas/
magi-wise-men-or-kings-its-complicated.html. (accessed
December 28, 2017).

Barbet, Pierre. *A Doctor at Calvary: The Passion of our Lord
Jesus Christ as Described by a Physician.* Fort Collins:
Roman Catholic Books, 1953.

Barna Group Staff. "The Priorities, Challenges, and Trends in
Youth Ministry." *Barna.com.* The Barna Group, April 6,
2016. https://www.barna.com/research/the-priorities-
challenges-and-trends-in-youth-ministry/. (accessed
November 12, 2017).

Bauckham, Richard. *Jesus and the Eyewitnesses: The Gospels as Eyewitness Testimony.* Grand Rapids, MI: Eerdmans, 2006.

Ben-Sasson, Haim Hillel ed. *A History of the Jewish People.* Cambridge: Harvard University Press, 1976.

Bergeron, Joseph W. "The Crucifixion of Jesus: Review of Hypothesized Mechanisms of Death and Implications of Shock and Trauma-Induced Coagulopathy," *Journal of Forensic and Legal Medicine* 19 (2012):113–116.

Bergeron, Joseph W. and Gary R. Habermas, "The Resurrection of Jesus: A Clinical Review of Psychiatric Hypotheses for the Biblical Story of Easter." *Irish Theological Quarterly*, 80, no. 2 (2015) 157–172.

Berman, Rochel. "Dignity in Terrorism" excerpt from chapter 8 in *Dignity Beyond Death: The Jewish Preparation for Burial,* Brooklyn: Urim publications, 2005.*kosherfuneral.com.*ChevraKadisha of Florida, http://www.kosherfuneral.com/dignitybeyonddeath.html (accessed March 3, 2018).

Biblical Archeology Society Staff, "Herod's Death, Jesus' Birth and a Lunar Eclipse," www.biblicalarcheology.org, October 7, 2017, https://www.biblicalarchaeology.org/daily/people-cultures-in-the-bible/jesus-historical-jesus/herods-death-jesus-birth-and-a-lunar-eclipse/. (accessed June 22, 2018).

Birnbaum, Yochai and Michael Fishbein, Carlos Blanche, and Robert Siegel, "Ventricular Septal Rupture after Acute Myocardial Infarction," *New England Journal of Medicine* 347, no. 18 (2002): 1426-1432.

Bivin, David. *New Light on the Difficult Words of Jesus: Insights from His Jewish Context*. Holland: En Gedi Resource Center, 2005

Blomberg, Craig L. *The Historical Reliability of the Gospels*. Downers Grove: Intervarsity Press, 2007.

Blomberg, Craig L. *Can We Still Believe the Bible?* Grand Rapids: Brazos Press, 2014.

Boston College staff. "The Birth of Jesus: Two Gospel Narratives." *Bc.edu*. Boston College, http://www.bc.edu/schools/stm/crossroads/resources/birthofjes us/intro/the_dating_of_thegospels.html. (accessed November 3, 2017).

Breuer, Josef and Sigmund Freud, *Studies in Hysteria*. New York: Basic Books, 1957.

Brickner, David. "The Mystery of the Passover Cup," *jewsforjesus.org*. Jews for Jesus, March 1, 2002. https://jewsforjesus.org/publications/newsletter/newsletter-mar-2002/the-mystery-of-the-passover-cup/. (Accessed February 13, 2018).

St. Bridget of Sweden. *The Prophecies and Revelations of Saint Bridget of Sweden,* Chapter 10. http://www.saintsbooks.net/books/St.%20Bridget%20(Birgitta)%20of%20Sweden%20-%20Prophecies%20and%20Revelations.html. (accessed February 23, 2017).

Brown, Michael L. *60 Questions Christians Ask About Jewish Beliefs and Practices*. Bloomington: Chosen Books, 2011.

Bruce, Frederick Fyvie (F.F.). *New Testament History*. New York: Doubleday, 1971.

Burkett, Delbert. *An Introduction to the New Testament and the Origins of Christianity*. Cambridge: Cambridge University Press, 2002

Catholic Answers staff. "Origins of Peter as Pope." *Catholic.com*. Catholic Answers, August 4, 2008. https://www.catholic.com/tract/origins-of-peter-as-pope. (accessed January 3, 2018).

Chilton, Bruce David and Craig Evans. *Jesus in Context: Temple, Purity, and Restoration*. New York: Brill, 1997.

Cohen, Mitchell J, and S. Ariene Christie, "Coagulopathy of Trauma," *Critical Care Clinics* 33, no. 1 (2017): 101–118.

Colson, Charles. "Watergate and the Resurrection of Christ" from a speech delivered at the National Religious Broadcasters Convention, Feb 1984. Baylyblog.com, David and Tim Bayly, April 24, 2012. http://baylyblog.com/blog/2012/04/chuck-colson-resurrection. (accessed April 3, 2017).

Cook, John Granger. *Crucifixion in the Mediterranean World*. Tubingen: Mohr Siebeck, 2014.

Crandall University Staff. "The Jerusalem Temple and the New Testament." *www.mycrandall.ca*. Crandall University, November 6, 2014.

http://www.mycrandall.ca/courses/ntintro/jerusaltempl4.htm. (accessed January 31, 2017).

Craughwell, Thomas J. "A Plot to Seal Lincoln's Body: A posthumous kidnapping attempt shaped the Secret Service." *usnews.com*. June 24, 2017, https://www.usnews.com/news/articles/2007/06/24/a-plot-to-steal-lincolns-body. (accessed May 10, 2017).

Dando-Collins, Stephen. *Legions of Rome: The Definitive History of Every Imperial Roman Legion.* London: Quercus, 2010.

Dionysius of Halicarnassus. "Roman Antiquities." VII, 69:1-2, *uchicago.edu*. Bill Thayer, University of Chicago. http://penelope.uchicago.edu/Thayer/E/Roman/Texts/Dionysiu s_of_Halicarnassus/7C*.html. (accessed September 23, 2017).

Draper, Jonathan A. *The Didache in Modern Research*. Leiden: Brill Academic Pub, 1996.

Durant, Will. *Christ and Caesar: the History of Roman Civilization and of Christianity from their beginnings to A.D 325.*vol. 3 of *The Story of Civilization.* New York: Simon and Schuster, 1944.

Dutton, Richard. "Pathophysiology of Traumatic Shock, "*International Trauma Care* 18, no. 1 (2008): 12-15.

Editors of Encyclopaedia Britannica. "Caesarea: Ancient City, Israel." *www.britannica.com*. Encyclopaedia Britannica, February 18, 2015. https://www.britannica.com/place/Caesarea. (accessed January 23, 2017).

Edwards, William and Wesley Gabel, and Floyd Hosmer, *On the Physical Death of Jesus Christ*, Journal of the American Medical Association 255, No. 11, 1455-1463.

Ehrman, Bart D. *Misquoting Jesus.* New York: HarperSanFrancisco, 2005.

Eusebius, *Church History*: L.1, C22. http://www.documentacatholicaomnia.eu/03d/02650339,_Eusebius_Caesariensis,_Church_History,_EN.pdf. (accessed June 14, 2017).

Eusebius, *Ecclesiastical History*, Book IV, chapter 15:4, in Arthur Cushman McGiffert, *Nicene and Post-Nicene Fathers, Second Series*, Vol. 1. Philip Schaff and Henry Wace, eds., (Buffalo: Christian Literature Publishing Co., 1890) *www.newadvent.org.* http://www.newadvent.org/fathers/250104.htm. (accessed December 15, 2017).

Eusebius. *"The Writings of Papias"* in *Ecclesiastical History,* book 3, chapter 39. http://rbedrosian.com/Eusebius/euch3.htm. (accessed December 28, 2017).

Louis Feldman, "Financing the Colosseum" *Biblical Archaeology Review*, 27, no. 4. (2001):20-31, 60-61.

Evans, Craig A. *Jesus and His Contemporaries: Comparative Studies*. Leiden: Brill, 2001.

Foster, RC. *Studies in the Life of Christ: introduction, the Early Period, and middle Period, the Final Week.* College Press Pub

Co, 1995

Gonzales, E. and E.E. Moore, H.B. Moore, M.P. Chapman, C.C.
    Silliman, and A. Banerjee, "Trauma-induced Coagulopathy:
    An institution's 35 Year Perspective on Practice and
    Research." *Scandinavian Journal of Surgery* 103, no.2 (2014):
    89–103.

Gregory, Andrew. "The Reception of Luke and Acts in the Period
    Before Irenaeus." *Tyndale Bulletin* 53, no. 1 (2002): 153-156.

Grout, James. "Alexamenos Graffito" in Encyclopaedia Romana,
    University of Chicago, Penelope.uchicago.edu., April 1,
    2017,
    http://penelope.uchicago.edu/~grout/encyclopaedia_romana/gl
    adiators/graffito.html. (accessed January 11, 2018).

Gualdi-Russo, Emamuela, et al., "A multidisciplinary study of
    calcaneal trauma in Roman Italy: a possible case of
    crucifixion?" Archaeological and Anthropological Sciences,
    (April 2018): DOI: 10.1007/s12520-018-0631-9

Guyton, Arthur C. and John E. Hall. *Textbook of Medical
    Physiology*, 12th ed. Philadelphia: Saunders, 2011.

Haas, N. "Anthropological Observations on the Skeletal Remains
    from Giv'at ha-Mitvar." *Israel Exploration Journal* 20, no. 1/2
    (1970): 49-59.

Hachlili, Rachel. *Jewish Funerary Customs, Practices and Rites in
    the Second Temple Period*. Leiden: Brill, 2005.

Habermas, Gary R. "Experiences of the Risen Jesus: The

Foundational Historical Issue in the Early Proclamation of the Resurrection." *Dialog: A Journal of Theology* 45 (2006): 288–97.

Habermas, Gary. *The Historical Jesus: Ancient Evidence for the Life of Christ.* Joplin: College Press, 1996.

Habermas, Gary and Michael Licona. *The Case for the Resurrection of Jesus.* Grand Rapids: Kregel, 2004.

Hengel, Martin. *Crucifixion in the Ancient World and the Folly of the Message of the Cross.* London: Fortress Press, 1977.

Hess, John, et al., "The Coagulopathy of Trauma: A Review of Mechanisms." *Journal of Trauma Injury, infection, and critical care* 65, no. 4 (2008): 748–754.

Hirsch, Emil G. and others, "Weights and Measures" Jewish Encyclopedia.com http://www.jewishencyclopedia.com/articles/14821-weights-and-measures#217. (accessed April 2, 2017).

Holden, Joseph M. and Norman Geisler. *The Popular Handbook of Archaeology and the Bible.* Eugene: Harvest House, 2013.

Horsley, Richard and Jonathan Draper. *Whoever Hears You Hears Me: Prophets, Performance, and Tradition in Q.* Harrisburg: Trinity Press, 1999.

Horsley, Richard. *Bandits, Prophets, and Messiahs: Popular Movements in the Time of Jesus.* Philadelphia: Trinity Press. 2000.

Holoubek JE and Holoubek AB. "Blood, sweat and fear. A classification of hematidrosis." J Med 1996;2(3-4):115-33

Hynek, Rudolph W. *Science and the holy shroud, an examination into the sacred passion and the direct cause of Christ's death.* Chicago: Benedictine Press; 1936.

Iraneus. *Against Heresies*, book 3, chapter 1:1, in *Ante-Nicene Fathers*, Vol. 1. Translators Alexander Roberts, James Donaldson, and A. Cleveland Coxe. (Buffalo: Christian Literature Publishing Co., 1885.) https://en.wikisource.org/wiki/Ante-Nicene_Fathers/Volume_I/IRENAEUS/Against_Heresies:_Book_III/Chapter_I. (accessed December 28, 2017).

Jackson, Wayne. "Did Jesus Eat the Passover Supper?" *Christiancourier.com*, Christian Courier Publications. https://www.christiancourier.com/articles/390-did-jesus-eat-the-passover-supper. (accessed April 5, 2018).

Jackson, Wayne. "Jesus' Prophecy and the Destruction of the Temple." *ChristianCourier.com*, Christian Courier Publications.https://www.christiancourier.com/articles/1302-jesus-prophecy-and-the-destruction-of-the-temple. (access April 9, 2018).

James, M.R. "The Acts of Peter", in *The Apocryphal New Testament* (Oxford: Clarendon Press, 1924). Kirby, Peter. "historical Jesus Theories." Early Christian Writings. http://www.earlychristianwritings.com/text/actspeter.html. (accessed March 1, 2017).

Jewish Encyclopedia editorial committee, "Covenant" in Jewish Encyclopedia, vol. 4, 318-322 (New York: Funk and

Wagnalls, 1906), *JewishEncyclopedia.com*
http://www.jewishencyclopedia.com/articles/4714-covenant.
(accessed March 20, 2018).

Jones, Ron. "The Hebrew and Greek Gospels Written by Matthew
the Apostle of Jesus Christ." Ron Jones and the Titus Institute.
Hebrew Gospel.com.
http://hebrewgospel.com/Matthew%20Two%20Gospels%20M
ain%20Evidence.php. (accessed 1/2/2018).

Johnston, Bruce. "Colosseum 'built with loot from sack of
Jerusalem temple'" *www.telegraph.co.uk.* The Telegraph, June
15, 2001,
http://www.telegraph.co.uk/news/worldnews/1311985/Colosse
um-built-with-loot-from-sack-of-Jerusalem-temple.html.
(accessed March 1, 2017).

Josephus, Flavius. trans. William Whiston, *The Works of Josephus:
Complete and Unabridged.* Peabody: Hendrickson Pub Inc.,
1987.

Josephus, Flavius. The Antiquities of the Jews, book 18, chapter
3.3, trans. William Whiston, (London: Blackie and Son 1866).
https://en.wikisource.org/wiki/The_Antiquities_of_the_Jews/
Book_XVIII. . (accessed January 8, 2018).

Josephus, Flavius. *The Life of Flavius Josephus*, William Whiston
translator. 75.
http://www.perseus.tufts.edu/hopper/text?doc=Perseus:abo:tlg,
0526,002:75 (accessed March 23, 2017).

Josephus, Flavius. *Antiquities of the Jews*, book 20, chapter 9:1.
https://en.wikisource.org/wiki/The_Antiquities_of_the_Jews/
Book_XX. (accessed January 8, 2018).

Jung, Carl G. *Contributions to Analytical Psychology. Vol 9.* New York: Harcourt, Brace, 1928.

Juvenal, G.G. Ramsay trans. *Satires of Juvenal.* London: William Heinemann, 1918, 3.34-37. Harhttps://en.wikisource.org/wiki/Juvenal_and_Persius/The_S atires_of_Juvenal/Satire_3. (accessed March 29, 2018).

Komoszewski, J Ed, M. James Sawyer, and Daniel B. Wallace, *Reinventing Jesus: How contemporary skeptics miss the real Jesus and mislead popular culture.* Grand Rapids: Kregel, 2006.

Komski, Jan "Administrative Punishment – a painting by Jan Komski," *remember.org.* http://remember.org/komski/komski-paintings1-009. (accessed November 3, 2017)

Kostenberger, Anreas and Michael J. Kruger. *The Heresy of Orthodoxy.* Wheaton: Crossway, 2010.

Kreeft, Peter. *Fundamentals of the Faith: Essays in Christian Apologetics.* San Francisco: Ignatius Press, 1988.

Kreeft, Peter and Fr. Ronald Tacelli. *Handbook of Catholic Apologetics: Reasoned Answers to Questions of Faith.* Downers Grove: InterVarsity Press, 2009.

Kruger, Michael. *The Question of Canon: Challenging the Status Quo in the New Testament Debate.* Downers Grove: Intervarsity Press, 2013.

Lash, Neil and Amy. "The Lord's Right Hand – April 2016." Jewish Jewels, April 1, 2016. Jewish Jewels, http://www.jewishjewels.org/news-letters/the-lords-right-hand-april-2016/. (accessed March 21, 2017)

Leale, Charles A. "Lincoln's Last Hours." Speech delivered to the Commandery of the State of New York, Military Order of the Loyal Legion, Feb 1909. p. 11. https://archive.org/stream/lasthours00lealrich/lasthours00lealrich_djvu.txt. (accessed May 12, 2017).

Lewis, Clive Staples. *Mere Christianity.* New York: Harper Collins, 1980.

Lewis, Clive Staples Lewis. *Surprised by Joy: the shape of my early life.* London: HBJ pub, 1955.

Le Bec, "The Death of the Cross: A Physiological Study of the Passion of Our Lord Jesus Christ." *Catholic Medical Guardian* 3 (1925): 126–132. (Originally published in French, *La Revue de Philosophie.* March/April 1923).

Licona, Michael R. *The Resurrection of Jesus: A New Historiographical Approach.* Downers Grove, IL: IVP, 2010.

Ligouri, Alphonsus. "St. Ignatius of Antioch," *Roman Catholic Saints.* Catholic Vitality Publications. http://www.roman-catholic-saints.com/st-ignatius-of-antioch.html. (accessed March 29, 2018).

Lucian of Samosata, "Trial in the Court of Vowels", *Sacred-texts.com.* http://www.sacred-texts.com/cla/luc/wl1/wl110.htm. (accessed January 10, 2018).

Mackay, Christopher. *Ancient Rome: A military and political history*. Cambridge: Cambridge University Press, 2004.

Maglie, Roberto and Marzia Caprioni, "A case of blood sweating: hematohydrosis syndrome" *Canadian Medical Association Journal*, 189, no. 42 (2017):E1314. doi: 10.1503/cmaj.161298

Manning, Scott. "Process of copying the Old Testament by Jewish Scribes." *Scottmanning.com*. Historian on the Warpath, March 17, 2007. http://www.scottmanning.com/content/process-of-copying-the-old-testament-by-jewish-scribes/. (accessed February 12, 2017).

Manonukul, Jane et al. "Hematidrosis: a pathological process of stigmata. A case report with comprehensive histopathological and immunoperoxidase studies," *American Journal of Dermatopathology* 2. (2008): 135-139

Martyr, Justin. "First Apology", chapter 35, trans. Marcus Dods, (Edinburgh: Clark, 1867). *Ante-Nicene Christian Library*, Wikisource.org. https://en.wikisource.org/wiki/Ante-Nicene_Christian_Library/The_First_Apology_of_Justin_Martyr. (accessed January 8, 2018).

Justin Martyr, *First Apology*, 67, https://en.wikisource.org/wiki/Ante-Nicene_Christian_Library/The_First_Apology_of_Justin_Martyr. (accessed December 28, 2017).

Marucchi, Orazio. "Archeology of the Cross and Crucifix", in *The Catholic Encyclopedia*, vol. 4 (New York: Robert Appleton Co. 1908). http://www.newadvent.org/cathen/04517a.htm. (accessed December 13, 2016).

Maslen, Matthew W. and Piers D. Mitchell. "Medical theories on the cause of death in crucifixion." *Journal of the Royal Society of Medicine* 99, (2006): 186-187.

Mauck, John W. *Paul on Trial: The Book of Acts as a Defense of Christianity*. Nashville: Thomas Nelson, 2001.

McDowell, Josh and Bill Wilson. *Evidence for the Historical Jesus: a compelling case for his life and his claims*. Eugene: Harvest House, 1988, 1993.

McGovern, Thomas. Lesson 2 in online course "Another Doctor at Calvary," *Catholic Distance University*. https://cdu.catalog.instructure.com/browse/cma/courses/another-doctor-at-calvary. (accessed May 3, 2016).

Montefiore, Simon Sebag. *Jerusalem: The Biography*. New York: Alfred A. Knopf, 2011.

My Jewish Learning Staff, "What does It Mean to Be a Rabbi?" *myjewishlearning.com*. My Jewish Learning,https://www.myjewishlearning.com/article/rabbi-teacher-preacher-judge-but-not-priest/. (accessed February 21, 2018).

O'Connor, John. "Report of first doctor to reach shot Lincoln Found" June 5, 2012. Yahoo News. https://www.yahoo.com/news/report-first-doctor-reach-shot-lincoln-found-175353998.html?ref=gs. (accessed May 12, 2017).

Pascal, Blaise. *Pensées*, 800, 801. *Gutenberg.org*, Gutenberg

project, April 27, 2006,
http://www.gutenberg.org/files/18269/18269-h/18269-h.htm.
(accessed January 12, 2018).

Pascal, Blaise. "Of the Necessity of the Wager", in *Pensées*
(Thoughts), trans. William Finlayson Trotter, (London: Collier
and Son, 1910), Section 3, 233: 84,85. (Originally published
in French, 1670).
https://en.wikisource.org/wiki/Blaise_Pascal/Thoughts/Section
_3. (accessed 1/5/2018).

Pearse, Roger. "Constantine banned crucifixion – sources,"
www.roger-pearse.com. Roger Pearse blog, February 16,
2015,http://www.roger-
pearse.com/weblog/2015/02/26/constantine-banned-
crucifixion-sources/. (accessed June 21, 2016).

Pliny the Elder, *The Natural History*, 22: 4, trans. John Bostock
and H.T. Riley (London: Taylor and Francis,
1855).*www.perseus.tufts.edu*. Perseus Digital Library, Tufts
University,
http://www.perseus.tufts.edu/hopper/text?doc=Perseus:text:19
99.02.0137:book=22:chapter=4. (accessed February 20, 2018).

Powell, Doug. *Holman Quicksource Guide to Christian
Apologetics*. Nashville: Holman Reference, 2006.

Prasad, Abhiram, Amir Lerman, and Charanjit S. Rihal, "Apical
ballooning syndrome (Tako-Tsubo or stress cardiomyopathy):
A mimic of acute myocardial infarction." *American Heart
Journal* 155, no. 3. (2008): 408–417.

Praveen, B.K. and Johny Vincent. "Hematridosis and hemolacria:
A Case Report." Indian Journal of Pediatrics 79, no. 1

(2012):109-111.

Quintilian, Lewis Sussman translator. *The Major Declamations ascribed to Quintilian.* Bern: Lang, 1987.

Rees, W. Dewi. "The Hallucinations of Widowhood." *British Medical Journal* 4 (1971): 37–41.

Rees, W. Dewi. *Pointers to Eternity.* Talybont: Y Lolfa, 2010.

Rocca, Samuel. *The Army of Herod the Great.* Oxford: Osprey pub., 2009.

Ritmeyer, Leen. "Twelve-year-old Jesus in the Temple at Passover," *www.ritmeyer.com*. Ritmeyer Archaeological Design, April 7, 2017.https://www.ritmeyer.com/2017/04/08/twelve-year-old-jesus-in-the-temple-at-passover/. (accessed February 8, 2018).

Ritmeyer, Leen. "The 'Gold of the Temple' and Financing the Colosseum 1," *thelampstand.com.au*. The Lampstand, 22 no. 4, July 6, 2016.https://thelampstand.com.au/the-gold-of-the-temple-and-financing-the-colosseum1/. (accessed February 7, 2018).

Roger, Raymond N. *A Chemist's Perspective on The Shroud of Turin.* Self-published, Joan Rogers and Barrie M. Schwortz., Lulu, 2008.

Routledge, robin. "Passover and Last Supper," *Tyndale Bulletin*, 53, no.2 (2002): 203-221.

Sadock, Benjamin J, Virginia A. Sadock, and Pedro Ruiz, Kaplan and Sadock's Synopsis of Psychiatry, Behavioral Science/Clinical Psychiatry, 11th ed. (Philidelphia: Wolters Kluwer, 2015)

Sanborn, Earl. "Clinico-pathologic aspects of traumatic wet lung." *American Journal of Surgery*, 87, no. 3 (1954): 457–461.

Santala, Risto. "Paul's Childhood Education," *www.RistoSantala.com*.http://www.ristosantala.com/rsla/Paul/paul05.html. (accessed February 2, 2017).

Sanders, E.P. *Judaism: Practice and Belief, 63 BCE-66CE.* London: Trinity Press International, 1992.

Schaff, Philip. "Latin Christianity: It's founder, Tertullian," Christian Classics Ethereal library, June 1, 2005. http://www.ccel.org/ccel/schaff/anf03.v.iii.xxxvi.html. (accessed, November 29, 2017)

Schafer, Peter. *History of the Jews in the Greco-Roman world.* London: Routledge, 2003.

Schechter, Solomon and Wilhelm Bacher, "Gamaliel I", *Jewish Encyclopedia*, http://www.jewishencyclopedia.com/articles/6494-gamaliel-i. (accessed January 12, 2017).

Schreiber, Martin A. "Damage Control Surgery," Critical Care Clinics, 20, (2004): 101-118.

Schwartz, Seth. "Political, social and economic life in the land of Israel," in Steven T. Katz, and others, eds., *The Cambridge*

History of Judaism. vol. 4, The Late Roman-Rabbinic Period. Cambridge: Cambridge University Press, 2006.

Scott, J. Julius. *Jewish Backgrounds of the New Testament.* Grand Rapids: Baker Books, 1995.

Seales, William Brent and others., "From damage to discovery via virtual unwrapping: Reading the scroll from En-Gedi." *Science Advances*, September 2016, http://advances.sciencemag.org/content/advances/2/9/e160124 7.full.pdf. (accessed September 23, 2017).

Seneca, Annaeus. "Of Consolation: To Marcia," XX. Wikisource , https://en.wikisource.org/w/index.php?title=Of_Consolation:_ To_Marcia&oldid=7922787. (accessed January 11, 2018)

Slick, Matt. "When were the Gospels written and by whom?" Christian Apologetics & Research Ministry, CARM.org. https://carm.org/when-were-gospels-written-and-by-whom. (accessed November 3, 2017).

Sozomen, *Ecclesiastical History*, trans. Edward Walford. London: H. Bohn Pub., 1855.

Staff contributor. "Archeology of the Cross and Crucifix." *Newadvent.org.* Catholic Encyclopedia, online. http://www.newadvent.org/cathen/04517a.htm (accessed December 22, 2016).

Staff writer, "April 2018 – Sun in Jerusalem." *TimeandDate.com*, https://www.timeanddate.com/sun/israel/jerusalem?month=4. (accessed January 23, 2018).

Staff writer, "Historic Average, Jerusalem, Israel," *Intellicast, The Authority in Expert Weather.* http://www.intellicast.com/Local/History.aspx?unit=F&month =4. (accessed December 5, 2017).

Staff writer, "Jerusalem Climate History," *myweather2.com.* Weather2, http://www.myweather2.com/City-Town/Israel/Jerusalem/climate-profile.aspx. (accessed April 18, 2018).

Staff writer, "The Herodian Period: 37 BCE – 73 CE" Israel Ministry of Foreign Affairs, 2013, http://www.mfa.gov.il/mfa/aboutisrael/maps/pages/kingdom% 20of%20herod-%2030%20bce%20to%2070%20ce.aspx/ (accessed July 3, 2018).

Stewart, Roy A. "Judicial Procedure in New Testament Times." The Evangelical Quarterly 47, no. 2 (1975): 94-109.

Stott, John. *The Cross of Christ.* Downers Grove: InterVarsity Press, 2006.

Strong's Exhaustive Concordance, "apologia", *biblehub.com.* Helps Ministries, Inc., http://biblehub.com/str/greek/627.htm. (accessed December 6, 2017).

Strong's Exhaustive Concordance, "Apostolos", *biblehub.com.* Helps Ministries, Inc. http://biblehub.com/greek/652.htm. (accessed December 6, 2017).

Strong's Exhaustive Concordance, 4716, "stauros", *biblehub.com.* Bible Hub, http://biblehub.com/greek/4716.htm. (accessed January 11, 2018).

Strong's Exhaustive Concordance, 4616. "Sindon", *biblehub.com*.
Bible Hub. http://biblehub.com/greek/4616.htm. (accessed
January 9, 2018).

Stroud, William A. *Treatise on the physical cause of the death of
Christ and its relation to the principles and practices of
Christianity*. London: Hamilton and Adams, 1847.

Tacitus. *The Complete Works of Tacitus*, Moses Hadas, editor,
Alfred John Church and William Jackson Brodribb translators.
Toronto: Random House, 1942.

Tacitus, Annals 15:44 in *The Works of Tacitus*, Alfred John
Church and William Jackson Brodribb translators, (London:
Macmillan, 1864, 1877). http://www.sacred-
texts.com/cla/tac/a15040.htm977.(accessed January 8, 2018).

Teeple, Bryan and Jason Caplan, and Theodore Stern. 'Visual
Hallucinations: Differential Diagnosis and Treatment."
Journal of Clinical Psychiatry 11 (2009): 26–32.

Tertullian, *The Apology of Tertullian*, W.M. Reeve translator,
(London: Griffith Farran, 1889) 53.
http://www.tertullian.org/articles/reeve_apology.htm.
(accessed December 21, 2016).

Tieu, Brandon H. and John B. Holcomb, and Martin A. Schreiber.
"Coagulopathy: It's Pathophysiology and Treatment in the
Injured Patient." *World Journal of Surgery*, 31 (2007): 1055-
1064.

Tzaferis, V. "Jewish Tombs at and near Giv'at ha-Mivtar,

Jerusalem," *Israel Exploration Journal* 20. No. ½ (1970): 18-32.

Vincent, Jean-Louis and Daniel De Backer. "Circulatory Shock." *New England Journal of Medicine* 369, no. 18 (2013): 1726–34.

Wallace, Daniel B. "The Gospel according to Bart," *Bible.org*, April 24, 2006. https://bible.org/article/gospel-according-bart. (accessed October 23, 2016).

Wallace, J. Warner. *Cold-Case Christianity: A homicide detective investigates the claims of the Gospels*. Colorado Springs: David C. Cook, 2013.

Wallace, J. Warner. "What does 'Gospel' Really Mean?", ColdCaseChristianity.com, May 16, 2014, http://coldcasechristianity.com/2014/what-does-gospel-really-mean/. (accessed December 6, 2017).

Wallace, J. Warner. "What Was the Shape of Jesus' Cross?," *coldcasechristianity.com*. Cold-Case Christianity, January 8, 2018, http://coldcasechristianity.com/2018/what-was-the-shape-of-jesus cross/?utm_source=feedburner&utm_medium=email&utm_ca mpaign=Feed%3A+ColdCaseChristianity+%28Cold+Case+C hristianity%29. (accessed January 11, 2018).

Wallace, J. Warner. "The Problem with the Christian Explanation." ColdCaseChristianity.com. August 24, 2017 http://coldcasechristianity.com/2016/the-problem-with-the-christian-explanation/?utm_source=feedburner&utm_medium=email&u tm_campaign=Feed%3A+ColdCaseChristianity+%28Cold+Ca se+Christianity%29. (accessed March 3, 2017).

Wallace, J. Warner, "Was John Describing Something He saw, or Was He trying to Make a Point?" *ColdCaseChristianity.com.* Cold Case Christianity, August 17, 2016. http://coldcasechristianity.com/2016/was-john-describing-something-he-saw-or-was-he-trying-to-make-a-point/?utm_source=feedburner&utm_medium=email&utm_ca mpaign=Feed%3A+ColdCaseChristianity+%28Cold+Case+C hristianity%29. (accessed June 1, 2017).

Weir, Erica. "Mass sociogenic illness." *Canadian Medical Association Journal* 172, no. 1 (2005): 36. doi: 10.1503/cmaj.045027. (accessed January 5, 2018).

Wikimedia Commons contributors, "File:NinthAvStonesWesternWall.JPG," *Wikimedia Commons, the free media repository,* https://commons.wikimedia.org/w/index.php?title= File:NinthAvStonesWesternWall.JPG&oldid=200746420 (accessed April 10, 2018).

Wikipedia contributors, "Koine Greek," *Wikipedia, The Free Encyclopedia,* https://en.wikipedia.org/w/index.php?title=Koin e_Greek&oldid=819246217. (accessed January 11, 2018).

Wikipedia contributors, "Lagerordnung", Wikipedia, The Free Encyclopedia, July 8, 2017, https://en.wikipedia.org/w/index.php?title=Lagerordnung&old id=789597052. (accessed August 17, 2017).

Wikipedia contributors, "Strappado", Wikipedia, The Free Encyclopedia, November 24, 2017, https://en.wikipedia.org/w/index.php?title=Strappado&oldid=

811789389. (accessed December 6, 2017).

Wohlgemuth, Isaiah. "Hallel," *myjewishlearning.com*. My Jewish
    Learning, https://www.myjewishlearning.com/article/hallel/.
    (accessed January 23, 2018).

Wilson, Marin R. *Our Father Abraham: Jewish Roots of the
    Christian Faith*. Grand Rapids: Eerdmans, 1989.

Wright, Nicholas Thomas. *The Resurrection of the Son of God*,
    volume 3 of *Christian Origins and the Question of God*.
    Minneapolis: Fortress Press, 2003.

Zias, Joseph and Eliezer Sekeles, "The Crucified Man from Giv'at
    ha-mivtar: A Reappraisal." *Israel Exploration Journal*, 35.
    No. 1 (1985): 22-27.

Zugibe, Frederick T. "Death by Crucifixion." *Canadian Society of
    Forensic Science Journal* 17, no. 1 (1984) 1–13.

Zugibe, Frederick T. *The Crucifixion of Jesus: A Forensic Inquiry*.
    New York: M. Evans and Co., 2005.

IMAGE INDEX

SCRIPTURE INDEX

Note: Scripture index entries are listed as follows:

Book and Chapter

Verse .... Page Number

166

hypothermia, 156, 157, 158, 159, 162, 163

hysteria, 189, 194

I

I AM, 6

Ignatius of Antioch, 79, 218

Irenaeus, 30, 31, 34, 35, 213

Isaiah, 43, 56, 66, 115, 229

J

James, 26, 30, 33, 47, 82, 89, 94, 107, 124, 170, 171, 174, 188, 192, 195, 196, 197, 198, 213, 215, 217, 232

Jerusalem, 20, 27, 31, 35, 36, 37, 38, 39, 40, 41, 55, 56, 58, 59, 61, 62, 63, 65, 67, 71, 73, 74, 76, 77, 78, 82, 84, 89, 91, 94, 99, 100, 102, 105, 119, 125, 133, 134, 150, 152, 162, 163, 167, 182, 195, 198, 210, 216, 220, 224, 225, 227, 231, 232, 233

John, 2, 3, 4, 5, 6, 7, 12, 13, 14, 15, 22, 28, 29, 30, 32, 33, 35, 36, 42, 44, 45, 46, 52, 57, 59, 61, 63, 65, 69, 71, 72, 73, 75, 81, 82, 83, 85, 87, 89, 92, 94, 108, 114, 117, 120, 121, 123, 125, 127, 132, 136, 140, 142, 143, 148, 149, 151, 157, 158, 160, 161, 162, 163, 165, 171, 173, 174, 178, 179, 180, 182, 183, 185, 189, 195, 210, 213, 214, 220, 221, 225, 226, 228

John the Baptist, 3, 57, 65

Joseph of Arimathea, 61, 183, 184, 185, 196, 197

Josephus, 25, 26, 35, 36, 38, 39, 57, 62, 63, 73, 77, 82, 91, 94, 111, 135, 179, 196, 216

Judaism, 8, 33, 39, 58, 62, 84, 223, 224

Judas of Galilee, 62, 63, 64, 72, 73

Judea, xx, 20, 21, 24, 26, 27, 31, 38, 56, 62, 84, 119, 196

Julius Caesar, 52

Jung, Carl, 217

K

King James Version, 49

King of the Jews, 56, 88, 160

Koine Greek, 106, 228

ABOUT THE AUTHOR

Joseph W. Bergeron, M.D. has been a practicing physician for over 25 years. He has authored peer-reviewed journal articles on the death and resurrection of Jesus. His particular area of interest is in the medical aspects of Christ's death and the disciples' belief in his resurrection. He also volunteers with Ratio Christi Campus Apologetics Alliance.

Joseph W. Bergeron

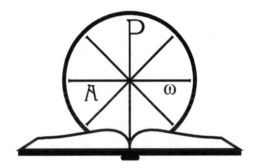

St. Polycarp Publishing House

CPSIA information can be obtained
at www.ICGtesting.com
Printed in the USA
BVHW040956270519
549329BV00019B/572/P